REMEMBERING WITH GRANNY

by

Alma D. Worthington

Derryberry Publications

Tallahassee, Florida

1995

Published by—Derryberry Publications
4772 Charles Samuel Dr.
Tallahassee, FL 32308

Additional copies or bulk quantities at discount prices should be directed to Nancy Jeter, Publisher

Book and Jacket Design by
Douglas M. Eason—Havana Florida

Contents

Dedication
Preface

Dedication

I dedicate these stories to my two children, Jimmy and Nancy, who have brought me much joy and who have encouraged me to keep writing even though I can no longer see well to write legibly.

To my very best friend, my sister, Evelyn, who participated in these experiences with me and has helped me rekindle these fond memories of our childhood.

To Doreen Roberts, who continued persuading me to write down my memories of the past, "the good old days".

Love, Granny

Preface

I was born in Columbia, Tennessee, Maury County, on March 27, 1916, the sixth of twelve children. My parents were very poor in material possessions but very loving, caring and rich in other ways.

My father's name was Gideon Blackburn Derryberry, Sr. and my mother's name was Nannie Fox Derryberry. They were hard working, God fearing people. They reared ten of twelve children they bore. They celebrated their sixtieth wedding anniversary on April 11, 1966, and all ten living children attended. This was the last time we were all together.

Most of the names in this book are relatives. I am listing my brothers and sisters by their first names only and in order of their birth: Mary, Cornelia, G.B., Jr., Frances, Evelyn, Alma (Author), William (Bill), Charles, Sarah, and Ruth,

My first husband, Teddy E. Johnson, died in 1959. Harvey B. Worthington, my second husband, died in 1984. Jimmy and and Nancy are my children. My grandchildren are: Ted, David, Cathy, Mark, Brian, Ben and Linda. I have nine great-grandchildren: Jessica, Cassady, Josh, Allison, Chance, Gavin, Colton, Megan and Kaylee.

Many times over the years I have told my children and grandchildren the experiences of the hard times, the fun and the lessons we learned from our poverty and from the love and Godly training our parents showed us. My children have urged me many times to write these stories down for them so these wonderful memories would not be lost as time goes on. They always delighted in hearing of these happenings and would ask me to tell them over and over. When my oldest grandson, Ted, was small and was visiting us, he would always say, "Granny, let's sit on the porch and tell me about the good old days." Doreen Roberts, my dear friend, asked me to write some of my memories for the church bulletin.

All of this inspired me to continue writing these stories. Due to my failing eyesight, I am being inspired and aided by my beloved daughter, Nancy, who decided she wanted to compile them into a book for others to enjoy and learn from. I hope that the reader of this book will feel even a little of the joy, love and fun in reading it as I had in living it and in writing my remembrances of times past.

Granny

Chapter 1

The Depression Days
Hardships and Blessings

Many have asked me what it was like living in the time of
the depression. It's an experience you almost have to live to believe. There were some good times and some bad. It seems the
poor families survived it better than the wealthy. Perhaps because it wasn't such a drastic change in their way of life.

I'll tell you of the bad things first.—Wearing second hand
clothes which were made over to fit or left too large for you.
Wearing shoes which have holes all the way through the soles
into which you put pieces of cardboard to help keep your feet
warm. Sometimes you tie pieces of heavy cloth around your
shoes for extra warmth, especially if you don't have socks.
Walking miles to school and sitting all day with wet feet; walking to town, to the store, or to church in the freezing cold or the
blazing sun. Sleeping three in a bed to keep warm. Making lye
soap and using it for everything from doing the laundry to
washing dishes and from baths to washing hair. (There wasn't
enough money to spend on soap.)

Finding a penny or picking cherries or strawberries for one
cent a quart and giving it to Dad to help buy food or coal. I remember the good feeling it gave me to know I was contributing
to help the family survive, sometimes not knowing where the
next meal was coming from but trusting all the same that it
would be there on the table.

Dressing and going to bed in a cold room, knowing you
would get up and dress in the morning in this same cold room
with no heat. Sitting around the fireplace studying by a kerosene lamp or shelling dried peas which were salvaged from the
garden before the frost came. Canning and preserving every edible thing during the summer. Saving everything—papers,
strings, cardboard boxes, bags. A piece of cardboard keeps a lot
of cold wind out of a broken window. Newspapers layered

between quilts adds warmth. Everything had a use.

Few parents could afford to give their daughters a large formal wedding. The weddings were small and simple, the cost was very meager compared to wedding expenses of today. The money was needed to survive and to set up your home. Usually the couple would ask another couple to stand up with them and the four would go to the preacher's house or to the Justice of the Peace for the wedding. But the love, sincerity and happiness was no less for this custom—maybe it was even greater because of it.

Your first home was a rented two room apartment, perhaps even sharing it with another couple, and buying very little furniture, just the absolute necessities. I remember the pride we took in paying $1.00 down and $1.00 each week until this furniture was paid for. Only then would we move to a three room apartment and purchase more furniture. We planned and grew together and seldom had to worry over having more debts than we could pay. However, occasionally if something came up that kept us from having the $1.00 payment one week, we would go to the dealer and tell him our plight and he allowed us to catch up the next week. We never ignored the missed payment therefore we were never refused credit nor did we get into arguments over indebtedness.

A depression means closed businesses and consequently people out of work. Men had to leave their families and hop trains going from state to state looking for work. The stock market crashed, banks failed having no federal insurance for their depositors' money. Thus, many people lost all their possessions. Many committed suicide, unable to bear their losses. This is just a sampling of the bad side of a depression.

Now you are probably wondering what possible good could there be among all these hardships. First, it brought people back to God. People began to depend more on God and less on their ability to be self-sufficient. You witnessed God keeping His promise to provide your daily needs. You saw friends, neighbors and even strangers caring for one another and sharing whatever they had. You saw people eating less in order to give to someone who had none. You saved any portion a child might leave on his plate for there would be another child who had none and would eat it.

Families and neighbors worked together harvesting crops,

building barns, repairing equipment, etc. You saw women sharing cooking, sewing, tending children, helping with the ill or with the women who were giving birth. All rejoiced together and sorrowed together. You saw children respecting their parents and teachers, and parents having time to sit down and listen to, advise and enjoy their children. You saw two families move into one house to share and conserve heat and food. You saw families taking in and caring for their elderly relatives.

Like the children of Israel in the Bible, people began turning back to God, going back to church and the church growing. You saw people gathering together for Bible studies and prayers and neighbors joining in.

People had time to appreciate the quietness and stillness of the night and to sit on the porch counting the stars and meditating on the great love of God. You could take a man at his word, knowing he would keep it. Trusting your fellow man and him trusting you.

You learned to be grateful for the bounty of God's blessings.

Chapter 2

Our House-Our Home

Our house sat in a newly developed part of Columbia, which at that time bordered on Duck River. This area was known as Riverside. Not many houses were in Riverside but it is thickly populated today. We played all over the area, gathering wild flowers in the spring and in the fall hiking in the wooded areas, picking up chestnuts, hickory nuts and walnuts. The bridge over the river was an old iron bridge that shook when a horse and buggy went over it, so much so that as children we were afraid it would fall. In the winter when we walked across the bridge the north wind was freezing cold. The river flooded often so the first street after crossing the bridge was about two city blocks away. This was the street our house was located on. Thus the back of our property bordered on Duck River. We had lots of rich river bottom on which to plant crops for much of our food.

Our house was a two story house with large rooms; two bedrooms upstairs, one downstairs, a parlor, dining room and kitchen, front porch, a large back porch and a long side porch. The smallest children always slept on one of the beds in the room with Mother and Dad and graduated to an upstairs room when the next baby arrived. With ten children, this was the arrangement for a long time. No one had a room all to themselves as so many children have today. We were only able to have the necessities in the bedrooms. Each bedroom had two double beds, and we slept two and sometimes three to a bed. There also was a dresser or a washstand and a trunk, in which we kept our clothes, but no other furniture.

Our furniture was rather crude then—but so much of it is found in antique stores today! The beds had either iron, brass or oak headboards. Our chairs were straight chairs with cane bottoms. Our dining room table was an old homemade one. In the kitchen was a large wood range, a pie safe and two homemade tables. On one table were buckets of water used for cooking. The other table was used for preparing food. At the end of this table was a flour barrel. Mother had to buy flour in a 100 pound bag. This was dumped into the flour barrel. She kept her bread trough, rolling pin, sifter and biscuit cutter in the barrel. Then she turned the dough board over the top of the barrel for a cover. I remember there were always good biscuits in the warmer of the stove. We knew there would be something in the oven to eat after school.

The floors were bare except for a linoleum in mother's bedroom and in the dining room. The house was kept spotless. At the end of every wash day the floors were scrubbed with the soapy water left from washing clothes and then thoroughly rinsed.

There was no indoor plumbing or electricity so that meant we had an outhouse, used kerosene lamps for lighting and fireplaces for heat.

Dad was short in stature but mighty in his faith and protection of his family. He was a good Christian man whom everyone respected and looked up to. He loved God and taught his children to love God also. He lived his life daily as a wonderful example for others. Dad was a song leader for gospel meetings and new congregations of the Church of Christ throughout the state of Tennessee. He worked at many different jobs, doing whatever manual labor he could find and did not owe a debt to anyone when he died. Dad's example of willingness to work taught us valuable lessons in working and paying our debts and not having others pay our way for us. He taught us to play together and work together.

Mother was a tall and stately woman with the face and disposition of an angel. I do believe she possessed almost every trait of the virtuous woman in proverbs 31. To know her was to love her. We obeyed Dad out of fear of punishment and respect of his authority as our father. We obeyed Mother because we wanted to please her and not disappoint her. She never raised her voice at us but spoke firmly when necessary. And believe me, there were many times when she would have been justified in yelling at us!

We wanted her affection and received it. She never said an unkind thing about anyone and would not permit us to either. I remember when we began to tell something she would say, "If you are going to tell something good, continue, if it is not good, it is better left unsaid." In addition to taking care of the daily household chores and a family of ten children, she often did sewing and quilting for others and took in laundry. She was always willing to care for those who were sick and needed help. She made all of our clothes. She was a much loved lady and gave us by her example an almost endless list of the kind of person we should be.

Our house, with all of its inconveniences and very little heat, became one of the warmest homes a child could grow up in. You see, there is a difference in a house and a home. A house is tangible—a home is intangible. A house is physical—a home is spiritual. A house is built by man—a home is built by God.

A house is costly—a home is priceless. A house is cold and unfriendly—a home is warm and filled with love. A house is filled with material things—a home is filled with respect, compassion, and care and concern for one another. Not everyone can afford a house—anyone can have a home. A house has parents who spend much time trying to buy bigger and better things for their children—a home has parents who are there for their children, to advise, comfort, to discipline and to teach them God's word. It requires money to build a house—it requires love and patience to build a home.

Mother and Dad made our house a home

Chapter 3
My Dad

He was only about five feet tall, but he was one of the tallest men I ever knew. He loved his family and never failed to let us know it. I will always remember how safe and secure I felt when Dad was around. He was a peaceful man, but he would fight quickly if needed in defense of his children.

Dad was a stern man in discipline and never wavered or compromised in his punishment when we disobeyed. Sometimes he would postpone a whipping two or three weeks, but we knew he would not forget it. That waiting time was worse than the whipping. About the time we thought he had forgotten, he'd say, "Let's get that whipping over with." I've wondered later in life if he did that to keep from punishing us in anger. Ephesians 6:4," And, father, do not provoke your children to anger; but bring them up in the discipline and instruction of the Lord."

We had so much fun with Dad. He played games, sang, had Bible studies with us, and helped us with our homework, although he did not have a high school education. All the kids in the neighborhood loved him, he invited them to play with us, too. He was known all over the county and state for his ability to lead singing. He learned new songs by the shaped notes and that's the way he taught it.

We used to start playing around at night after we went to bed and would begin laughing and giggling. Dad would call us down only twice. The third time he would say, "If I hear you again, I'm coming up there." By then we couldn't stop, it seemed to make everything funnier and make us laugh more. Then we'd hear him coming up the stairs two at a time. (Though it seemed like he came up in only two steps.) So you couldn't blame it on someone else and try to get away from a spanking. Then things got plenty quiet!

When we were dating, Dad was strick on our curfew. Ten

o'clock was bedtime. If the boys didn't leave by five minutes after ten, he would call, "Bedtime." If, in five minutes more they hadn't left, we would hear Dad's shoe hit the wall. (Our second notice!) In five more minutes the other shoe would hit the wall. (Our third notice!) By then the boys left in a hurry. They learned his tactics quickly and would always say, "Let's wait for the second shoe to hit."

Dad's shoes, although used as warning signals, were very remarkable. They would look very odd to most of the present generation. They were black and high top, laced up about half way. Just above the ankles there were little hooks on each side and the shoe strings crossed back and forth across the tongue to the top where they were tied. Usually there was a knot or two in the strings where they had been broken and tied back together. His shoes were well worn, sometimes re-soled and slightly run over at the heel. He wore the same pair every day, including Sunday, until they were no longer wearable or repairable. The only change was that on Sundays they were polished and shined like a new silver dollar. When Dad came home tired on a cold winter night, I loved to take off his shoes and bring in a pan of hot water by the fire and soak and rub his feet while listening to his sighs of comfort.

Dad was our pal, our protector, our disciplinarian, our friend, and we love and respected him for it.

Chapter 4

Making Something From Nothing

Mother was an identical twin and she also had twin brothers, Wilburn and Willie. Mother, whose name was Nannie, and her twin, named Fannie, dressed alike all their lives. If any of their children bought material for a dress, they bought enough for two. It delighted Mother and Aunt Fannie to have dresses alike. They fixed their hair alike, weighed the same most of the time and went shopping together to buy shoes and hats. Few people in town could tell them apart. Their voices even sounded a lot alike. Some of their grandchildren called them Grandmother and 'nother Grandmother. When they married, they had a double wedding and their husbands made them each a rolling pin, which was the custom on those days.

They each could take nothing and make

Aunt Fannie and Mother

something out of it. Both of them were blessed with many abilities. I remember their sewing and beautiful handwork. Boxes of outgrown clothes were given to us by relatives and neighbors. When Mother and Aunt Fannie finished ripping them apart, cutting them down, and remodeling them, it would made a dressmaker envious. Mother would make the boys' shirts from the tails of men's shirts which had the collar and cuffs worn. She made their pants from the legs of men's pants that were worn around the pockets and cuffs. She made dresses and coats for us girls. She usually added some fancy little trim and hand stitching on the collar to make it special.

The feed she bought for our cow came in one hundred pound cloth sacks. If she couldn't buy two sacks alike (which was the amount she needed for a dress) she made a trip to town and could always find a matching solid color piece of material to go with it. And like waving a magic wand, she would soon turn out one of her originals. She never used a pattern. We would show her a picture and she could copy it.

Mother had a knack for making us feel special when we put on a new dress she had made. She would say, "Oh my, you look so pretty." And even though it was originally a feed sack, we felt dressed up in it. As we thanked her for it, she replied, "Thank God for your pretty dress. All things are made by God." She gave praise and honor to Him.

She sometimes earned money by sewing for others in the neighborhood. All of this was done on a treadle Singer sewing machine.

There was a flour mill in our town named Blue Seal Flour Mill. Their logo was a big royal blue seal shaped just like a legal document seal. No amount of soaping and scrubbing completely removed that bright colored seal from the sacks. These were the days before bleach. Mother also bought the flour in one hundred pound sacks and she collected a lot of them. From these flour sacks she made all of our underwear (bloomers) and slips, they were so soft and white. What wasn't used for underwear was made into dish towels and these were what she taught us to embroider and make fancy stitching on.

Mother had a catchy little way to tell us we weren't sitting lady-like without embarrassing us. She would say, "Alma, your blue seal is showing. " I would very quickly sit up straight and tug at my dress. How we hated those blue seals!

Some of the sacks she would cut in half and iron on a pretty stamped design. Then she showed us how to make the various stitches. After that she taught us to hem them with the feather, blanket or some other stitch. She would say, " If you are going to use flour sacks to dry your dishes on, they might as well be pretty." As we got older she gave us some of them to put in our hope chest. They were so pretty I didn't even mind if the blue seal showed a little. After we went to work we continued to do this handwork on other linens. I have many beautiful framed pictures on my walls today that I would never have made had Mother not taken the time to teach us this almost non-existent art. She also taught us to knit, hemstitch, do drawn work and sewing. I so enjoyed the work that I never ceased doing it until I lost my sight. My sisters continue to make beautiful things.

One beautiful kind of handwork that mother did that I never accomplished was quilting. Aunt Fannie was always there to aid her with quilting also. Mother had a quilt frame that hung from the ceiling so she could pull it up out of the way when we were all home and the space was needed. Then it was lowered to just the correct height when she was ready to quilt again. She also quilted for other people. She received $1.00 for a plain quilt and $2.00-$2.50 for a fancy quilt. People charge one hundred dollars or more today for quilting.

Mother's only social life, besides going to church, was neighbors coming in to visit. They always pitched in and assisted her in whatever she was doing, quilting or canning. She never had time to stop and visit, that is unless there was sickness in the neighborhood, then she would go and offer her services sometimes returning with an armful of dirty clothes to wash and iron.

Mother lived to serve her family, her neighbors and God for 88 years.

Chapter 5

The Most Beautiful Doll

I remember my first and only doll. When we were very young, our Christmas gifts consisted of one piece of warm clothing, a bushel each of apples and oranges for the whole family, some nuts and hard candy, and one game we could all play together. There were ten living children and during the depression days I'm sure even this took much sacrificing.

Right in the middle of the ten were three of us girls with only 12 to 18 months difference in our ages. One Christmas, a local men's club chose to play Santa to us. We each received a doll and a doll buggy. We did nothing all day but push our dolls up and down the sidewalk. Frances received the doll with brown hair, dressed in bright yellow. Evelyn got the black-haired doll in blue and mine was a curly-haired blonde in a pretty pink dress. That was the most beautiful doll in all the world and I was the happiest little girl. Mother warned us not to leave our dolls around where the younger children could get them.

One day while I was upstairs, my youngest brother, Charles, was up there also but I didn't know it. I suddenly looked around just in time to see him holding my doll by the hair through the rails of the banister. I ran to grab it, reaching out just as he let go. I was too late. I don't know which was more broken...my doll's head or my heart. I cried for days. Mother consoled me that maybe someday she could get me another doll, but in my child's mind, I knew it could never be. That day never came; there were too many necessary things needed for the family. I picked up all the pieces and put them in a shoe box and kept them under my bed. I never knew what happened to that box. I imagine my mother's heart was as broken as mine because she couldn't afford to buy me another doll, so she probably threw the box away hoping I'd forget about it. My little brother put his arms around me and told me he loved me. That made me feel better and I realized it was my fault...not his.

Sometimes it is hard to put our grievances and hurts 'under the bed.' All too often, we bring our problems on ourselves and blame others. But even though I'm past seventy years old, I would still love to have a little blond-haired doll in a pretty pink dress.

Chapter 6

Surrey Rides

Riding in a surrey can be lots of fun...that is, if it isn't your only means of transportation and if the weather is agreeable for open air travel.

I remember our Sunday morning rides to worship in a surrey. We lived about ten miles from the church building. In the springtime it was lovely, we felt like we were floating on fresh air.

During the summer it was fine going to church, but hot and sticky going home on dusty roads in the middle of the day when we were hungry. Mother usually had a biscuit or tea cakes in a sack to tide us over.

But the surrey rides during the short days of the winter months were the most memorable ones of all. Our grandparents lived next door to the church building. Regardless of the weather, we made that ten mile trip every Sunday. I remember our regular Saturday night ritual. Take baths, lay out clothes for Sunday, get our lesson and polish our shoes. Mother packed a suitcase with fresh clothes for the youngest children. They were usually just wrapped in blankets and carried to my grandmother's house in their nightclothes and changed there. We put bricks in the ashes in the fireplace to heat during the night...and then early to bed. Sunday morning, we were up at dawn. There was always hot biscuits, butter and jelly for breakfast. We would dress while Dad hitched up the horse and surrey, wrapped the hot bricks in rags and put them on the floor of the surrey to keep us warm. We had a big lap blanket over us and usually were fairly comfortable. In fact, we were packed in so tight, we kept each other warm.

I remember the thrill of seeing Granny's house come into view. The aroma of coffee, hot bread and bacon as we walked into her house was mouth watering. I can almost smell it now! She always gave us something warm to eat while Mother dressed the smaller ones. Dad led singing and went right on to the church building as soon as he unhitched the horse and put the bricks in the fireplace to warm up for our trip back home.

Granny fed us our dinner before we started back. We had no lights on the surrey and the weather was uncertain so we could not stay for night services.

This was the one big event of the week and we all looked forword to it with joy.

I have often wondered how many mothers today would go to that much effort to get their children to Bible school or worship services.

I wonder...

Chapter 7

A Mother Hen Gathers
Her Chicks

My mother was a courageous and brave woman. I think there were only two things she ever feared. One was that her children would be hungry or cold and the other was storms. Dad assured her that God would supply our daily bread. In spite of her concern of where the next meal would come from, she never turned anyone away who asked for food. During those days many men were going from town to town seeking any kind of work so they could send money home to feed their children. They did not ask for a free handout; they asked to cut wood, repair the house, clean out the barn or repair fences— anything. We didn't have the work for them for we had plenty of hands to keep the work done. Nor did we have money to pay to have it done. Almost every day, as we sat down to eat, one or two such men would knock at our door. Mother always asked how long it had been since he had eaten. Usually it was two or three days. We then heard those (then) dreaded words, "We don't have much, but we will share what we have." She would bring a clean plate to the table and take a portion from each of our plates to feed the man. I'm afraid our hearts were not as big as hers because we would almost count the beans to make sure our portion was not reduced by more beans than the other one's. Beans, potatoes and cornbread was our usual dinner, plus butter and milk. Sometimes the pantry looked pretty bare, but before the next day, someone brought in something they couldn't use. We may have been a little reluctant at first to share our small portion, but as you watched the man consume his food with such hunger, you had to feel happy and know you had helped by sharing. I remember thinking, "This is some-body's daddy." Mother usually asked him about his family and some stories were pretty sad. We gave thanks that our daddy was home.

I remember we jokingly teased that our food was blessed twice. Dad gave thanks before we ate and, without fail, when Mother finished eating, she sat up straight and said, "Thank God for another good meal." Peter told the lame man who lay at the gate of the temple asking for alms, "...silver and gold have I none; but such as I have give I thee..." This was Mother. She was willing to give what she had. These times were stormy weather.

Mother simply could not take those thunder storms that came up in the night. I think at the first clap of thunder her feet hit the floor. At the second clap she was walking from window to window. At the third clap she was calling us (all of us) to come downstairs until the storm blew over. We sleepily obeyed and she sat us all around on her bed while Dad slept on and she continued walking from window to window. The older kids kept begging her to let them go back to bed, but she said if we blew away she wanted us to all be together! When I was small, I curled up at Dad's feet and went back to sleep because I knew Mother would catch me as I blew out the window past her! But as I grew older I joined the others in begging her to let us go back to bed. "Just a little longer," she'd say. To us it was the best kind of weather to sleep with the pitter-patter of rain on a tin roof.

Can you imagine all those kids sitting around on your bed at midnight? Can you imagine thinking you could hold on to ten kids if the house did blow away? Can you imagine a father sleeping through all that—or even putting up with it? Can you imagine so great a Mother's love.

"...As a Mother hen gathers her chickens under her wings...", that's how it seemed to me.

Through a child's eyes...
Katie, the little girl next door, heard Nancy reading part of this story as she typed it. After which she was asked to bring the story over to me. When she came in she said, "I want to read you a story, Great-Granny." Looking earnestly and somberly at the paper, this is the way she read it:

"The mother was afraid of the storm. She made all the children come downstairs and sit on her bed. The daddy was asleep on the bed. the little girl laid by her daddy's feet and went to sleep. She was not afraid because she knew her mother would catch her when she flew out the window. But the mother was afraid because she didn't want her children to blow away. Then the wind blew hard and the children were all holding hands and the children blew out the window and the mother held on to them and they all flew across the sky." "Wouldn't that be fun, Great-Granny?"

Now I know that what was reality to me as a small girl sleeping at her daddy's feet is the way a small child really sees it and the faith she has in her mother to protect her is very real.

Chapter 8

Our Toys

As I sat and watched some children playing with their battery-operated and high tech toys one day, I remembered about the homemade and make shift toys we used to play with. One really had to use his imagination and ingenuity to come up with some of our inventions. We seldom had a store bought toy. The boys usually had some marbles (most of which they found) and a ball. Sometimes they made a ball of old socks rolled and sewn together. If they were ever lucky enough to find an old skate or wheel of any kind, they brought it home and worked unceasingly until they constructed a scooter or a push wheel to run up and down the walk with. I remember one time they found enough wheels to make a wagon. We were the richest kids in the neighborhood riding in that wagon!

My nephew, Franklin, riding a scooter made by my brother Charles

At Christmas we usually got a deck of Rook or Flinch cards. We loved getting the cards because we knew Dad would play with us at night. In fact, we played with them so much they didn't last long. We saved all our tablet black and white cardboard we came across until we had enough to make us another deck. They were mean to shuffle! We just put them on the floor and stirred them round and round. Cardboard was a precious commodity in our house. It was used for many things from making toys to lining our shoes when the soles wore out.

The girls played mostly with paper dolls. We each had our own box of families. Again, we used cardboard and made our furniture. Most of our paper dolls were cut out of a Sears or Spiegel catalogue. Occasionally a neighbor gave us a magazine, The Pictorial Review. It always had a pretty paper doll with a complete wardrobe in it. This doll was always called Dolly Dimple. We were in heaven when we got one of those for our collection.

We usually had an old rope to jump and needed nothing but a rock or piece of glass to play hopscotch.

The most amazing thing was G.B. and Bill making a kite in the spring. I do believe they were professionals! They saved all the strong string they could get their hands on. One of them whittled out a good smooth cedar stick and the string was tied together very tight and rolled on the stick a certain way. Come spring and the kite making would begin! They would cut and smooth three long thin sticks which were notched on both ends and cross and tie them together. Then run a string all around the tied stick form. Then G.B. made his paste of flour and water. He spread newspaper out on the floor, lay the sticks on the paper and begin to cut and shape the newspaper around the stick and string. He folded it over the string and pasted it in place.

Meanwhile, Bill was tearing old rags into strips and tying them together for the tail, which had to be just the right weight and length to make the kite fly.

They tied the end of the twine to the center of the sticks. Then we'd all head to the garden to see if the kite would fly. They always flew it in the garden for there were no trees there and they had a long place to run to get it up. Occasionally it dipped and had to be brought down to shorten or lengthen the tail.

Once they got in in the air, we all laid down and watched it float higher and higher. We used to imagine we were flying on the kite and would tell all the things we could see. Sometimes it would go so high that we'd pretend we could see into Heaven and name the things we could see there.

Sometimes the string would break and the kite kept going higher and higher until we could see it no longer and we wondered how high and how far it went.

The next day it was back to the drawing board. Another kite was in the making as the boys discussed what went wrong and what they could do to keep from loosing this kite.

We just sat around waiting and wishing they would talk less and work faster so we could fly a kite.

I wonder today when I hear people murmur, "There is nothing to do" or "I have nothing to wear" or "I don't have money to repair or buy _____", how they would have survived in those days. Where is their imagination—to fly a kite and be content to see the wonder of God's creation? Where is their ingenuity—to entertain themselves and their children? The most self-satisfaction can be obtained by taking *nothing* and making *something* out of it. Being poor is not a bed of roses, but if we are taught to use it to our best advantage and be content and happy with what the Lord has given us, it is a rewarding experience.

We can grow in this ability also. We are taught to be content. Philippians 4:11—Paul said, "...I have learned to be content in whatever circumstances I am." We are taught to use our talents. Matthew 25: 14-19 — The man with the five talents and the man with the two talents used what had been given them and gained more and their master was pleased with them. Can't we be like Paul and the men with five talents and two talents?

Sometimes I think our life is like flying a kite. Everything goes well and we fly along in the breeze happy and content. Then the 'winds' of life get rough and our 'string' breaks and we do a nose dive right down to rock bottom. These are the times we need to lie down on the grass and look up to God's heavens and beautiful creations and see what we did wrong. Then start all over again, count our many blessings, thank God for them and try to a little harder to make a better 'kite' this time.

Chapter 9

Children of Yester-Year

Children should be seen—not heard! I'm sure this old rule is much outdated today. However, it was very much enforced seventy years ago. We had to wait our turn to speak, especially if older people were talking. "Let them finish and then speak", we would hear. Even if we got into an argument we were given an opportunity to speak our argument without interruption. We could not both talk at the same time. Then if it seemed foolish, Mother made us put our arms around each other and kiss and make up. Sometimes this was difficult to do and one of us wouldn't hug or kiss—Mother would make us do it over. She would say, "This is one of those things that is worth doing and you will do it until you do it right." And her ever watchful eye saw that it was done according to rule. Usually one of us would say something silly like, "Do it right this time, so I won't have to kiss you again!" Always, we would end up laughing and the fussing had ended. We still are the "kissingest' family you ever hope to see. Ask anyone who knows us.

Eight of the Derryberry children, about 1921. Mary, Cornelia, Charles, G.B., Alma, Evelyn, Frances and William

Children were usually given health preventive checks at
school by the Health Department. There were not so many pre-
ventative vaccinations as there are today. In fact, I remember
when the first vaccine for small pox was given. It was very
painful and made a huge sore and left a large scar on your arm.

I was never sick or got to miss school like the other kids.
When the others began getting sick from their vaccination, I remember thinking, "Now I'll get to stay in bed all day too." Well,
my vaccination just would not turn red and everyone else's began to swell. I scratched and pinched mine to try to make it get
sore. Nothing happened! A few weeks later the nurse came
back to school and vaccinated me again. "Ah-ha," I thought,
"Now I'll get to stay home and the others will have to go to
school." Just my luck! That one didn't take either! I guess I'm
permanently immunized because the vaccination never took on
me. I remember some of the girls who wore swim suits had
their vaccination on their upper leg instead of their arm so the
scar would not show when they wore their swim suits. The legs
of the swim suits were longer than they are today. I'm afraid
that would be to no avail today. In fact it is difficult to decide
where it could be put in order for the scar to be unseen when in
swim suits.

Another very obvious difference in present day children and
those of yester-year: Out of respect for their elders, children always waited for the older people to help their plates and eat
first. I remember we always had two tables full for lunch on
Sunday. Some of us always invited friends and there were
times Mother invited some of her or Dads family. Twelve could
be seated comfortably at one time. Mother sat the twelve oldest
ones at the first table. We kids went outside and played until
they finished eating. I was number six in the family line so I always had to wait to eat at the second table. We would get so
hungry and afraid they were going to eat it all up, sometimes
we would send one of the smaller children to peek in the window and see if they were almost through or if there was any
food left. After they finished the dishes had to be washed and
dried before the second table could be served because we didn't
have an abundance of dishes. By the time we sat down every
bowl was full again! I never knew how Mother could prepare so
much food and go to church with so many kids.

We jokingly said she must have been the woman in I Kings

17:10-16 who only had a handful of meal and a little oil in a cruse that she was going to use and she and her son eat, then die. But she did as Elijah told her, made it and fed Elijah, then she and her son ate and continued to eat for many days from the little she had. "And the barrel of meal wasted not, nether did the cruse of oil fail, according to the word of the LORD, which he spake by Elijah.

Chapter 10

Mother's Love And The Baby

She was a pretty young woman who lived next door to us when I was about ten years old. Her baby was about one month old when we noticed she cried a lot. People didn't have air conditioners then and windows were always open so we couldn't help but notice how the baby cried.

We had a baby sister about five months old, named Ruth, who never cried. We called her "Baby Ruth" as it was about the time the Baby Ruth candy bar was so famous.

One day the young mother came to our house crying. She told Mother she had just returned from the doctor and he told her that her baby was dying. Something was wrong with it digestive tract and the baby could not digest any kind of milk or formula they had tried. Medications did not help. The baby looked so fragile and tiny. The doctor told her their last hope was to find a mother who nursed her own baby who would be willing to nurse the sick baby too. He said the natural milk of a mother might be digestible.

The woman said she didn't have the heart to ask any mother to deprive their own child in order to save hers. Mother said, "You didn't ask me—just give me the baby." Mother took the baby, nursed and rocked her as she stroked her head and rubbed her tiny little hands, talking softly to her all the while, just as I had seen her do to her own babies. I knew as I watched her, that she had often times showed that tender kind of love to me and it made me so proud of her. But I remember thinking, "Maybe our Baby Ruth will get hungry."

The baby's mother must have read my thoughts as she said, "But your baby may get hungry now." Mother simply said, "God has fed my other nine children. He will feed mine and yours too."

The baby fell asleep and the woman kissed my mother and went home. She continued to bring her baby back at feeding time, day and night, until the baby was able to digest other food and be weaned from a mother's milk.

The baby lived to be a happy, healthy little girl and a playmate for Baby Ruth and we felt we had another little sister. Mother gave us a great lesson in sharing and trusting in God for our every need.

Matthew 6: 25-26, "For this reason I say to you, do not be anxious for your life, as to what you shall eat, or what you shall drink; nor for your body, as to what you shall put on. Is not life more than food, and the body than clothing? Look at the birds of the air, that they do not sow, neither do they reap, nor gather into barns, and yet your heavenly Father feeds them. Are you not worth much more than they?"

Chapter 11

The Happy Singing Family

I have many fond memories of my family that I will share with you. Six of us are still living and when we get together, there is always lots of laughs, hugs, kisses, games and practical jokes.

We were blessed with God loving parents who taught us the Word of God. They sang with us in everything we did...shelling peas, doing dishes, picking up potatoes, picking tomatoes and just sitting on the front porch on a hot summer night. We knew most of the hymns by heart. We had two complete quartets in our family. As soon as we finished one hymn, someone would start another. Our neighbors called us the happy singing family and often would come over and join in.

Mother, Dad, Grandpa Derryberry and eight of us children

I remember one night, after midnight, Dad came upstairs and awakened us. The elderly mother of the man next door was dying and she wanted us to stand outside her window and sing until she passed on. We were young and horrified. I was scared! This was a new experience. Dad assured us it would be what Jesus would want us to do. It would be comforting to a dying woman and her family.

We finished singing her favorite, The Old Rugged Cross, and as we began Nearer My God To Thee, the man came out to tell us she was dead and to thank us for helping her die peacefully. We all went back to bed but not until Dad prayed that peace and comfort be with the family.

I remember it was hard to get back to sleep. We were all sniffing and blowing noses. We didn't say a thing to each other but it was a great lesson in compassion for us all.

Later, this family began attending church. I do not know what happened to them, as they moved away and we lost touch with them.

I do not understand why some people today refuse to let their children be around sickness, old people or death. How can one teach a child to feel sympathy or compassion for others if they haven't experienced some of it? How can you teach them to trust in the Lord for peace and comfort?

I thank God every day for my godly parents and c hristian home. I hope I have instilled these same lessons in my children and grandchildren.

What kind of memories will your children have of you???

Chapter 12

Our Cellar

Before the days of refrigeration storing and preserving foods for the winter months and the year until the next crop season was much more difficult than it is today. There were few stores and they were quite scattered. It was impossible to run by the store every day for milk or bread as we do. So we had to have a supply of food stored up and on hand for use as we needed it. There were not big supermarkets—just little country stores. It was a treat for us to go there because the owner would let us select one penny piece of candy. We would usually choose a jaw breaker or an all-day sucker because they would last longer!

From early spring until frost Mother was canning and storing food in the cellar. She canned all of her vegetables in 1/2 gallon jars; fruit and preserves in quart jars; and jelly in pint jars. These quantities supplied her family best, since there were so many of us, and it didn't take so many jar tops. Onions and hot peppers were dried and tied together and hung on a rafter in the cellar. Potatoes, turnips, and rutabagas were spread out on cardboard on the ground of the cellar. Sweet potatoes were usually put in a deep hold and covered with dirt to keep them from spoiling.

But that's not all the cellar was used for. Our cellar was one happy place to play in for us kids. It was just a big dug out place underneath the kitchen with a dirt floor and dirt walls. It even had dirt steps going into it. It was as big as the kitchen and dining room above. It had a sloped entrance over the steps which had a hinged wooden door to cover it. We used to have great fun sliding down the door. We finally wore that door out—and the seat of our pants too! Then we started sliding down the steps and almost wore them out, but Mother needed the steps to get into the cellar so we stopped.

Without the door we found another way to use the entrance. We played church in front of it and the cellar was our

baptistry. G.B. did the preaching and Bill or Charles led singing. We set up boxes outside the door for seats and the Lord's
Supper. We had two or three baptisms every day, but—our con-
gregation got no larger! Dad had lots of song books he had been
given over the years, so he let us use some of his oldest ones. I
still have some of these old books.

I guess it shouldn't be surprising that we played church and
our cellar turned into a baptistry. We had no radios, bicycles, or
toys (expect those our ingenious brothers constructed out of
practically nothing), our imaginations entertained us. Church
and going to school was our entire social life. Eventually one
brother became a preacher and I guess we all taught Bible
classes.

Perhaps today's children should have cellars and play
church to use their imagination instead of so much television
and video games to occupy their time. I Wonder— — —?

Chapter 13

Sweeping The Floor

The old adage, "If you want something done right, do it yourself." didn't hold true at our house. Mother's philosophy was, "If you don't do it right the first time, you keep on doing it until you *do it right.*"

We always had certain chores to do all morning, but as soon as the dishes were put away after lunch and the floors were swept, the afternoon was ours. Then we hit the yard and all the neighborhood kids gathered.

Always, Frances washed the dishes, Evelyn dried and put them away and I had to sweep the dining room and kitchen floors. The sweeping had to be done after the other chores, so consequently, I was the last to get out and play. Mother always inspected our work to make sure we did it correctly. One day the kitchen didn't look very dirty to me, so I hurriedly swept the dining room very thoroughly, hoping Mother would only look at it, and was out of there—ready to play. It wasn't long before I heard Mother call me and I knew why. So I hurriedly swept the middle of the kitchen floor. Frankly, I was a little mad that she had called me in. I had not much more than joined the kids than I heard her call me again, more sternly this time. She said, "You can sweep the kitchen right this time or you can stay in here all afternoon. It's your choice." I was mad by now and I began sweeping like a whirlwind. I moved everything in that kitchen but the stove. I probably would have moved it if I could. It was a wood range so I took out the ashes and swept all the dust and trash off the stove. Then I picked up the wood box, dumped the wood on the floor, swept under the box, and picked up each stick of wood and hit it against the floor to knock off trash, then put it back in the box. I didn't leave one speck of trash in that kitchen. Then I called Mother to come and inspect. (I wanted to say, "Does this suit you?" But I knew better!)

I'll always remember her sweet reply, "It is a very good job.

Thank you. If you had done it right the first time, you would
have been playing by now and saved us both time and trouble."

I never half-did a job again. That was an invaluable lesson
to me. In every job I ever held I was commended for doing a job
right. That is part of redeeming the time.

Mother always gave us three chances to do a job right—
then the punishment! We have only one chance (one lifetime) to
live our lives right—then the punishment or reward! Think
about it! Parents have the right and are obligated to teach their
children to respect other peoples' property, to work and do a job
right, honestly, and to the best of their ability.

Chapter 14

Electricity — Let Your Light Shine!

The news of ice storms in the northeast and people being without electricity for a week, bring back many memories to me. One week without electricity! How accustomed we get to the luxuries of life. Did you ever wonder what it would be like to live all the time without electricity? We did just that until I was about twelve years old. I imagine only a few today know what it is like to live for a long time without electricity.

We had a kerosene lamp that hung on the wall in our kitchen. We had two other lamps that were carried from room to room as needed. Mother cooked on a wood range, which sufficiently heated the dining room long enough for us to eat. We knew not to be late when we were called to eat unless we wanted to eat in the dark and the cold, because the lamp had to be moved to another room and the kitchen cleaned before the fire went out. We bought the wood we burned so we had to use it sparingly.

Our parents' bedroom was where we all assembled after supper to do our homework and have our Bible study. There was a fireplace in their bedroom which was our only other source of heat except a fireplace in the parlor which was used only for company. Our chairs were placed in a semi-circle around the fireplace and the lamp was placed on the mantle. In that way we all were able to use the same light to do our work. We did our homework on our lap. Dad was always there to help us if we needed it.

When we finished studying, we ran upstairs, undressed in the cold and went to bed. When it was really cold, Evelyn and I would hop in the bed and undress underneath the covers. Our beds had cotton mattresses and springs which had to have wooden slats underneath the springs for support. I remember how we would often bounce up and down to knock out some of the slats so we could have a little more sagging in the middle of the bed. Then we would cuddle up in the hole in the middle of the bed and get warm quicker. We had no heat upstairs and often in the morning we would grab our clothes and get back under the covers and dress. We slept with so many quilts on the bed to keep warm we could hardly move. When one of us wanted to turn over to get our back warm, we would wake the other one up and both of us turn over. I don't know if the others did this or not, but Evelyn and I did everything together and just knew how each other thought.

I remember those wonderful mornings when the weather was extremely cold, Mother brought a large platter of hot biscuits and gravy or biscuits and butter and jelly into their bedroom and let us eat around the fireplace so we could be nice and warm when we left to walk the two and one-half miles to school. At that time school buses did not pick up children who lived within the city limits. Walking was our only means of transportation. We really didn't mind it so much, we never knew any difference.

The love and concern of our parents, getting up in the cold to have the room warm for us and giving us a good warm breakfast, warmed our hearts and souls. We knew they cared for us.

On the cold winter nights that we didn't have to study, we always had things to do. Our favorite activity was singing. We also played games, popped corn and cracked nuts.

I guess the greatest impression Dad made on my memory was his repeated statement, "I am not a wealthy man and probably will never be, but I am the richest man in the world because I have you children." He said, "The only thing I can leave you is our good name and the light of God's Word. You can keep the name good and pass both on to your children or you can bring shame on the name and God's light will go out. It is my prayer that you will keep it shining." This is the greatest gift and inheritance Dad could possibly have given us.

Matthew 5: 16, "Let your light shine before men in such a way that they may see your good works, and glorify your Father who is in heaven." Dad believed and lived this and Proverbs 22: 1-2, "A good name is to be more desired than great riches, Favor is better than silver and gold. The rich and the poor have a common bond, the LORD is the maker of them all."

Chapter 15

The Ice Wagon

It was fun on a hot day to follow the ice wagon to get the small chipped-off pieces of ice to eat and get cool. The man selling the ice didn't care, the small pieces would have melted and been wasted anyway. The 100 pound blocks of ice were stacked in the front of his horse drawn wagon and covered with a big canvas. He would pull one large block to the back of the wagon and chip it into two 50 pound blocks. Each of those was chipped into 25 pound blocks, depending on the amount of ice the customer wanted. The ice man, as he was called, traveled from house to house with his horse drawn ice wagon delivering ice to those who ordered it. This was the only way we had of keeping food cool.

The first thing each morning someone in each house hung out their ice card indicating how much ice they wanted the ice man to leave. The cards were about 12 inches square. There was a hole in each corner and the numbers 25, 50, 75 and 100 in respective corners. The cards were hung so that the number at the top indicated the quantity of ice you wanted. If you didn't need ice that day, you turned the ice card around and hung it backwards. Ice tongs were used to bring ice to the back door and it was placed in your ice box.

Our ice box held 100 pounds of ice. The ice was placed in the top part so there was little room left for food. It was necessary to keep a pan underneath the ice box to catch the water as the ice melted. This pan had to be emptied several times during the day or it would overflow on the floor.

Almost every Sunday Mother bought an extra piece of ice and made a freezer of ice cream for dinner. She mixed it up and one of us was designated to turn the crank. Remember, NO ELECTRICITY! The reward was great. Whoever turned the crank had the privilege of licking the dasher. Man, you haven't lived if you haven't licked the dasher of homemade ice cream! Mother removed the dasher then packed the cream firmly in ice and covered it tightly before we went to church. No one was late to dinner for sure on those days.

We didn't have to worry too much about preserving left overs. There simply were no left overs in our house. The first time I heard a teacher imploring the children at school to eat all their food so they could be a member of the clean plate club, I had to wonder if she had been snooping around our house. This, of course, happened when my children were going to school—not me!

These old ice boxes are rare today, but are expensive in antique shops. Isn't it odd that we threw away these old treasures for modern electrical appliances? Little did we know!

Chapter 16

All About The Outhouse!

Don't you hate standing in line? We must stand in line at the check-out counters, at restaurants, at the bank, at theaters, and sports activities. But did you ever have to stand in line on a cold winter morning in front of an outhouse? Inside where it's warm is different. But, OUTSIDE??

Our outhouse was slightly different from most I had seen. Ours had three holes. With twelve people using it there were times when the females shared their privacy and the males shared theirs. The door was at one end of the front so the small hole for the smallest children was directly in front of the door. The other two holes were for adults. There were cracks in the walls where the boards did not fit snugly together. The back end was not enclosed down low and I do declare the coldest wind, without fail, always came from that direction. There was a box in the far corner that held old newspapers and always a Sears-Roebuck catalog, if possible. It was much softer, except the colored pages, and we always liked to get it until you picked it up and some "jerk" had left only the colored pages. They were so slick, someone must have greased them! Every once in a while we had to go to the neighbor's house and ask if they had any old newspapers or catalogues. We couldn't afford to subscribe to a paper or magazine and this was our only tissue. It wasn't too bad though, because it offered us reading material also. A luxury, I suppose, for the outhouse!

I imagine we put on quite a show for our neighbors. Our outhouse was a good distance from our house, down in the edge of our garden. We had to go through a swinging squeaking gate to get into the garden. The outhouse could be seen from the windows of the neighbors on each side of us.

No matter how early you ran to go, the line had already formed. I do believe Dad camped out overnight because he was always there when we went down the first thing in the morning. This was an advantage to our brothers because they could walk right past us girls and go in and share with Dad. That made us stand there twisting and turning and jumping up and down and crossing our legs longer and longer! Then you would hear the gate squeaking again and look up, "Oh, no." One of the little ones running down the pathway right past you and straight in, no matter who was in there. They would invariably run out and not close the door securely and the wind would whip it open and whoever was sitting there was exposed to the "world" and shouting, "Somebody close that door." Sometimes, if Dad wasn't inside, we girls wouldn't close the door in our effort to make the boys hurry out. This was our way of getting even with them for getting ahead in the line.

We stood there and watched our neighbor go in and out quickly, one by one, and wished we had that luxury. And to think their outhouse had only one hole. WOW! What luck!!!

Anytime one of us had to go after dark, Mother always made another one go with her. One night after it had rained all day, Evelyn got the urge and Mother told me to go with her. I went in first and took the hole which was farthest from the door and left her the middle one. Suddenly, I heard Evelyn give out this blood curdling yell and before I knew what had happened, she was going through the garden gate like a streak of lightning! I was PETRIFIED! I remember thinking someone was in there and if I sat real still, they wouldn't know I was there and would leave. As I sat motionless, I could see the light from a flashlight coming out our back door. It was Dad—calling me as he "flew" down that pathway. Then I knew I was safe. He came in and looked around—nothing! Then he flashed the light down in a hole and there was the ghost—an old hen, soaking wet from the rain. Her wet feathers had raked across Evelyn's bottom and scared the daylights out of her—me too! We never had another night like that in the outhouse again.

I guess there are two morals to this story:
1. If you have an outhouse, don't take a laxative on a cold rainy day.
2. No job is complete until the paper work is done!

And speaking of bathroom chores...One of my grandchildren asked me, "Well, Granny, if you didn't have a bathroom, how did you take a bath?"

For sure, we didn't go dirty. In summer we drew a wash tub full of water early in the day and sat it out in the sun all day.

About dark we moved it in on the back porch. Mother put the smallest ones in first, I guess she thought they were less dirty. Then one by one, according to age, we each bathed—in the same water—or we could use cold water if we preferred to empty the tub and draw more water. Usually we preferred the warm used water.

Baths were different in the winter. After supper Mother would keep the wood range stove going and keep water on the stove. We took turns with a wash pan full of water and bathed our bodies in sections. Mother always said, "Start at the top and bathe down as far as possible. Then start at the feet and bathe up as far as possible. Then bathe possible."—This story has always gotten a laugh from my grandchildren and a "You're kidding?!"

Bathing got better when we got city water. G.B. piped water into the smoke house and installed a shower. We bathed there in the summertime. But when winter came, we still preferred the wash pan by the stove. But the ear and neck inspection never ceased.

As disgusting as it may sound, we played games down on the path going to the outhouse. There were flower bushes on the side of the path and we would pretend the path was our stage and the bushes the audience, the outhouse was our dressing room. We would pretend to put on a great performance on the "stage", singing at the top of our lungs and run back and forth to the outhouse pretending to change costumes. I've often wondered since what the neighbors must have thought about all the commotion going on around the outhouse. We had great imaginations when it came to finding things to play!

Chapter 17

Water, A Gift From God

How easy it is to get water today. We simply turn a spigot and there it is...hot, cold or warm. This was not so in the days gone by.

We read much in the Bible about wells—Rachel drawing water from a well for Jacob's camels, the many wells Jacob dug, Jesus talking to the woman by the well. These wells were dug deep through rocks until a stream of water was struck. The water was pulled up in buckets and poured into containers. A lot of effort went into getting water, which is very necessary for survival.

In early American history, the people settled near springs of water which were usually in the mountain side or hill. They built a small house, which was called a spring house, over the spring to protect it from animals and keep the water clean. The water was very cold so they would keep their milk, butter and other perishable food in a container and set it in the cold water. Sometimes in the summer they would put a big watermelon in the water to get cold. Of course it meant a trip to the spring house every time they needed food or water. Water was brought to the house in buckets.

We had neither a spring nor a well. Our water came from a cistern which was on a raised platform at the end of a big screened back porch. A cistern was installed over a deep walled up hole in the ground. Whenever it rained, the gutters were focused into a rain barrel outside so that the first water washed the dust off the roof into the barrel. From this barrel water was used for watering the animals, chickens, flowers and washing clothes. When the roof was clean, the gutters were rearranged so the clean water would run into the cistern. This was used for cooking, drinking and bathing. Not a drop was wasted. Water was never taken for granted as it is today. I do not remember our cistern ever going dry, but it sometimes got pretty low.

Whenever the water was low, Dad would turn the top back

and he or my oldest brother would go down into the cistern and clean it out. That was the deepest, blackest hole I have ever looked into. It looked scary and I used to dream of falling into it, but I never did!

Outside the cistern top was a handle attached to a big sprocket on the inside of which was a long chain. Cups were spaced about six inches apart on the chain. As you turned the handle, the sprocket would turn and lower the cups into the water. As the cups came back up, they were filled with water and brought to the top and emptied into a spout which emptied into a container underneath it. It took a lot of turning to fill a bucket of water. With a cistern, one is totally dependent on rain water. So, like Elijah, we often prayed for rain.

That old platform around our cistern was used for a lot of things. It was an excellent stage when we wanted to put on a show. We played with our paper dolls on it. I remember when I was too small to stand on the floor to churn butter, Mother placed the churn beside the platform and I stood on the platform so I would be tall enough to push the dasher up and down to make the butter (a tiring and despised chore with very good results). We sat on the platform and peeled potatoes and shucked corn for Mother, or washed her fruit jars in a big tub on her canning days.

Water is a necessary commodity to the physical life of every living thing and person. There was a sulphur springs about seven miles from our town. There were always people there drinking sulphur water for their health. Some bottled the water and carried it home with them. The smell of it was enough for me! Cups were always there for visitors.

I remember, when walking through the woods, playing on a farm, or traveling down a dusty road, seeing a cool springs under a tree or water trickling down a rocky hill and settling in a little clear pool at the bottom. There would usually be a tin or aluminum cup hanging somewhere near by. Travelers would stop and get a refreshing cool drink from the spring water with the cup. It was often referred to as the travelers cup. I remember Dad making such stops with all of us children in the wagon or surrey on the way to or from church or town.

This brings to mind two cups and saucers that were very special to me. One was a large china cup but the saucer did not match. It belonged to my grandfather and he would not drink his coffee from any other cup. He always stirred in the cream and sugar and then would pour some of the coffee into his saucer to cool and sip it from the saucer. I never understood how he raised that saucer to his mouth without spilling the coffee.

The other cup and saucer was a tiny china cup and saucer which I imagine came from a child's tea set. Nancy was about four years old and we had carried her to her first auction sale with us. She watched and listened to the buyers bidding. When they held up the little cup and saucer, she yelled, "$1.00." The auctioneer looked at me and smiled. I nodded yes, thinking someone would bid higher. But no one did, so she made her first purchase at the auction. After the sale, several people told me they had wanted the cup and saucer but they would not bid against her. I suppose she still has the cup and saucer. I know she still goes to auctions and yard sales and still can't resist bidding. Her motto at yard sales is. "I look as I walk, I speak when I see it; if I don't, it's gone."

We often forget water is a precious gift from God when it is so plentiful and so easy to obtain today.

Chapter 18

An Allowance

In their effort to get an increase in their allowance, one of my grandchildren asked me, "How much allowance did you get when you were growing up, Granny?" I said, "Honey, you don't want to know. I didn't even know the meaning of the word then." "Well, how did you get your spending money?" I began to ponder this question—the quantity was so small. Sometimes we found a penny. Sometimes someone would give us a penny. Evelyn and I would hide our pennies underneath the rug in the parlor until we accumulated a dime. The other kids would immediately spend theirs on a jaw breaker or an all day sucker. After Evelyn and I had a dime, we went to the corner grocery store and bought one big dill pickle for 5 cents and asked the man to cut it in half. Then we picked out five cookies at 1 cents each. They had big tin boxes with glass windows so you could see and choose the cookie you wanted. Then we walked very slowly back home, eating as we walked, the cookies and pickle together. We wanted to make sure it was all consumed so we wouldn't have to divide it. After all, we reasoned, the others had enjoyed their treats that they bought with their money.

Mary would sometimes give us a nickel to do special things for her. She was working then and I imagine this was her way of helping us along. In the summer she had prickly heat extremely bad on her back. I always had long nails and she would give me a nickel to scratch her back until she could go to sleep. Remember, there was no air condition or fans at that time.

One summer Mother was pretty sick with one boil after another underneath her arms. She had to lay with her arms raised to have any comfort. Dad got a good old colored couple to help us out with washing and ironing. We called them Aunt Hattie and Uncle Bill. Aunt Hattie stayed with us for a week or two. She was really partial to me and would always make the others do more chores than I had to do. After she quit staying at the house she carried our clothes to her house to wash and iron until Mother was well. She and uncle Bill always brought the clothes home on Saturday, driving a horse and buggy. When I'd see them coming, I always made two glasses of ice water and carried them a drink to the buggy. Uncle Bill always gave me a nickel. One day Evelyn saw them first, so she carried the water. Aunt Hattie told her that was my job and gave me the nickel anyway. The money went under the rug (our hiding place) for Evelyn and I to spend together, so it really didn't matter.

I guess our strangest way of getting money not many would do. Baby Ruth was still in diapers and she was a cute baby and just about every one was constantly giving her a penny. She immediately put them in her mouth. Evelyn and I watched and eventually she would swallow the penny. The next day, we'd volunteer to wash the diapers and retrieve the penny! We'd wash it off very well and head to the parlor, raise the rug and count our pennies to see when we could go to the store again. As strange as it must have seemed to Mother, she never questioned our willingness to wash Baby Ruth's dirty diapers. We told no one our secret—for fear they'd try to take over our ingenious way of getting money!

I was once shopping with Nancy in the mall. Three boys in their teens were approaching us. One dropped a coin, looked down, saw it was a penny and then kept going without picking it up. As I came to it, I bent down and picked it up. Nancy exclaimed, "Mother." I said, "If he doesn't want it, I'll take it and put it under the carpet." Now, she picks them up too. We were taught, "If you take care of the pennies, the dollars will take care of themselves."

Chapter 19

A Trip With My Dad

Years ago few people had means of transportation. Products were mostly sold by door to door salesmen. Then on a regular schedule, the manufacturer would send a repairman to call on the buyer for servicing and any repairs the equipment might need. Dad used to work as a repairman for the Singer Sewing Machine Company. The sewing machines were the old treadle type—before the electric machine. The company furnished him with an old Model T-Ford to travel his route for repairs. In rainy or cold weather Dad had to put up curtains for protections for there were no windows and of course, no heater or air condition. He never had to worry about a speeding ticket!

I remember one day he was going to a little town about twenty miles from our house. Mother's twin sister, Aunt Fannie, lived there and he was planning to service her sewing machine. I asked to go spend the day with her. I will never forget that long, slow trip. It was a warm breezy day. With the breeze blowing in my face, I got so sleepy. I could hear the tires playing The Old Rugged Cross over and over. I asked Dad if he could hear music. He said, "No." I said, "Listen, it's coming from the wheels." So I began humming the song so Dad could hear it too. Dad began singing it with me. "Sure is," he said. "I didn't notice it." After a while he said, "Listen, it's changed songs." And he began humming, On Jordan's Stormy Bank. He kept adapting other songs to the hum of the tires and I never could figure out how those tires knew so many hymns. Dad only said he guessed it listened while parked at the church building every week! The hum fit every song that we sang.

Our singing was temporarily stopped when we came upon a car pulled off to the side of the road. During those days, you never passed anyone in trouble without stopping and offering help. Dad helped him fix a flat tire and we resumed our journey and singing. Aunt Fannie carried me to the fair, which was just a little way from her house, while Dad serviced and repaired the sewing machines in town. It was quite late when we got home and those tires hummed all the way back. A "good samaritan" stopped to help us on our return trip home. Our radiator was hot and Dad had to stop. A man stopped, then drove on and brought us some water back for the radiator. It is so sad that it is not safe today to stop and help each other. It was a part of our life then.

I sometimes wonder if the high tech vehicles of today bring as much happiness and sweet memories as those slow moving ones of yesteryear. Instead of feeling the fresh air blow on your face, you constantly hear—"It's too hot, turn on the air-condition," or "It's too cold, turn the air off." Then when you exit the car, your glasses fog up and you can't see a thing. Instead of hearing the tires hum and singing hymns with your Dad, you have to listen to the kids argue over which station to listen to and, "Turn the radio up, I can't hear it." And instead of being a good samaritan and showing love toward your fellow man, you are trying to speed around a stopped car for fear that someone in the other car may have a gun pointed in your direction. Somehow, I'm thankful that I lived most of my life in those "inconvenient days" when people loved people and had time to show their love for God and mankind.

I am thankful for a Dad who had time and patience to listen to a small child's unusual imagination and play along with it instead of putting me down and saying something that would make me feel stupid. It is important that parents spend some time alone with each of their children. It leaves such happy memories from an important time in a child's life. The little insignificant, seemingly unimportant things in a child's life are the very things that they reflect on when they are an adult. Not the expensive material things bought for them.

I recently read this little saying:
"One hundred years from now, it won't matter how big your house was; how much money you had in the bank; what kind of car you drove; how important your job was; how many vacations you had; or if you owned a boat. What will matter is if you played an important role in the life of a child."

What do you think?

Chapter 20

Our Front Yard, Everyone's Playground

We must have had the cleanest front yard in town when I was a kid. Every morning during the summer, when Mother assigned each of us our chores for the day, one was designated to sweep the yard. That's right...sweep the yard.

Every time Mother bought a new broom, the old one became the yard broom. And we wore out lots of brooms on wooden floors, never having heard of a vacuum cleaner.

Our front yard was used so much that not a sprig of grass grew in it. It was worn and swept right down to the very hardest surface. Thus Mother made us sweep it daily to remove any Hopscotch sticks or Hull-Gull rocks or marbles that might cause us to fall or get hurt on. Our front yard was the playground of the neighborhood. Dad used to laugh and tease the neighbors about having to cut their grass and he didn't have to. I remember Mother's only prize flowers were some salvia planted close to the house, so we could watch the hummingbirds late in the evening, and a couple of ferns she kept on the porch.

Our back yard was not a playground because it usually held a washpot and tub, a wood pile, a coal pile, and always lines and lines of clothes drying in the sun and breeze.

I remember three huge water maple trees in our front yard. They furnished lots of shade in summer and lots of fun in the fall. The leaves were beautiful and when they began to fall, we made a game of seeing who could catch the most, the prettiest or the biggest one. Then we would rake up a big pile and jump in them or cover each other up. It is characteristic of water maple trees to grow big roots near or on top of the ground. Those caused lots of stumped toes and falls. Anytime we could catch Mother and Dad where they couldn't see us, some of us would stand guard while our oldest brother got the axe and cut out the roots and covered the holes with dirt. Our parents didn't want us to do this for fear of killing the trees. But those dear old trees just grew taller and fuller every year in spite of our continual surgery. I used to think they really loved children playing beneath them.

Every Sunday afternoon our yard became a baseball field. Our umpire and manager was Dad. He loved playing with us and we loved it too. All the kids in the neighborhood came when the game began. One Sunday afternoon as Mother was sitting in the swing on the porch, I heard her say, "Daddy, what do you suppose the neighbors think of you out there playing like a child?" I will never forget his response. "I really don't care what they think...I know where my children are, what they are doing, and what they are saying."

We would play until about 5:00 o'clock, when you'd see Dad look at his watch and say, "Okay, everybody, it's time to get cleaned up and go to church. Go ask your mother if you can go and be back in thirty minutes." Most of them came back and were ready to go. Dad lined us up and we'd start the two and one-half mile march right through the middle of town, singing Onward Christian Soldiers or We're Marching to Zion. Even today when I go back on visits, I see a few of those now gray-haired children still "Marching to Zion." They often mention the fun we had in our grass-less front yard.

Oddly enough, the house is torn down now and the property sold with surrounding property on which a school now stands. So children are still enjoying the playground...only it's in the back yard and grass is growing in the front yard.

Do you know where your children are, what they are doing, and what they are saying? Do you know who they are with?

Chapter 21

Fun Things We Did

A simple piece of wrapping string could furnish hours of fun for us kids. Dad saved every bit he came across and always gave us a piece when we asked for it. Sometimes we got a large button from the sewing machine drawer. We ran the string through the holes of the button and tied a knot in the string. Then we centered the button and holding the ends of the string in each hand, we twirled the button round and round to twist the string. Then we pulled the ends in and out in see-saw fashion to make the centrifugal force keep the button going in motion. The game was to see who could keep their button going the longest time.

We often put big colorful buttons or wooden thead spools on a string for the baby to play with. They loved chewing on the bright buttons and spools and crawling after the spools as they rolled on the floor.

We made see-saws of string by putting the string around our wrist and pulling it off in a certain way. It took two to play this game. We would see-saw the string back and forth until the string broke in half. We used string to make crow's feet, a Jacob's ladder and other string designs and games.

Have you ever played with a June Bug? This was another way to use string. We'd catch June Bugs—they are so pretty—and tie a string loosely around one of its legs. We would hold the other end of the string and let it fly as we ran in whichever direction the June Bug flew. When it came down, we untied it and let it go then use another bug to do the same thing. We rotated them so we would not hurt them.

The boys used to empty spools more than we did. I never knew how they made crawler tractors out of the spools but it was fun to watch them race the tractors or see which one could go over an object without turning over. The best I can remember, they notched the spool all around both ends. Then took a pencil and rubber band and somehow twisted it around and around, put in on the floor and it crawled along like an army tank. The notched edges kept if moving. Another way they used them was to take four spools, then fasten two together by inserting a stick through the holes in them making a wheel base, then fasten a flat piece of wood on the sticks making a small wagon. They tied a piece of string to it and the smaller children played with it until it fell apart.

We often used spools to blow bubbles. Sometimes we found a small piece of hollow cane and stuck it in one end of a spool like a pipe. Then we blew the bubble out of the top of the spool. Just a small piece of soap softened in a little water furnished lots of bubbles and fun. Again it was a contest to see who could blow the biggest bubbles and who could make their bubble go the highest. They were so pretty with the sun shining through them. We would watch them sail away as we sang, "I'm Forever Blowing Bubbles." Mother emptied lots of spools of thread and had neighbors saving spools for us also.

Pieces of hollow cane made great peashooters. This, of course, was something the boys liked to do. Sometimes they shot huckleberries through them if they had no peas. It could really sting too if they hit you!

One morning recently as I sat and watched a big butterfly perched on my hummingbird feeder drinking the sweet nectar, I remembered all the fun we had chasing butterflies. There was a large field across the street from our house where wild shasta daisies grew in large clusters. There were so many butterflies that it sometimes looked like there was a butterfly for each bloom. They were not easy to catch. About the time we reached for her wings, she sensed the danger and flew to another bloom. They were so colorful and pretty flying over the yellow and white blossoms. We were told if you caught a butterfly and kept it in a box, you would get a new dress that color. We believed it—but it never came true. Nevertheless, we spent many afternoons chasing butterflies and picking daisies. We gathered arms full and took to Mother and elderly women in the neighborhood. We gathered white clover galore, then tied and looped them together to make bracelets, rings, head bands, belts, anklets, etc.; each one trying to out dress the other one. This sometimes filled an entire afternoon.

Bill and G.B. could go down by the river and do things, but the girls were not allowed to go there. If the boys discovered a nice grapevine swing not too near the river and promised to watch out for us, occasionally we could go swing a while. That was one of our highlights.

In the spring and summer, Mother let us go along the fence rows looking for asparagus or polk greens. Both grew wild and it was food for the table. We also took an extra bag and gathered green apricot and hollyhock blooms which made beautiful little people or dancers if we wanted to put on a show. We turned one flower upside down, this made the skirt and had two little feet sticking out. Then we pulled the petals from another bloom and inserted the stem into the top of the skirt. We had so many pretty colors. They just didn't last long.

The boys always had a sling shot they made from a forked piece of wood and a strip of rubber inner tub. They would target shoot tin cans, but always away from a house or people. This was usually at the river playground when no one was around.

In the winter months we were allowed to play in the snow having snowball fights and building snowmen. At night we made snow cream and sat around the fire eating it.

We turned down chairs and made a train and took long trips using our imagination and talking about all the places and things we knew we would never see. Finally the engineer would screech the train to a stop. We all got out, a new engineer climbed in the engine and shouted, "All aboard", and we all hopped in again after obtaining another ticket.

One thing I'll never forget. When we began running short of our playhouse dishes, Frances and Evelyn would tell me we had to have dishes. My job at meal time was drying dishes. The cry for more dishes meant I had to 'accidently' drop a dish while drying them so we could have more in our playhouse. The secret was well kept and I was never punished for this. Mother would say, "Be a little more careful, honey, I don't have many." I always felt guilty even though I was careful to select a dish that was already cracked. I gave Mother more dishes after I went to work trying to make up for it and finally admitted it to her one day. She only laughed and said, "You little rascal."

This is only a few things children did to have fun for such a small price and we were drawn closer together in the family unit by using our imaginations and playing together this way.

Chapter 22

Wash Day Revolutionized

It is a real crisis today when our washing machine breaks down. Not many women of today have experienced a wash day of scrub boards and boiling kettles of water in the yard. It was an all day, back breaking chore. Many times I have watched my mother do this. The older children helped her while the younger ones made a play house of bricks and boards and cooked dinner of greens (any kind of weeds), potatoes (rocks), and made mud pies (for dessert) in jar tops and broken dishes which we found in the trash pile.

Dad was out early building a fire under the three legged iron kettle, which he filled with water and lye soap. Mother scrubbed the worst soiled spots on the scrub board and dropped them into the boiling water. They kept boiling and were stirred with a long stick until clean. Then they were dipped out of the kettle and placed into a tub of cold water where they were scrubbed another time, if needed. Everything went through three tubs of water. The final tub of water had blueing in it. This was an agent which helped whiten the white things and brighten the colored things by removing any remaining soap scum; we had no bleach then. When heavy clothes were wrung out by hand, it was very difficult to get all the water out. Then came the starching. Mother made a large pan of starch from lump starch mixed with water. Spray-on starch was not yet invented. Shirts, pants, dresses, pillow cases, and embroidered scarves were all starched and ironed to perfection. We did not have many clothes but when we left for school or church we had to pass Mother's keen eye of inspection for cleanliness and neatness. Clothes had to be hung on the line to dry, so rainy weather was a major problem.

Oh, Happy Day—when the washing machine was invented! Although it was not the automatic machine of today, it was indeed a major improvement over the kettle and scrub board. In those days salesmen would bring new appliances to the home for demonstration. Once Mother saw the washing machine, she refused to let that machine leave the house! She decided she could do the laundry for two families and let the money for that make the payments on the washing machine. We had electricity by this time. The biggest problem with this was that one of the families had three grown boys, which meant much additional ironing of shirts and white duck pants, which was the fad of the day for families of means.

Mother kept one of us older girls home from school on wash day to help her because there was so much laundry. This is where Evelyn and I had to pitch in. We took week about staying home to help with the washing and ironing. The week Evelyn stayed home, I carried her homework to her teacher to be graded and brought home her assignments for the following day. She did the same for me, so we managed to keep our grades up and in good standing.

The washing machines were very unlike those of today. The inside remained still and the entire tub made a circular motion, twirling the clothes back and forth against the stationary center. The clothes were removed one by one from the machine and placed through the wringer. Then the wringer was rotated back over the first tub and the clothes wrung into another rinse. All the clothes were put through three rinses, the final one was blueing and then starch for the pieces that needed it. So there was still much manual labor even with a washing machine!

As soon as the clothes began to dry, we began ironing. Again—no electric iron! But as soon as the washing machine was paid for, we got an electric iron! Wow! We had five or six flat irons so the fire had to be continually burning in the wood range for the irons to be hot enough to do the ironing. Everything was ironed—even cup towels, shoots and underwear. Mother ironed the starched pieces and we ironed the unstarched, under the ever inspecting eyes our our dear Mother. "If it is worth doing," she would say, "it is worth doing right." How many times we heard this!

The ironing board was simply a padded, cloth covered board without folding legs placed across the backs of two straight chairs spaced apart the length of the ironing board.

What a happy, happy day—when those modern appliances came into our house!

Chapter 23

A Good Neighborhood

Even though we lived within the city limits, Riverside was very much like living in the country. There were two country stores in Riverside and not more than twenty houses, which were very scattered. Down by the river about two blocks from us was a slaughter house and meat packing plant. Once in a while Mother would send us down to buy a liver. A whole liver and heart was only twenty-five cents. We weren't too fond of it but I guess you learn to eat anything if your are hungry enough. One liver made several meals for us and eventually we all learned to tolerate it and most of us learned to like it. We raised chickens but that was saved to have on Sunday and special days. That was about the extent our our meat.

The rest of the community was ours to roam and explore as long as we did not go on anyone's property. So even though we didn't have a large yard, we had a big playground with lots of trees and wild flowers and things to do.

About six blocks from our house was a dam which furnished electricity for the town. There was a walk leading out to the power house. As we were older, we were allowed to walk out to the power house and make pictures. We always had others come home with us from church on Sunday. I don't know

Alma on a Sunday afternoon at the cemetery

how Mother cooked enough food, she never knew or cared who we invited. She just wanted us to come home for dinner. Then we could go together wherever we wanted as long as we were back home in time to go to church at night. No one had a car. It was walk, walk, walk, everywhere you went.

There was an old cemetery on the other side of town. Sometimes we walked to it, made pictures and read the epitaphs on the tomb stones.

In a small town during those days you were safe anywhere. We never locked a door, even at night!

Near the dam was a mill. Farmers brought their corn to this mill to be ground into meal and grits. The mill was run by the father of a friend I went to school with. They lived next to the mill and she often invited me over when we were kids. We were allowed to play in the mill as long as we stayed away from the machinery. There was a high stack of dried corn shucks piled to the ceiling. We had such fun climbing to the top of the shucks and sliding down.

There was a fenced pasture about four blocks from us. We had a cow, named Old Blackie, which stayed in the pasture. Every evening some of us had to go drive her home for Mother to milk. Then we drove her back for the night. This had to be done again every morning. Sounds like a lot of work, but milk and butter and bread was sometimes our meal—so we didn't mind. And to hear Dad give thanks for it made your heart fill with pride that you played a part in putting it on the table by driving old Blackie home or churning the butter.

It was truly a wonderful experience to be brought up in a community like Riverside.

Sunday afternoon date at the cemetery

Chapter 24

My Granny's Sunshine

The sunshine has a strange way of shining through my bathroom window and casting a reflection on the carpet just outside the door. It forms a small spot about the size of a nickel and looks like a piece of paper on the floor. One day as I walked by the door, I saw Evelyn bent over trying to pick it up. I said, "You can't pick up that sunshine. It will return again tomorrow." We had a good laugh over it. I can't count the times I've tried to pick it up myself.

This caused me to remember a time I visited my Granny. She was making some chicken soup to carry to a sick neighbor. As I watched, she handed me a pair of scissors and told me I could go out to her flower garden and cut some flowers and take them to the neighbor when she carried the soup. I remember the warm feeling of doing something nice for someone.

I asked Granny why it felt better doing a nice deed for someone else than when someone did it for you.

She said, "It is more blessed to give than to receive, my child." Then she said something I will always remember. "The sunshine you spread along your way will return to warm you some stormy day."

This is the way Christians should be, as Paul described to us the fruit of the spirit in Galatians 5: 22,23—"But the fruit of the spirit is love, joy, peace, patience, kindness, goodness, faithfulness, gentleness, self-control; against such things there is no law."

Some of the happiest days of my life are the days I spent with my Granny. Granny was a wonderful, loving, Christian woman. She was very short, probably not five feet tall, but that never detracted from her Christian beauty.

How I loved her bedroom. She had an oak bed with a high rolled headboard and footboard. On it was a feather mattress which was fluffed so high it looked like it almost reached the ceiling and a pretty quilt she had made herself. She had a beautiful marble top dresser with a marble shelf and another shelf across the top of the dresser. There was a big high-back rocker for Paw and a small one for Granny.

The thing I liked best in her kitchen was the pie safe. It smelled so good and there was always something good to eat in it.

There was a long back porch which was very high off the ground. Paw's grapevines grew all the way up to the top of the porch and we could stand there and eat grapes and spit the seeds on the ground. I remember Granny had a big rooster in the backyard. He would fight anyone who dared come into his territory. Granny kept saying she'd make dumplings out of him some day...and she did!

During the summer months, I would often walk the three miles to her house to spend the day. I especially loved to go when their meeting was in progress. She lived next door the the church building.

Christians who lived during those days would be shocked at our little three or four day meetings of today with only one service a day. Their meetings were always from ten days to two weeks. They would have three services a day: 11 a.m., 3 p.m., and 7 p.m. At the morning service, the minister would cut his sermon short and let everyone quote a memory verse and give the scripture. You had to memorize a new one daily. Granny made sure I knew one each time. She sat me down and read it over and over until we could both quote it. I would always try hard to memorize it before she could. I usually did (or at least she made me think I did) and then she would brag on me and tell Paw I was smarter than she was. I remember the pleased look on her face and her sweet smile when I quoted my verse.

In her older years after Paw died, she came to live with us. She had beautiful white hair that was so long she could sit on it. I would often brush it, which she loved. I was in my teens by this time. She shared the girls room and slept with me. Some nights when I had a date, I came in after she had gone to bed. I would be cold when I got into bed and Granny would always say, "Put your feet next to mine and I'll get them warm for you." Sometimes I wouldn't because I didn't want to get her cold, so she would put her feet against mine. Then she would say, "Say your prayer and have a good sleep."

She always told me my dress was pretty. Often I'd remind

her of the patches on it. "But," she said, "it is so fresh and clean. your mother works so hard to starch and iron your dresses. That makes them so pretty one doesn't even notice the patches. Anyway, true beauty comes from within. Pretty is as pretty does." She could always say the right thing to make one feel good.

Today, when I think of my Granny, I am reminded of I Timothy 1: 5 and the faith of Timothy's grandmother and pray that my grandchildren will have the same fond memories of me.

Chapter 25

A Guilty Conscience

I have always admired (almost envied) anyone who could draw anything they wanted to draw...just make a few curves here and there and make it look like something. I never had a bit of talent along this line. When I was in the seventh grade I had a friend who was very gifted at drawing. Her name was Kathryn and she lived next door to me. Just show her a picture and in a matter of a few minutes, she could duplicate it. She was always drawing pictures for me and I kept them all.

One day my teacher, Miss Foster, announced that the two seventh grade classes were going to have an art exhibit at the close of school and invite all the parents. They were going to give extra points on the subject of our choice for each poster or paper each pupil made for the exhibit. We could earn as many points as we wanted to.

Somehow, I got the stupid idea that I could put one of Kathryn's drawings at the top of a poster board and print my caption underneath the picture and 'rack up' a few extra points on history, which was not a favorite subject of mine. So I proceeded to do just that. I knew Kathryn would keep my secret. In fact, she thought it was funny to fool the teacher. I knew in my heart this was dishonest, but I told myself I put it together and did the printing so it was my poster.

Well, it backfired on me! One day, Miss Foster announced we were going to make a calendar. Two students would make one month; one would do the picture for the top and the other would make the numerical part for the bottom of each poster. We got October. My partner told me I'd have to do the drawing. No problem! I got Kathryn to draw me a Halloween picture with ghosts and pumpkins and black cats, etc. We were the first to finish.

Time was running out to turn them in. The girls who had September were as 'talented' at drawing as I was. One day, Miss Foster asked me if I would draw their picture for them. I

said, "Sure.", planning to take it to Kathryn. Then she said,
"I'm sure you won't mind staying a few minutes after school
and drawing it so they can finish it tonight." She would accept
no excuse I tried to give her for not being able to stay after
school. My heart almost stopped. There was nothing to do but
try. Somehow, I felt she knew I had not drawn all those pictures. I remember how many times my mother had said, "Be
sure your sins will find you out."

Well, I began drawing and praying with every stroke. I
promised myself I would never pull a dishonest trick like this
again if I could just get this picture completed. It was a little
girl sitting at a school desk, and she had a face—I could never
draw faces! I thought, "Why couldn't she choose a school house
with trees in the yard (which I could draw)?" I don't know how
long it took me. It seemed like six hours, but somehow I got
through it. It wasn't too bad but it certainly did not look like
Kathryn's art. When I gave it to Miss Foster, I couldn't look her
in the eye. I was more sure than ever that she knew my secret,
but she didn't accuse.

The next morning, I found an apple and a Milky Way candy
bar on my desk. I picked them up and carried them up to Miss
Foster and told her they were not mine. She said the girls
brought them to me for drawing their picture. I would not accept them but I sure wanted that candy bar (because we never
had much candy). I told her I did not deserve them. I guess I
was punishing myself for being dishonest. She smiled sweetly
at me. It was then that I knew she knew. She had, in kindness
and love, taught me a lesson I would never forget, without a
harsh word or embarrassing me in front of my friends.

The moral of the story is when your conscience has been
trained right according to God's word...don't go against it. How
can it hurt so bad when you go against your conscience?

Chapter 26

Exploring the Attic

Did you ever explore the attic? An old attic that was filled from top to bottom and bulging walls with exciting things like old hats, out of date clothes, toys, books and pictures from days gone by. Sometimes we would sit up in the attic for a long time reading from the old books.

Our attic was as big as two rooms. It was over both our kitchen and dining room. Mother had two large baskets in the attic. In one she put old clothes that someday might be some good to someone; the other was for rags. (You simply didn't throw away anything in those days. We could always find a use for things in one way or another.) The first basket is the one that gave us the most joy. Whenever Mother would leave home for a while, we headed for the attic. We dressed up in the things from the old clothes basket until we knew it was time for her to come home. The old hats were the weirdest. Dad always wore a derby hat, a vest, suspenders and shirts with celluloid detachable collars. (I don't know how he could turn his head in those stiff collars—not to mention sing in them.) They attached to his shirt with a collar button in the back of the neck of the shirt, which had no sewn on collar. The reason for him wearing this type of shirt was because at times he would be gone from home for two to four weeks in a gospel meeting to lead singing. He could wash the collar daily without laundering the whole shirt. He didn't own many shirts and laundries were non-existent then and it was difficult to keep clothes clean. Dressing up and exploring the things in the attic was a real fun thing to do, but we made sure everything was back in place by the time Mother got home.

When we had to buy a new mattress, we always saved our old ones. They would be stacked in the attic for storage. When we had company overnight, Mother would drag out one or two of these mattresses and make beds on the floor for us kids. The company slept on our beds.

The upstairs was strictly our territory to keep clean, make beds, and bring down dirty clothes. Every so often Mother went up for inspection and things had sure better be ship-shape!

Evelyn and I shared a bedroom with one double bed. In the summer Evelyn and I often got the idea to put all those mattresses on our bed. (They were cotton mattresses, not the box spring we have today.) So we would roll them up and pull and tug until we had them stacked on top of each other, getting our bed higher and higher until we could reach up and touch the ceiling. We would probably have broken our necks had we fallen out of the bed, but we didn't think of that then. We just giggled and laughed about it all day. It was so hot that close to the ceiling so we took a piece of ice to bed with us to rub on our face and arms to cool us. When inspection day came Mother always said, "You two girls march right upstairs and make your bed right—right NOW!" That didn't keep us from trying it again. She never really punished us for it. I guess she knew we were having fun. Every child should have the joy of having an attic to explore and play in on a rainy day!

How exciting it is to explore the Bible with the intensity we explore an old attic! The joy we could find if we have the desire and the eagerness of that child exploring the attic. Not just open the book, look in and then close it—but search out its treasures, really read it. Let yourself be carried back to the days of that year and re-live it in your mind with Moses and Abraham and others. Fight the battle of faith with Paul and the apostles. "Dress yourself up" in the gospel armor of God: "...that you may be able to resist in the evil day, and having done everything, to stand firm. Stand firm therefore, having girded your loins with truth, and having put on the breastplate of righteousness, and having shod your feet with the preparation of the gospel and peace; in addition to all, taking up the shield of faith with which you will be able to extinguish all the flaming missiles of the evil one. And take the helmet of salvation, and the sword of the Spirit, which is the word of God". Ephesians 6:13-17.

What treasures to be found!

Chapter 27

Pillow Park

There was a park near our home. It was not a recreation park but was used for community activities. Only one house stood between our house and Pillow Park; and there was a high wire fence separating the house from the park. The river was on another side and high board fences were on the two sides bordering the streets. They obstructed the vision of anyone outside from seeing in. We were delighted that the wire fence was between us and the park because we could sit on the side porch and see all the activities going by. There were two buildings in the park. The National Guard met in one, the other was used for various community meetings. During the summer, baseball was the main activity in the park. Dad and the boys loved to sit on the porch and watch the games. Other men in the neighborhood would often join him and he would jokingly tell them he was going to have to start charging admission.

Pillow Park was where the county fair was always held. We seldom got to go but we sat on the porch and in our imagination we would ride the ferris wheel and the merry-go-round. We could hear the music and would often go up and down and round and round in our pretense of riding. There were times the manager of the fair and his wife would ask around the neighborhood about a room to sleep in for the week to get out of a tent. In our parlor we had a leather couch which made into a bed. When the opportunity arose Mother rented this room to them. They always gave us passes to the fair. This was some kind of treat! Mother gave us each a dime out of the money she got from the rent of the room. Nothing at the fair cost more than a dime. I remember the fun we had making our decision on how to spend our dime. Frances, Evelyn and I always went together. We spent hours standing and looking at each thing carefully and then start at the beginning and go over it all again and again. We all wanted to ride the same ride because it was more fun that way. We would finally come to an agreement. Perhaps this was our way of making it last longer.

The most exciting thing was when the circus came to town! It, too, was held in Pillow Park. We sat on the porch and watched the elephants pull up the big tents. There was a fire hydrant right across the street from our house. A large gully ran along the side the road. After the circus was all set up, the workers brought all the animal cages up to the hydrant to clean them and wash the animals before the parade through town. We sat in our yard across the street and watched the elephants spray water on themselves. There was always a big hippopotamus that they put in the ditch filled with water. The elephants would spray water on him. He had a grand time in the water, and so did we watching him! The tigers, lions and monkeys were not too happy with the water, so they finished them first and carried them back to the park. We knew when they finished washing the elephants and horses that the parade would soon being. So we ran down the street and across the bridge so we could get a good place to see the parade going and coming back. I think my favorite thing was the steam calliope. I never grew tired of hearing that music. When I hear one today it still brings back fond memories.

The park held a scary memory also. Many times the gypsies came to town and camped there. We were told so many stories of how they would steal and kidnap children. We were warned not to go near them. One day Mother sent me to the store, which was three blocks from our house and past the park. She did not know the gypsies were in town at that time. Charles, my youngest brother who was about five years old, went with me. When we walked in the little country store there were gypsies every place. They went in stores in a group and scattered so the clerk couldn't possibly watch all of them at once. I don't know how I turned Charles's hand loose, but I happened to look out the window and saw him going across the street—a gypsy on each side holding his hands. I screamed, "They've got my brother.", and ran out the door. A man ran out behind me yelling, "Turn that boy loose." They did and I grabbed Charles and kept on running and did not stop until we got home. I did not even get what Mother sent me for, but she said that I did the right thing.

Gypsies traveled around lots during those days. Once Dad ran a creamery where farmers brought in cream to sell. He tested it for quality, paid them and resold it for butter, ice cream, etc. One day some gypsies came in while Dad was bent over the table writing a check, one slipped Dad's wallet out of his hip pocket. The man waiting for the check saw it and told Dad. He went after the gypsy and a policeman was right there and made them leave town. Dad laughingly said the joke would have been on the gypsy because his wallet was always empty.

It was great fun living next to Pillow Park—it provided us with many hours of entertainment and most of it was free! My daughter says the story of Pillow Park always makes her smile!

Chapter 28

A Scary Moment

I do not relish writing this memory, but it definitely is a sign of those times in which I grew up. It was near Christmas and I was about eight years old. Dad had carried us to church or some kind of program or class.

The courthouse is built right in the middle of town with an entrance on all four sides and a street running directly toward each entrance and circling around the courthouse making a square, thus called the town square or courthouse square.

To go home from church we had to come down one of those streets and circle around part of the courthouse and go down one of the other streets toward home.

This particular night as we got within a block of the courthouse, we noticed a lot of people screaming and yelling. A man was approaching us and Dad asked, "What's going on up there?" The man said, "They found the man who raped the little girl and have hung him from the courthouse." Very quickly Dad said, "Don't look children.", as he turned us down another street away from the angry mob. It was too late for me as I immediately glanced up and saw the chillingly evil scene of angry, uncontrollable people, some dressed in white hooded sheets. I didn't understand. I'll never forget the cold chill that ran down my spine when I saw that man hanging by his neck. It haunted me for days. I could not walk by that side of the courthouse for a long time so I always took the longer route around the block.

I remember the Halloween night of that same year. We didn't go out trick or treating as other kids did. We were sitting around the fireplace doing our homework. There was a knock on the door. When Dad opened the door someone with a white hoods over their head just walked right in. When I looked up and saw it, all the scene at the courthouse flashed in my memory and I remember thinking they were coming to get Dad. I began to scream and cry and ran over into the corner behind the bed. I must have scared the others for they all jumped up and followed me. Mother followed us trying to comfort us. She wore long, full dresses and long aprons and she staunchly took her stand in front of us spreading her dress and apron for protection. I positively knew no one would get to us through that outstretched dress and determined mother, but Dad was still out there with that white hooded figure! What about him? Dad kept yelling for her to get out, she was scaring the children. He knew it was a neighbor woman but there was too much noise and confussion for us to hear him and she later told him that she thought we were pretending and was sorry for scaring us. Dad finally had to pick up the broom and seriously threaten her to make her leave. He knew we were truly scared.

We can make such deep impressions on our children. These impressions will follow them through life. The impressions can make them a social misfit and a danger to others and eventually destroy their souls. Or can impress them and form them with loving, caring feelings and self-confidence leading them to live a good life, one of following Christ who will guide them safely Home at the end of time.

Which impressions are you making?

Chapter 29

School Days

School days are the happiest days of our life, but the trouble is we don't usually realize this until much later in life. We fail to take full advantage of the present because we are too anxious to get into the future.

There were very few school buses during my school years. The children out in the country rode school buses. Some kids in town were fortunate that their dad owned a car and carried them to school. Although most walked regardless of the distance or weather. I guess the distance we walked was two and a half or three miles one way. It was very difficult to get there by 8:30 a.m. As we ran out the door Dad always shouted, "You better not be late." So we ran most of the way and arrived at school completely breathless. We went straight to our first classroom and at 8:30 a.m. the bell rang for us to go to chapel. We marched into chapel to the tune of one of John Philip Sousa's marches. Always in a straight line and no talking! The boys went in and sat on one side of the auditorium and the girls entered separately and sat on the other side. Then we sang a hymn, had a scripture reading, a brief inspirational talk, a prayer and one or two patriotic songs or ballads. We recited the Pledge of Allegiance, any necessary announcements were then made and we marched back to our classroom in the same manner that we had come. We never had a religion or a doctrine taught, just good morals and inspirational talks. We had about five subjects and would change classes at the sound of the bell. Glee Club, drama and art classes were after school. Fees were charged for art classes. School ended at 3:30 p.m. and by the time we walked home it was 4:30. We always had homework in every subject.

Always—the boys and girls were separated in the classrooms, in study hall, in the lunch room, and on the playground. In the classroom the boys sat on one side of the room and the girls sat on the other. We had separate playgrounds, the girls' area on higher ground than the boys' section. Some of the girls would sit up on the hill and watch the boys play ball, some would walk around and some sat in a group talking girl talk.

We were in deep trouble if we were ever caught slipping a note to one of the opposite sex, but you better believe we found ways to do it without getting caught. Everyone knew who liked whom and would never tell a note was passed if they knew it, and would even assist if necessary. Many times I'd feel a foot on the side of my seat and reach down without even looking and pull the note out of the side of a person's shoe. Slowly raise my hand to my desk and very casually glance down to see whose name was on it. Then put it in the side of my shoe and put my foot on the seat in the direction the note was to travel. Sometimes the note would go completely across the room in this manner—from one shoe to another. Sometimes we would swap a book before class and suddenly notice we had Bob's book (whoever the note went to) during class and raise a hand to tell the teacher, "Somehow I have Bob's book—does anyone have mine?" Always Bob had it, so we'd swap books, leaving a note inside of each book. The trouble with this one was, you couldn't keep using it on the same teacher. She'd wise up sooner or later. There were many other devious ways, but the fun was in fooling the teacher, not in writing the note.

I remember a "love" experience when I was in the fifth grade. There was a boy who sat one seat ahead of me in the opposite row of desks. He often looked back and winked or smiled. I was so excited about it! However, the girl who sat behind me thought he was flirting with her. We often discussed it as we walked to and from school—each thinking we were *The One,* and secretly laughing at the other. On Valentine Day, when the valentines were handed out from the beautifully decorated box, I received a big valentine. It wasn't one of those ten for a nickel ones, which were the ones usually given. It wasn't one of those three for a nickel ones. It was a WHOLE NICKEL one! It was even in an envelope—AND—it was from George! Now I knew I was *The One.* That afternoon as we walked home, we couldn't wait to show each other our valentine. Suddenly, we looked at each other in surprise. He had given her a nickel valentine exactly like the one he gave me. Both were signed, "Love, George." Boys! How fickle! We decided we would tear them up on the count of three and put them on his desk the next day.

We counted to three—but neither of us could tear our beautiful valentine up. I guess each thought the other one would tear hers up, then we'd be first in George's eyes. But it didn't turn out like that, we both kept our valentine, laughed about it and were still good friends.

We did have a lunchroom, some would buy a lunch but most of us packed a lunch from home. Lunchtime for me was always a difficult time. In my teenage mind, when appearances and what others think of you is so important, I was embarrassed by what I had for lunch and how I had to carry it. Biscuit and gravy or biscuit and jelly wrapped in newspaper. Most of the other kids had sandwiches with real store bought bread wrapped in wax paper and carried in a brown bag or lunch box. So many times I just did not eat lunch and would be starving when I got home. Now I realize and appreciate the effort and struggle my parents put forth to provide that food for us. And I am certainly not ashamed. I soon grew out of that and learned to be grateful for what we had.

I do remember an incident in geometry class one day. Mr. Mathis game us four problems every day for homework. The following day everyone was sent to the blackboard at the same time to work the problems. We were numbered alternately, 1-2-3-4, and had to work the problem coinciding with our number. If he saw anybody who didn't complete the problem, he'd make you get up in front of the class and explain the problem. His idea was if you couldn't do the problem, you hadn't done your homework and you'd get a zero for the day. One night I had a terrible time understanding a problem and no one could explain it to me. Wouldn't you know it, that's the problem that I had to write on the board! It completely stumped me! I didn't want a zero for the day, so I decided to try to bluff my way through it. I began to write it on the board and give some explanation. Somehow, as I was explaining the problem, it suddenly came to me like a bolt of lightning! A light bulb went off in my head, I understood it, and I picked up the chalk and completed the problem. I lucked out on that one and I think we both were surprised. I was relieved. That experience taught me never to say I can't until I tried.

We had excellent teachers and we were taught to respect them. At home we were never allowed to speak disrespectfully about a teacher. If there was a teacher we didn't like, we were told by Mother and Dad that we must try a little harder in that class and the teacher would notice and reward our efforts— then we would like her better. It never failed either!

The main difference in the schools then and now is the subjects taught. We were taught the 3 R's—reading, 'riting, and 'rithmetic. We had all the basic studies taught in classes today. In addition we had spelling and penmanship classes from first grade to twelfth grade. Glee Club and art classes were optional. We were not taught sex education and free sex. We were taught high morals and respect for self and others. Pregnancy of teens and single women was looked upon as a disgrace. It was unheard of among teens and if an older girl became pregnant, she was sent away to an aunt or near relative until the baby was born. The girl felt disgraced and she sometimes moved to another town to escape those who knew her and to begin her life anew. Abortion also was rarely heard of and was a reputation destroyer. I am happy those things were not taught in our classes, but glad to see that there is more love and understanding shown today, although I believe there should also be more restraint used in these relationships and some degree of disgrace felt.

Little emphasis was placed on sports, unlike today where it is a major part of school. We did have basketball (girls and boys) and football. We had no computers or calculators to aid in mathematics. Everything had to be committed to memory and problems solved from that. I remember how Dad saved every piece of paper that had no print on the back. He insisted we do our math problems on the back of scrap paper, let him check it and make corrections. Then we copied it on tablet paper to turn in for grading. We were graded on neatness, and this saved paper also. It was extra work but paid off in grades.

Field Day was an event we all strived to participate in. The teacher of each grade chose the two students she considered the best in each subject. They were tested against each other and the best was chosen to represent their school in that subject against every other school in the country on Field Day. The second student was an alternate. We were all anxious to bring awards for the best back to our school. It was an incentive for hard work and better study. The only thing I was ever chosen to represent our school in was writing (penmanship) and I was very proud of that. We had lots of memory work to do in literature. Even in grade school we committed many poems to memory, most of which I can still recite. I feel very fortunate to have been educated during those days. One went to school to learn and we were never permitted to forget it.

One of the fun things of school days was our autograph books. These could be purchased for ten cents at Woolworth and were the fad of teenage girls in the 1930's. Every girl just had to have one. We carried it everywhere we went and asked everyone to write in it—especially the boys. The boys would write mushy, gooey things in it about love. Later we girls would get together and read each others' book. Much to our disgust, some boys who didn't have much imaginations would write the same love message in every girl's book. Nevertheless, we had so much fun reading them and tried to make each other believe the messages were really meant for us. I still have my autograph book and have let my children and grandchildren read it to me again. This was more fun than the original readings because they believed I had a lot of male admirers. While most of the messages were lovey-dovey, one autograph stood out for being so different. It was dated 1935 and read simply:

Miss Alma Derryberry, I think you and your sisters, Evelyn, Frances, and Mary are the nicest girls I ever met.

T.E.J.

I'll have to admit, I was a little disappointed that this message wasn't a little more lovey-dovey because I really liked this boy more than the others. Guess what? This is the boy I married in 1936, Ted, and he was a wonderful husband and father.

It isn't so bad being poor when you are small and when almost everyone around you is poor too. You simply accept it as the natural scheme of things. However, when you get in high school, you begin to notice what pretty dresses the other girls wear. These differences gave me a funny feeling—an inferior feeling. Mother made our clothes. We had two school dresses and one Sunday dress each. Frances, Evelyn and I were about the same size so we began to swap dresses every few days so we would have six changes instead of two. We learned to keep our feet flat on the floor so the holes in our shoes would not be noticed. We stopped carrying a lunch and just did without until we got home. We pretended not to be hungry. But, oh how good those other kids' lunches smelled. During those days, many kids finished eighth grade and quit school to go to work. Times were hard and financial help was needed at home. My two oldest sisters did this, even though Mary, the oldest, graduated at the top of her eighth grade class. Her greatest desire always was to be a nurse. We could always go to Mary for advice. Mother was so busy caring for the family—washing, ironing, cooking, and sewing we didn't want to bother her with our problems, so we went to Mary for advice. Mary was our confidante. One day I told Mary that I thought I would quit school and get a job after I finished the eighth grade. I was tired of not being able to look like the other girls in class. I remember well the little talk she gave me. First, she told me she had not quit—that she was still going to be a nurse. She just had to postpone it a little while. She told me she understood my feelings about those things for she had been there herself. Then she said, "We are just going to figure out other ways you can surpass those other girls, then they will notice you. Now, show me your prettiest smile." I grinned. "You know," she continued, "there isn't another girl in that school that has a smile like that. Now you start practicing that smile on everyone you meet. They will smile back at you. Your smile will never wear out and people will never get tired of looking at it." Then she said, "You have another thing that God gave you which only you can make better. That's your brain. You're going to have to work hard at it, but you can be the smartest girl in your class. Then they will come to you for help regardless of what you wear. People will respect you for what you are—not what you have or wear." I took her advice, I started smiling and people always smiled back. I began feeling more confident and I studied hard. Some nights I would rewrite a paper two or three times so I could turn it in flawless. By the end of the year most of the girls in pretty dresses would sit at the same table as me during study period and ask me to help them in algebra or to diagram sentences. I never figured out how Mary worked things out, but she was in nursing school before I finished high school. Again, she graduated from nursing school at the top of her class. I'll always remember two very special things people always have said about her, "Mary always smiles" and "Mary is everyone's confidante." One thing is for sure—she helped me at a time of crisis during my school days.

Chapter 30

Rejected—Forgiving and Caring

I used to tell the children the story about The Ugly Duckling. He had five little brothers and sisters. They were all soft and fluffy and a pretty pale yellow color. But one little duckling was different. He walked different, quacked different and was not at all like his brothers and sisters. So they began to make fun of him, pointing at him and laughing. They would never play with him—they rejected him! Even his own Mother rejected him. She would not find food for him as she did the other ducklings. He had to find his own food and play all alone.

One day the ugly duckling decided he would never treat anyone like he was being treated. He would use the rejection he felt to his advantage. He would be so nice and friendly and good to every animal in the barnyard, even his brothers and sisters, that they would have to notice him and like him. And this he did. Very soon all eyes were upon him. He grew up to be the most beautiful duck in the group. Even his family noticed and tried to emulate him because he was always happy and he never forgot the feeling of being rejected.

Sometimes our young people feel rejected by their peers because they are different. They feel pressured to be like their school mates—to dress like them, to do the things they do, go to the places they go for entertainment, and use the language they use. It is hard for us to remember, the things that make one feel accepted now are not the things that make one beautiful and Godly in later life. I have even seen many adults go deep in debt trying to be accepted by rich friends only to end up with a broken home and financial difficulties. Today's pleasures are tomorrow's woes and may cost you a lifetime of misery.

The feeling of being rejected is a very real hurt. I remember my first feeling of rejection from seventh grade. When I was in the first grade there was a family who lived near us who had only one child. Her mother came over to ask if her daughter could walk to school with us as school was about two and a half miles from home and she didn't want her to walk alone. We became staunch friends and walked to and from school together every day. She always had a nickel to spend on the way home. We came right through town and would stop in Woolworth and buy candy. She always gave me a piece of her candy. I never had a nickel to buy candy and share with her and I felt very bad about this.

When we were in seventh grade another family moved into the neighborhood; they had two daughters. One of the girls was our age and she too had a nickel every day and the three of us walked together for a while. We always waited inside the door at school for each other. One day I kept waiting for a long time and neither girl came. I ventured outside to look for them and saw them running across the street, looking back over their shoulders as they ran faster and further away from me. Of course, I felt it was because I could never give them some candy in return. I walked home alone very slowly. They kept looking back but did not wait for me. I did not even want to walk with them. I had been rejected by my best friend over a nickel piece of candy! As I came near the front of Woolworth store, I glanced up just in time to see them peeking out, looking in the direction I was coming. Then they ran back into the store and I went on ahead of them. I would never have taken the candy had I known their offer wasn't sincere. I have never wanted to take a piece of candy from a friend since then.

Dad had always taught us to respect our poverty and be thankful and share what we had. So I assumed everyone did this. They used to sell suckers on a long stick with a small sucker on each end. If I had a penny and someone was with me, I would buy this sucker instead of the big sucker. Then I would break the stick in half and give half to the one who was with me. Although it's a bad feeling to be rejected, one forgives and forgets.

Jesus did. He was rejected by his own people, Luke 9:22-26.

Chapter 31

A Narrow Escape

Probably from the beginning of time parents have exasper-
ated their children with repeated warnings of protection, "Lock
your doors", "Don't drive fast", "Don't pick up strangers", etc.,
etc. We, as teens, got it from our parents also, though slightly
different. We heard, "Don't get in a car with anyone you don't
know", "Never take money from anyone if you haven't earned
it", "Never stay around anyone who's drinking", "Don't walk
alone at night", etc. We, just like kids of today, rolled our eyes
and shrugged our shoulders and said, "I know"—only we never
let our parents see or hear us.

Surprisingly though, those warnings saved me from what
could have been a terrible fate, which all happened so innocent-
ly. I probably was about ten or twelve years old. I remember
one hot summer day Mother sent me to carry Dad's lunch to
him since he worked only about a mile from home. I sat and
cooled down as Dad ate his lunch so I could carry his plate back
home. As I left he followed me to the door. I was just a short
distance from the door when a car pulled up to the curb and a
man asked if I wanted a ride. I replied, "No thanks", since I did
not know him. Dad yelled, "It's OK, Alma, it's Mr. T____." So I
proceeded to get in the car. We had gone about two blocks when
he laid a dollar in my lap. I said, "What's that for?" He said,
"Oh, just buy you a soda or some candy or whatever you want."
Being naive, I said, "I'll give it to Mother to buy me some school
clothes." "Oh no," he said, "don't tell her about it. Spend it on
yourself." Immediately that little red warning flag flashed before me and I knew this man was up to no good and I threw the
money back to him. He tried to force me to take it and I told
him I would throw it out the window if he put it in my lap
again, so he stuck it in his shirt pocket.

By this time, we were at the street on which we lived, but
he made no attempt to turn. I said, "I live two blocks up the
street. Just stop and I'll walk." "I'm just driving on out to

Third Avenue. I will turn by your house and I'll be headed back
to town.", he answered. I knew the neighborhood well and
knew this was true, so I said no more. However, when he arrived at Third Avenue, he continued to drive. Again, I asked
him to let me out and I'd walk. This time he assured me that he
had some cattle just a little further out and wanted to check on
them while he was that close. He stopped at a barn and went
in. This is when I should have gotten out and ran but I believed
him. When he returned to the car, I smelled a strange, strong
odor. Another red warning flag flashed. Although I had never
smelled whiskey, I knew this was it and I was scared stiff. He
still didn't head back toward home. Instead, he continued in
the opposite direction and turned up a little dirt lane and
stopped. Then he tried to kiss me. I have always had long nails
and I flew into him. They were my only weapon and I used
them. I clawed and scratched at his face, bringing much blood,
until he let me alone and took me home.

I remember when he pulled up in front of our house, Dad
and Mother were at the curb. Before I could open the door, Dad
had gone around the car, opened the door, had this six foot man
by the collar, and dragged him out of the car saying, "What
have you done to my girl?" Mr. T____ began pleading, "I did not
harm her, Mr. Derryberry, honest, I didn't." Dad said, "Looks
like she harmed you a little and if she says you harmed her, I'll
get you worse!" I ran in the house crying and didn't come out of
my room for two days. Evelyn stayed with me a lot, but I
couldn't even talk to her about it.

I'm sure you are wondering how this could have happened
when Dad told me it was okay to ride with him. Well, there
were two brothers in town who could have passed for twins.
One was a very respectable insurance salesman, the other was
a bootlegger. This was during prohibition days and liquor was
illegal. Dad thought it was the insurance man when he okayed
the ride. He realized he had made a mistake before we got out
of sight so he closed the shop and rushed home. I'm sure he
went through torment before I arrived home.

Some years later, this same man was caught trying to harm
a child across the street from us and later served time in prison
for raping a fourteen year old girl. I had a very narrow escape
thanks to the continued warnings of my parents. Mothers and
fathers must continue to warn their children of the dangers out

there. The flag will flash at the appointed time and may save a life.

Chapter 32

Friends

Mother used to say that she went from room to room counting heads before she went to bed. If one child was missing she searched until she found him and saw him safely tucked in bed.

I used to think Dad counted heads before we went to church. He'd get us all lined up and away we would march, Mother and Dad carrying the two smallest ones.

Dad was named Gideon, for Gideon in the Bible. I remember sometimes as we marched down the street we would meet someone who would say, "Here comes Gideon and his 300." Dad would reply, "I can have more than 300 today, come and join us and we will fight together." I did not understand the significance of this at that time and it really provoked me as I thought we were being made fun of. Since I've learned better, I'm proud to be a soldier in Gideon's army. Dad trained some good soldiers for the Lord's work, song leaders, preachers, teachers, and Mothers and Fathers. He was later called affectionately "Mr. Gid" or "Brother Gid".

The Tennessee Orphan's Home was located near the church building. Those children really loved to sing. Most of them called Dad "Uncle Gid". They frequently asked Dad to come teach them some songs. We loved to go with him and visit the children. We made many good friends this way. I especially remember one girl who was deaf and couldn't speak. She had such pretty curly hair and such a happy smile. Her name was Alma, the same as mine, and we became good friends. She taught me how to talk with my hands so we could converse.

I made another good friend named Stella. She never ceased talking. Together we could get into more mischief. I last saw her at our 50th class reunion where she made the statement that in our junior year someone had written her an anonymous note telling her that she was keeping company with the wrong person and was going to get into trouble. She wanted to thank that person for being concerned about her. Then she asked,

"Was that you, Alma?" I said, "No, I was the person you were keeping company with—remember?" I hope we can be together again at our next reunion. Once when Stella visited me, we had some new baby chickens. She fell head over heals in love with the soft yellow chicks. She begged Mother to give her one. Mother couldn't resist her pleas even though she knew Stella had no place to keep it. She put it in a box in her room at the orphan's home. Every afternoon I went by the orphan home to see the chicken. The chicken was about fryer size before the Matron discovered Stella had a chicken in her room. It was as much fun to us seeing how long we could keep the secret as it was for her to have a pet.

I remember the race the girls ran at recess to be first to find a shade tree to sit under while eating lunch. Stella and I never seemed to get there first. So we decided we would just plant us a tree. We found one about one foot high and planted it in the school yard, even staked it so someone wouldn't cut it down when cutting the grass. Every day we sat on either side of that little tree to protect it. We took cups of water and poured on it, laughing all the while and kids commented on us going to the drinking fountain so often. I do not know if the tree still stands today, but the school building did until 1994.

It is so easy and rewarding to make friends among those who are lonely and less fortunate than we are. It makes for a life-long remembrance.

"A man that hath friends must shew himself friendly: and there is a friend that sticketh closer than a brother." - Proverbs 18:24. This is one of the lessons we learned as children by our parents example as well as being taught by them. The greatest friend we can have is Christ. In John 15:12-15, Christ tells us, "This is my commandment, That ye love one another, as I have loved you. Greater love hath no man than this, that a man lay down his life for his friends. Ye are my friends, if ye do whatsoever I command you........"

Chapter 33

First Aid

During my younger days, doctors were few and located far apart. Our town was fortunate to have a doctor locate there. Most people had no transportation to the doctor's office, except to walk. If one was too sick to walk, the doctor made house calls. He brought his little black bag and most of the time had a variety of cure-all pills, which usually made you well. He received small pay and sometimes none, but received much pride and satisfaction in helping his fellow man. His job was tough for he was on call day and night. Neither distance nor bad weather hindered his answer for a distress call. Most babies were delivered at home by a mid-wife unless there were complications.

I've heard Mother tell of the bad flu epidemic of the early 1900's when so many died with it. Everyone in our family came down with it at the same time except Mary. She was in her early teens at the time but she nursed us all back to health. Perhaps that is why she later became a nurse.

After that Frances and I had double pneumonia. There were no miracle drugs then. A pneumonia patient had to have lots of fresh air. Mother said Granny came over to help her with Frances and me. It was winter, they moved a bed on the front porch and hung quilts all around the bed to keep us out of a draft. They kept a fire going all night in the fireplace and they took turns going in to get warm. One of them, wrapped up in quilts, sat beside our bed day and night for 10 days to keep us covered and watch our temperature. The belief was if the temperature broke in ten days the patient lived. If not—death. Mother said she would never forget the night Granny came in and said, "They will live, their fever has broken." What wonderful advancements the world of medicine has made today!

Many other old remedies worked that sound ridiculous today. We often woke in the middle of the night crying with the earache. Mother roasted an onion in the hot ashes in the fireplace, squeezed the warm juice into a teaspoon and dropped the juice into our ear. The pain left soon and we could get back to sleep.

When we woke up with a cough, we were given a teaspoon of sugar with a few drops of kerosene on it. For a sore throat, a mixture of sugar, vinegar and black pepper boiled together and we'd take a teaspoon of it. I don't know if it really helped, but the pepper burned your throat so we thought it did. A baby with the croup had his chest rubbed with warm camphorated oil and a warm flannel cloth placed over his chest. If you stepped on a rusty nail or a piece of glass and cut your foot, the foot was soaked in a pan of kerosene and wrapped in a bandage from a piece of old worn out sheet. Old sheets were always saved for bandages because they were soft and white. Every home had cloverine salve, paregoric, peroxide and iodine.

Every spring we were given a tonic of sulphur powder and molasses. This tonic was supposed to get rid of the winter blahs and get us into action for spring and summer.

To remove a wart all you had to do was pick it until it bled, put the blood on a kernel of corn and toss it to the chickens, but you must not look to see which chicken ate it! For a boil, which was very common during those days, a piece of fat meat was placed on it to draw it to a head so it could be opened and drained. How painful that was!

Some of these remedies sound crude and unreal. But it was the only first aid kit we had. There was no 911 or rescue squad to call. So you did whatever worked successfully and these usually did— or at least so we thought! Anyway, something kept us alive and reasonably well.

Chapter 34

Marshall Fox

My memories would not be complete without writing something about Marshall. He was my first cousin on my mother's side and the only one near my age. So there was a certain bond between us. We played together a lot. When we were small we lived in the country in a small community about six miles from Columbia. Marshall's dad was named Wilburn and he had a twin brother named Willie, they were Mother's brothers. Mother also had an identical twin sister, so that was two sets of twins in her family. I'm sure they could have told many stories of their lives. Marshall's dad ran a little grocery store next to our house and my dad worked for Uncle Wilburn in the store. They lived across the road from the store up on a hill. There was a large pasture in front of his house where he kept quite a few cows and one bull. We were all scared of the bull. When I went over to play with Marshall, Mother always came out to see where the bull was and always cautioned me to walk —not run —so I would not attract the bull's attention. She always stood and watched me across the field. It was all I could do not to run as fast as I could, I was so scared.

There was a sty over the fence at the road and at the house. A sty is two or three steps built up to the top of the fence and down on the other side. This prevented opening and closing gates or climbing a fence. Often Marshall and I would just sit on top of those steps and talk. I dreamed for years of that old bull chasing me across the pasture.

Marshall thought no one in the world could make tea cakes (sugar cookies) like my mother. Quite often we would see Marshall coming across the field with a little hobo-looking pack tied to a stick and carried over his shoulder. In it he had flour, sugar, eggs and butter. He was coming to get Mother to make him some tea cakes. As soon as Mother saw him coming, she quit whatever she was doing and started a fire in the stove. We played while she baked his tea cakes, then she carefully put them in his hobo pack and he headed back across the pasture. I walked to the sty with him and stood there until he got on top of the sty on the opposite side of the pasture. We waved at each other and went on our way.

About five years ago I was visiting in Columbia. Marshall was visiting his brother there also. Marshall was a professor and administrator at University of Tennessee in Knoxville at that time. He came by to visit and he still talked about Mother's tea cakes.

By the time we were teenagers we moved into town and Marshall's family moved to a farm. I always called and invited Marshall to come in town and go to any party that I was invited to.

His parents always brought him and they visited with Mother and Dad while Marshall and I went to the party. Marshall didn't have many friends his age to socialize with in the country. He was one of my best friends and my favorite cousin.

Chapter 35

Special Treats

Have you ever watched a T.V. show where they talk in Japanese or German or some other foreign language? You are so busy reading the translation underneath the picture, that you can't see what is going on. If you have, you can understand what the silent movies were like. We never attended many movies. It was a rare treat even though you could see a matinee for a dime.

When talking movies came in there was a big promotion in our town to get people to attend movies more. One of the contests was for the largest family and the prize was a week's free pass for the entire family. Guess who won? We did! We were jumping with joy. WOW! An entire week of going to the movies!!

It was the custom of the theaters then to show the same movie Monday and Tuesday, another one on Wednesday, and another one on Thursday and Friday. Every Saturday a western/cowboy movie ran continuously from 1 p.m. to midnight. No movies ran on Sunday. You could watch the same movie four times each, two matinees and two at night on Monday and Tuesday; a different movie four times on Wednesday; and another one four times on Thursday and Friday.

Saturday we could see the same cowboy movie four times if we wanted to. And that's exactly what we did! Every day we kids were there at 1 p.m. and sat through the movie twice. Then go home to eat supper and go back to see it twice at night.

Then back the next day to see the same movie four more times. Mother gave us permission as long as we did our chores at home. She didn't know how fast we could work! And neither did we! A talking movie was something else! There was always a cartoon and a news report. Remember, this was before radios, so the theater and newspaper was the only means of knowing what was going on in the world.

I guess the manager of that theater didn't make any money

off of us. All those movies and not even a bag of popcorn bought. What cheap skates!

Another special treat we occasionally enjoyed was the Chatauqua. The Chatauqua was a traveling tent show that came to town once a year. It consisted of slap-stick comedians, who blackened their faces, wore top hats, black suits, white gloves and shoes. They cracked jokes and did the soft-shoe tap dance. There were also magicians, clowns, a band, dog tricks and some other forms of entertainment. Someone usually gave Dad passes. This was great fun.

Then came the RADIO! A neighbor, Mr. Smithson, had the first radio I ever saw, I guess one of the first in town. It was a monstrosity with wires and knobs. He had it setting on a table and he sat in front of the table with some sort of head gear on to hear it. Only the person wearing the head gear could hear it.

So he would relate whatever was said to others around. I remember during the famous Max Schmelling boxing matches, which was all the excitement of the neighborhood, all the men gathered around Mr. Smithson's window outside and he would re-broadcast to them. Honestly, you would have thought they had a ringside seat. I remember Bill saying, "There's Dad yelling about that fight and he'd be taking his belt off to me if I was fighting."

It wasn't too long before better radios came out. When I got my first summer job in an ice cream store, I bought our first radio. It was a Majestic table model and I paid $1.00 down and $1.00 a week—no interest then! We spent many happy family hours sitting around it listening to Jack Benny, Fibber McGee and Molly, Fred Allen, One Man's Family, The Hit Parade, etc. There were so many good clean programs to listen to then, unlike the majority of today's T.V. programs.

One other very special treat I remember is getting to ride in the rumble seat of a Ford Coupe. One of the boys Frances dated had such a car. All the kids loved them. We were never permitted to date in a car unless another couple was along. Sometimes Ted and I had the honor of being asked by Frances to go with them. I know we weren't really wanted, but their desire to go on a date overwhelmed unwanted company! How do I know? Because sometimes I was on the other side of the fence and had to ask unwanted company to tag along. Company rules, you know! That (the company) being Mother and Dad!

Chapter 36

Some Funny Happenings

He was tall and a good looking young man. Every morning when he left for school every hair was in place. He saw to that. His clothes were starched and ironed to perfection and he had on a 25 cent tie from Woolworth. However, there were numerous little neat patches on his pants and shirt, but no dirt. This was his senior year in high school. Who would have thought it, Bill Derryberry was listed in his class book as the "Best Dressed Boy" in his class. It doesn't always require name brand clothes and high prices! We were poor but Mother saw to it that we were clean and neat and not ashamed of who we were or what we had.

* * *

Togetherness? Well, I guess! Ruth and Sarah were always in the bathroom (in later years when we had one) or outhouse at the same time. Anytime one went, the other went too. They would just sit and talk. Even after we all left home when those two came to Mother's house, they would head to the bathroom to tell secrets. Sometimes one of us would be forced to run them out, only to find them standing outside the door, waiting to go back in and finish their conversation. I never understood why they didn't find a more enjoyable place for their conversations.

* * *

G.B. was the prankster, the one who was always coming up with mischievous ideas, then talk us into carrying them out and get in trouble. In the winter Dad always left his shoes and socks sitting near the fireplace so they would be warm from the stoked fire in the morning when he put them on. I remember a little mouse that came out and played around the fireplace (to warm up I guess). One night Dad set a trap for the mouse and he and Mother went on to bed, leaving us sitting around the fire doing our homework. (Much to his regret later.) He told G.B. if the mouse was caught before we went to bed, to take it out and reset the trap. After Dad had gone to sleep we heard the trap snap and we had a mouse. G.B. dared me to put it in Dad's shoe, convincing me it would be funny to let him find it in the morning while putting on his shoes. It sounded pretty funny to me at the time. Dumb me!! So I took the dare and took the mouse by the tail and dropped it in Dad's shoe, giggling all the while. The next morning I didn't think it was so funny when one by one Dad asked us, "Who put the mouse in my shoe?" There was no way I could deny it because there were too many witnesses, everyone now sitting in the room had seen me put the mouse in Dad's shoe and all eyes now focused on me. I never saw so many accusing eyes! Besides, I knew I'd be punished for lying. G.B. had the last laugh—I got the punishment. In the end (literally the end) I got warmer than the mouse or Dad's shoes! You see, in our home we didn't blame someone else for something we did. If we knew better than to do something and then did it anyway, we were guilty and took the punishment for it. We were taught that you make your own decisions to do right or wrong and take the responsibility for your actions. Don't blame your mistakes on others.

* * *

Girls always wore cotton hose that came above the knee when I was young. Getting her first pair of silk stockings (not nylon, which had not yet been invented) was a very special event to a girl. One day Mother came from town with a pair of silk stockings for each of us, Frances, Evelyn and myself. They were only 25 cents a pair but that was a lot of money to Mother. I was about 12 years old and could hardly wait until Sunday which was the only day we were allowed to wear them. She gave us a little talk about taking care of them, "Take them off as soon as you come from church so you won't ruin them. If you don't, the next pair of silk stockings you will have to buy yourself." I was the little hardhead who didn't obey. I wanted all the kids in the neighborhood to see I had silk stockings. I ran down an alley and slipped on a rock, tearing the entire knee out of one stocking as I fell. I still have two dark scars on my knee which reminds me that I bought my second pair of silk stockings out of money that I earned. And I didn't wear them for play!

* * *

Of course I don't personally remember the stories of me when I was a baby, but I've heard them told many times.

The horse ran away with Dad one day, throwing and injuring him quite severely. Mother's brother came to get her and carry her to the hospital. I was a baby and was asleep in the bed. They loaded the other children in the wagon and took off. They were almost in town and suddenly Mother looked around and asked, "Who's got the baby?" Of course no one did! In the excitement they had left me asleep on the bed and had nailed the door shut.

Another time when I was still very small, our house caught fire. Everyone ran outside and were pouring buckets of water on the fire. Suddenly, a cousin who was visiting, remembered I was inside. She ran inside and rescued me. I later told Mother, "You can't get rid of a bad penny." Of course she denied that I was a bad penny and most especially that she didn't want to get rid of me.

* * *

I used to love to dress Ruth for Sunday School when she was small. Mother made her the prettiest dresses and I couldn't wait to fix her up. I curled her hair and she looked like a doll except she was too pale. So I proceeded to commit a great big "No-No", I got into my older sister's make-up (my first mistake), I put rouge on her cheeks and lipstick on her lips. I thought my handiwork was so beautiful so I told Ruth to go show Mother how pretty she looked (my second mistake). Then I followed her to get my praise (my third mistake). Mother took one look, her mouth flew open and with hands on her hips she said, "Young lady, did you put make-up on Ruth's face?" Suddenly my handiwork wasn't so pretty as I answered, "Yes Ma'am." "Well, you go wash it right off and then come and show me how pretty she looks. And don't you dare ever do that again", she continued, as I left the room. I didn't!

* * *

When Bill and I worked at Woolworth together, the boys in the stockroom were forever pulling pranks on the girls. We seldom permitted them to get one on us—at least not for long. One morning the boys rolled up some greenish cellophane paper, put some black markings on it, fastened baby rattles to it and tied a long string on one end. It resembled a snake. They placed it underneath the stairs. One by one as the girls went to the basement to get needed supplies, the boys slowly maneuvered the snake from underneath the stairs with the long string. It looked so real and scared the girls silly. I kept hearing the girls scream and knew the boys were up to their old tricks. I finally persuaded one of the girls to tell me what was going on so I could think of something to get even with the boys. So when I went down, at just the right spot the snake came crawling out, I fell on the floor in a pretense of fainting. The boys were scared stiff. They ran for some water but just as they got back I raised up and said, "Don't you throw that water on me." One of them said, "We ought to let you have the whole bucket full." That didn't stop the prank playing though.

Chapter 37

Vacations

We never had a vacation as a family. In fact, I don't remember my parents ever taking a vacation until all the children were grown and gone from home. After I was married and we moved to Florida, they came to spend three or four weeks with us almost every year. I guess this was their first vacation.

When I was about eight years old, Mother began allowing me to spend a week in the country at Uncle Wilburn's house. This was Marshall's father and mother. These were some of the most cherished days of my early childhood. A child sees and does things on a big farm they never have the opportunity to do in city life.

Uncle Wilburn lived in a big southern, colonial type house with a huge front porch with large round columns. There was a big shady yard to play in and a shallow brook nearby where Marshall and I spent hours playing in the water. It was a little brook that ran down the hillside from a spring. The water was cool and clear and weeping willow trees along the edges of the brook made a cool delightful place on hot summer days. We'd hold bottles under the water listening to them gurgle as they filled to see which could fill a bottle the quickest. We found pretty smooth rocks and would build a dam across the brook to make deeper pools of water. Then catch minnows and put in the pool of water. There was always something exciting to do.

As one entered the house, you walked into a long wide hall. The parlor was at one end and the staircase and a bedroom at the other end of the hall. This is the room I always slept in on a high bed with a feather mattress. The window in this room looked out on a very large barn. Every morning I was awakened by roosters crowing, pigs squealing, turkeys gobbling and mooing of cows as they were being driven to the barn to be milked. As soon as I woke, I jumped out of bed and ran to the window to see all of Mother Nature coming alive. It was a wonderful feeling just to stand and watch.

I usually dressed and waited around in my room until I heard Marshall up. I could smell ham and biscuits cooking. Aunt Gordie always asked us if we wanted to eat with them or go up in the peach orchard and cook our own breakfast. We always chose the latter. She fixed our little basket of ham and biscuits and gave us a skillet, eggs and a jar of milk and off we would go. Marshall started a little fire to cook our eggs while I picked a couple of big peaches and went into the tomato patch and got a ripe tomato. Of course it was almost dinner time (lunch) by the time we finished eating and playing and got back to the house. This may have been her way of keeping us out from under foot and it sure worked fine for us.

There were big stacks of hay we could slide down and a barn loft we climbed up in and looked for new hen or guinea nests. Aunt Gordie always let us gather the eggs in the afternoon so we were aware of looking for new nests. Every time we heard a hen cackle we'd look to see where she came from.

Sometimes they wanted the cows put into another pasture where there was more grass and water. Marshall had a big collie dog and we took her to go do the chore and it amazed me how that dog kept the cows together as we drove them along.

One outstanding remembrance I have of that long front hall in the house was the player piano that sat there. There were stacks of rolls of music on top. When I thought no one was around, I really put on quite a concert. I put on the song I knew, walked halfway up the stairs, made my own introduction, walked to the piano, took a bow and began playing and singing. The words were right on the rolls of music. Then I got up and made my bow. I was just so certain that I could hear the applause and, "Encore!", yelled. I loved that player piano.

After supper we all sat on the porch talking about the events of the day, watching the light of day gradually slip into the darkness of night. The bright sun changing to the shadowy moon and stars twinkling in the darkened sky. The cows, chickens and animals all slowly quieted down for their night's rest. Then the night sounds; making the night come alive with frogs, crickets, owls and an occasional dog barking in the distance. Night noises that soothingly sing one to sleep.

This annual summer visit with Marshall was the highlight of my year. There is a great deal to be gained by experiencing farm life. It's almost like living a fantasy to a child. I wish every child could experience just one summer vacation like I had.

Chapter 38

The Dating Game

I'm sure our dating would sound very silly and be most boring to the youth of today, but we had so much fun. Very few boys had the luxury of owning a car or even the use of a car. Those who did were considered "fast" and self-centered so that a respectable girl would not go out with them. We walked wherever we went. We seldom had money for movies although they only cost 25 cents. So we walked to town to the drug store and had a coke or ice cream at the soda fountain for 5 cents.

We had one firm rule we had to abide by, we always had to go in pairs. Therefore, if a boy wanted to date one of us girls bad enough and another one of the girls didn't have a date, he had to bring a date for her or put up with a third person along on the date. So he would usually bring another boy and we'd double date. We used to laugh and say, "That's the only way Dad could get rid of us all." They always stayed and went to Bible class and church services with us on Sunday night. We had loads of fun walking.

One night G.B. and two friends had been frog gigging. They wanted us to get all our gang together and go up on reservoir hill and cook frog legs. There were about eight couples in our group and they all met at our house. Mother gave us our skillet, shortening and everything we needed to cook and we took off, everyone carrying something. The hill was the highest point in Columbia and was about two miles from our house. Just as we got to the top of the hill a sudden thunderstorm came up. We had to make a run for home. We arrived wet and hungry. Mother kindled a fire in the wood stove (remember we didn't have an electric stove) and cooked the frog legs for us. She even made hot biscuits and gravy! The kids thought this was the best party we ever had.

I remember another party G.B. instigated. He and a cousin had worked all summer on our uncle's farm. In the fall our uncle gave a wiener roast for all his nieces and nephews. G.B. and my cousin talked him into letting them plan the route of a possum hunt over the farm before we ate. They knew that farm like the backs of their hands. They carried us through barns, over haystacks, across creeks, and through cow pastures. They had the only lights and they could see to step over cow patties and let us step in them. We had to step on rocks going across the creek. The girl ahead of us complained she couldn't do it, she was afraid she would slip and fall in. Her date was going to be the gentleman and said he would carry her over the creek. He picked her up and started across, he slipped on the rocks and they both fell in. My date asked me if I wanted him to carry me over and I quickly replied, "No, thank you." After that evening we girls planned the parties.

Almost every Friday night one of the girls had a party. We all went in couples. It was a good way to meet

Clide and Evelyn, Alma and Ted

new friends because if we didn't have a date the word got around and someone brought you a date. That is the way I met my future husband. Evelyn and Clide were going and I mentioned that I wasn't going because I didn't have a date. Clide and Ted were boarding in the same boarding house and Clide said he would bring Ted for me. We hit it right off. We all played silly little games all evening like Spin the Plate, Post

Office, Hull-Gull, and Button, Button Whose Got the Button.

It was strange about Evelyn and me, I guess one thing that made us so close was the closeness of our ages. We shared everything, slept together, played together, shared secrets and dated together as we grew older. I introduced her to Clide whom she later married. He used to come into the Bluebird Ice Cream Parlor where I worked and sometimes walked me home after work. But he fell for Evelyn when he saw her, which didn't bother me at all since he later introduced me to Ted as my date at the party. We stood up with them when they were married at the preacher's house and they stood up with us when Ted and I were married at the court house by the Justice of the Peace. I remember Dad telling us children, "You are making your bed for life so make it good." Weddings were simple in my time and the cost was very meager compared to present day weddings. We were more interested in having enough money that we might rent a two room apartment and buy only enough furniture to get by temporarily.

Ted and Clide

Even then we weren't always able to get an apartment or furniture right away. Times were hard—everyone had very little money and couples just couldn't afford an apartment by themselves. We had learned years before how to make do with what we had or could afford. So Clide and Evelyn and Ted and I shared an apartment for a while. There were also a lot of fun times together. After Ted and I had a family and needed more room, we moved into a house about six miles from town. Every Saturday Evelyn and Clide went to the movies then rode the

Greyhound Bus to our house. They always brought something to cook for supper, we'd visit a while then Ted would carry them home. When we visited at their house and started to leave, Nancy pretended to be asleep so Evelyn would always say, "Just leave her, don't wake her up." The minute we were out the door she'd be up and playing with Clide and Evelyn. Of course we weren't fooled for long.

I am not exaggerating when I say Ted and Clide were as close as Evelyn and me. They were just like brothers to each other.

When Clide went to the service during W.W.II, Evelyn boarded at Mother's. We moved their furniture to our house to care for until he returned. The night before he left for the Army they spent with us. Nancy was just beginning to learn to walk. Every time they tried to go to bed Nancy crawled across the hall behind them. Clide stood her up, she hugged his leg and he walked her back to our room. As soon as he sat her down she crawled back and would beat him there. This continued until he taught her to walk that night. She and Jimmy have always loved Clide and Evelyn like parents, in fact they've always called Clide and Evelyn their other Dad and Mom. The feeling has always been mutual. I'm sure because of the special bond between Evelyn and me, and Clide and Ted, a deep bond formed between the children and Evelyn and Clide.

So the dating game can lead to many years of friendship and love. I have often wondered why certain brothers or sisters pair off and seem closer. I guess the age differences play a part in it. Mary was already in nursing school and Cornelia was married by the time I was in high school. Charles, Sarah and Ruth were much younger and I can't seem to remember too much about their childhood. I do remember Ruth coming into the living room every time we had a date. The boys gave her a nickel to get her to leave the room. She was an entrepreneur very early in life. Bill and I never double dated but we worked together at the Bluebird Ice Cream Parlor and Woolworth's. We were supposed to come home together at night after work. Many times, if I had a date, he would ride his bike ahead and wait for me one block from home so we could go home together and not get into trouble with Dad. So we got to be close and good pals, and have continued so.

I guess basically teens and the dating game haven't

changed too much. It just seems worse when our children play the dating game than it did when we were the culprits.

Chapter 39

The 5 And 10 Cent Store

Most couples have a song that they call "our song". This may sound crazy to the present generation, but our song was, "I Found A Million Dollar Baby In The 5 & 10 Cent Store". You see, I was working at F.W. Woolworth's 5, 10 & 25 cent store when Ted and I met. "Nothing over 25 cents" they advertised in those days. They soon added $1.00 on that slogan. I guess there are really no more 10 cent stores as they were generally called. They were not at all like our present day Wal-Mart or K-Mart.

Woolworth's was the focal point of our town, it was the appointed meeting place when you planned to meet someone. Every Saturday farmers and their families came to town to purchase their week's supply of needs and to sell their wares. They would spend the day, Mothers shopped with the children while the men visited the farm supply stores and livestock barns or just stood around on the court house square lawn talking and comparing crop news. At a designated time each family met at Woolworth's and went home in time to feed the hogs and chickens and milk the cows. Even though we didn't know their names, we knew who belonged to whom because we saw them come and go together every Saturday.

The young men always dressed up and stood on the outer edges of the sidewalk in front of the store, watching all the girls go by. The girls, dressed in their finest dress and high heeled shoes, walked up and down the street as if in a parade. My counter was the very first one as you came into the store— there was a door on either side of the counter—so I could see everyone come in and go out, in addition to people strolling up and down the sidewalk outside. They came in one door, walked all the way to the back of the store, back up the other aisle and out the other door.

There were three long counters the length of the store and three counters wide. There was a cash register on each counter so that purchases were paid for at the individual counters, not at the front of the store as is done today. Three or four girls were behind each counter so one did not have to seek out a clerk. The customer paid the clerk and she rang the sale and wrapped the package.

The counters were flat on top so the merchandise could be displayed in little bins divided into sections to fit the product. My department was cosmetics and toilet articles. Merchandise was displayed on both sides and at the ends of the counter around our walking area. We handled almost every available article needed in toiletries in small sizes—from 5 cent bars of all kinds of soap, dental supplies, cosmetics, to men's hair tonics and razor blades.

This was the largest department in the store. Underneath the counter was our understock. From this we had to replace what was sold from the top of the counter. All shades, sizes and colors must be kept available for sale at all times. Extra stock was kept in the basement. The first thing I did every morning was to fill the top of my counter from the understock and write an order for things I needed from the basement. Two stock boys worked in the basement where they checked in the freight, marked the merchandise and filled our orders and brought them to each counter. My brother Bill was one of these stock boys.

Every other week I had to inventory my department in the basement, check sales for the past four weeks and write up orders to firms from which we ordered. We had to order enough to keep at least four weeks supply at all times. This took quite some figuring. Each department had an inventory book to maintain showing items in stock and on order. This book was used once a week by the manager to check our counters and make sure every item was on display at all times. You never knew when you would be checked. The inventory book also contained the percentage profit each item paid. We were taught to place the highest profit paying items nearest the front edge of the counter in the largest displays and to push that brand. In other words if a customer asked, "Which is the best nail polish?", I was to say the name of the 58% one instead of the 38% one. Therefore we had to remember the percentage profit of most of our articles. This was no easy job.

The hours were long—from 8:30 a.m. to 6:00 p.m. every day except Wednesday and Saturday and closed on Sunday. During the summer months we closed at noon on Wednesday, Saturdays we closed at 10 p.m.—with 1 hour for lunch and 30 minutes for supper. And there were no coffee breaks! Remember, this was before forty hour work weeks and before social security and minimum wage. My pay ??? My starting pay was $8.00 a week. After social security came in, we were raised to $9.00 a week. The only benefit was one week paid vacation after one year's work. Out of my pay I gave $5.00 at home to help feed the family. With the balance I bought my clothes and lunch. Hamburgers were 10 cents and hot dogs were 5 cents, which is what I usually ate, or carried a sandwich from home. I had one charge account where I could buy shoes and clothes. I bought only one thing at a time and paid $1.00 every week until it was paid off. Then I would buy another. No interest was ever charged.

In spite of the hard work, low pay and long hours, I will always value the discipline and invaluable training I got in this job. I learned inventory control, profit paying purchasing and customer service that I carried with me in much higher jobs. Later (when we moved to Florida) I worked as a clerk and buyer for Belks and as a fashion coordinator and buyer of ladies' and children's clothing for William's Department Store. In this job I made trips to New York and Atlanta as buyer for the store. I could never have accomplished all this without the hard work and discipline I was taught from childhood and through the further training I received at Woolworth's. And who knows .... I may never have been the "Million Dollar Baby found in the 5 and 10 cent store!!"

My first job was at a quaint little ice cream store with round ice cream tables and chairs, called the Bluebird Ice Cream Parlor. One of the brands we carried unique from any other was the Bluebird Special. It had chunks of colored pineapple in it. When we had a new flavor of ice cream come in I'd always take some home to Mother. We could eat all we wanted while working but had to pay for the cones. To save money we'd use the ice cream wrapping papers, fold them so they'd hold ice cream and eat it out of that.

Instead of coming packed in containers as they are today, we filled the quart or pint containers according to the order we had. People phoned orders in and Bill (my brother, who also worked there) would deliver them on his skates, carrying the ice cream packed in two or three paper bags for insulation. Sometimes he'd skate two or three miles to make a delivery. Cars would also drive up for ice cream, the boys would go out to the car and take the order then deliver them back to the car. Instead of using rounded ice cream scoops as we have today, we used a big slanted spoon and stacked the ice cream on the cone in a slant; we'd really pack it on high—all for a nickel. Mother would ask me to bring her a cone of ice cream home and surprise her with the flavor. So I'd stack spoonfuls of different flavors in a cone and wrap it in several layers of paper wraps and take it to her when I got off work. Sometimes she'd be in bed but she would get up and eat her ice cream. It thrilled me to do something special like that for her and see her so pleased to get it and enjoy it so.

Alma

Chapter 40

Hog Killing Time

Ted and I once lived in a very small rural community named Neapolis located just north of Columbia, Tennessee, on Highway 31, which was then the principal Highway to Nashville. There were probably about twenty families living in Neapolis scattered throughout the community, most of them farmers. Even though Ted worked at Monsanta Chemical Company, he still had some cows, chickens, pigs and raised a very large garden.

This was at the early years of World War II and everyone had Victory Gardens, thus called because there was a shortage of food from sending food overseas. We also raised and preserved all the food we could.

The people were friendly and very helpful to one another with their crops, animals, children or anything that they needed assistance with. Once Ted suddenly became ill and had to be taken to the hospital. A neighbor knew I did not know how to milk. Even though he had a large herd to milk, he arose earlier than usual to finish his milking, then came down and milked our cows. We only had five. Then he fed our hogs. This he did morning and evening while Ted was sick.

There were milk trucks in those days which drove throughout the countryside and picked up the large metal milk cans which the farmers filled and set by the side of the road. They delivered it to the creameries and you would receive a check once a month.

There was a man who lived nearby who traded horses. Nancy loved to visit him because he let her sit on a horse; she still loves horses. One day she asked him if he would buy her a pink pony. He said he would if he ever saw one. She never ceased to ask him if he had found one yet—every time she saw him! As long as he lived, whenever he saw Nancy, he asked her if she had her pink pony yet.

Across the road from our house was a little country store.

On Saturday nights, all the community gathered in this little store and sat around and drank cokes and talked. This is where we received all the news of the day; all the gossip of the neighborhood too!

The center of the community was a small church and cemetery, and a two room brick schoolhouse. This is where Jimmy started school. It had only two teachers and went through sixth grade. During the war many teachers resigned and took jobs at war plants because the wages were so much higher, so there was a great need for teachers. One of our teachers resigned and the principal suggested that I go take the test and replace her. Nancy was almost four years old and he said I could bring her to school with me. If one could pass the test of 12th grade, they were eligible to teach grades 1, 2 and 3. I passed with a two year college average, so I taught until the war was over and they merged the school with a city school. This little red school still stands today and is on the National Historical Preservation list. It is really a unique little schoolhouse.

I will always remember an old Negro couple who lived down the road from us. Everyone called them Aunt Lavena and Uncle Algie. They were the kindest and best neighbors anyone ever had. Nancy and Jimmy loved to visit them, many times Nancy would stay with them while I went into town (Columbia). One day they gave the kids their choice of a litter of puppies. They named the dog Spot and when we moved to Florida we brought Spot with us. Each time we visited Tennessee, we went to see Aunt Lavena and Uncle Algie.

In their back yard they had a hog scalder. When the first real cold spell came, Uncle Algie told all the neighbors when he was going to fire up the hog scalder so everyone who wanted to kill their hogs could bring them over. Some scalded and cleaned theirs and then carried them home to cut up and trim. Others did theirs there so they could help clean up the mess afterward.

After the meat was cut each carried their meat home, the men going from home to home with each other to help get the meat on the house top. It was put on cardboard on the top of the house overnight to keep animals from getting it and so it would get cold all the way through. The next day the men helped one another trim off the fat for lard and cut up some lean for sausages. The women cooked out the lard in a large black kettle in the yard. Each made their own sausage at home later and also packed their own meat. Some packed their meat down in the corner of the smoke house with lots of salt. Later, after it was cured in the salt, they hung it from a rafter and smoked it with hickory wood. We preferred to sugar cure our meat so it wouldn't be so salty. We rubbed into each piece a mixture of salt and brown sugar and black pepper. Then we wrapped each piece well and put it in a croaker bag and hung it from a rafter, letting it drip for days. We left it this way for about a month. It was really delicious—never too salty.

I failed to mention how Aunt Lavena loved the chittlens. I detested this job and don't think I would have assisted anyone except Aunt Lavena in cleaning the chittlens. I refused to eat any!

Chapter 41

Pets

We often had a stray cat or dog come to the house. We wanted to keep it so bad and would beg for just one, but Mother would always say, "I'm sorry, children, it is just another mouth to feed and we simply can't." No amount of pleading or offering to feed it from our plates made her give in. She said we needed our food more than we needed a pet.

One day there was a little lamb in our yard. We never knew where it came from for no one ever claimed it. We had plenty of milk to feed it, so Mother let us keep it. We named her Mary. She followed us every place and was so cute especially as she ran and played with us. Whenever we played hide and seek, she would follow one child and just stand in front of where that child hid and bleat. She always told on someone. We kept Mary until she was quite large. None of us ever knew what happened to her. I imagine she ended up on our dinner table! If so, Mother was smart enough not to tell us for we wouldn't have eaten a bite if we had known.

* * *

Jimmy and Nancy always had a dog or a cat. One Easter Evelyn gave each of them a little colored baby chick. One of them grew into a very large white hen. She was named Peepsy. She would come to them when they called her and sit in their lap. One day she fell as she attempted to fly into the nest to lay an egg. The egg broke within her. We knew she would die from that, but we could not kill and eat her. I called Mother to see if she wanted her for dinner, which she did and invited us to dinner, but we declined.

The other little colored chick did not live but a few days. Jimmy and Nancy decided they would have a funeral and bury her. I heard them planning it as Jimmy told Nancy he would say the Lord's Prayer and she could sing a song. I asked if I could go but they said, "No. They put the chicken in a little box and dug a hole behind the hen house, then gathered some wild flowers. When they went for the funeral, I sneaked inside the hen house. Jimmy began and said the Lord's Prayer. Nancy, who was about four years old at the time, stood up and sang, "Don't Fence Me In". I left hurriedly before they could hear me laughing, it was so cute.

They had several dogs throughout their childhood, but I guess their favorite one was Spot, the one Aunt Lavina and Uncle Algie gave them. Spot lived for about 15 years and sympathized with Nancy and helped her through many childhood and teenage crises. Every child needs a pet and the responsibility of loving and caring for it.

* * *

It seems fitting to tell about another animal here, although it is not a pet, it is a part of my fond memories and an important part of Columbia. One doesn't have to be in Columbia long before they learn who is "King for a Day." It is the Mule. Columbia is the mule capitol of the world. Every first Monday in April is the celebrated Mule Day. The mule is honored with a big parade which is led by the King Mule pulling a float upon which the Queen of Mule Day and her court rides. All floats must be drawn by a mule or horse, no motor driven vehicle is permitted on the streets during the day.

I remember years ago every first Monday of the month farmers and traders met around the courthouse square to buy and trade mules. It was a big event and I can still smell the scent of the streets as I walked to school or work. People came from all over the U.S. to participate. They still do on Mule Day in April. The mule is a cross between the mare and the Jack.

Mules cannot reproduce and are not a beautiful animal with their long ears and short stocky legs. They are stubborn animals but they are strong, hard-working, tireless and know how to obey commands and get a job done. Mules were used for many jobs that now are done by tractors and trucks. There have been a few exceptional times that a mule could do a job that some modern machinery could not do. A few years back in the Columbia area, a large piece of machinery was unable to remove some huge rocks from a building site. A farmer heard of their problem and carried his team of mules to the rescue. After fastening the rocks to the mules with chains, the farmer gave his command. The mules dug their feet into the muddy soil and began their ceaseless pulling. One by one the rocks were removed.

This is a true example of how Christians are to work for the Lord. The mule is considered to be a dumb animal, but we as Christians can learn a great lesson from him by being tireless in our efforts to serve God. Galatians 6:9, "Let us not become weary in doing good, for at the proper time we will reap a harvest if we do not give up."

Chapter 42

My Prodigal Daughter

I remember my Prodigal Daughter who was only about four years old at the time of this event. She was the first granddaughter in the family so was a little special among the grandsons. She was the apple of her daddy's eye. She could roll those big blue eyes and smile sweetly and twist her "big brother" around her little finger. She had a doting aunt (for whom she was named) and a very special uncle (whom she called Sonny). I realized very early that I must be the disciplinarian and hold the reins.

I never knew where she picked up the phrase, "If you don't give it to me, I'm 'gonna' run away." It always worked with her brother and I was having a problem with it before I heard her using it on other playmates. I had talked to her several times and had even spanked her for it. One day I told her the very next time I heard her say it, I would pack her clothes and let her run away.

One cold winter afternoon as she played with Jimmy, she tried me out. I asked her if she remembered what I told her. She replied, "Yes ma'am." I said, "Go get your suitcase." We packed several warm outfits. I put on her snowsuit and mittens.

We lived about six miles from town and often caught the Greyhound bus into town. It was about 30 minutes until time for the bus. I gave her two quarters, telling her one was to give the bus driver to carry her in. I put the other one in her pocket and told her not to spend it for anything. If she ever wanted to come back home, she could use this quarter to come back and we always wanted her to come home. Then I gave her $2.00, again cautioning her to use this for food only. When this was gone, she might get hungry because she was too little to get a job. I told her I would pray that she would find a warm place to sleep tonight.

Then I took her on my lap and told her the story of the Prodigal Son. When it was almost time for the bus I put on my coat to stand outside with her to wait for it. I picked up her suitcase, took her hand and started to the door. I could feel her pulling back as I noticed (through my own tears) the tears roll down Jimmy's cheek.

Suddenly, her tears came. She said, "Mama, please don't make me go." I picked her up and assured her I wasn't making her go. It was she who wanted to go. She said she changed her mind and didn't ever want to go and would never say that again. We took off our coats and I took her on my lap as we sat by the fire and rocked. Then she said, "Will you tell me the story again?" I picked up my Bible and read it to her. Jimmy stood by listening, "Boy, it's for real," he said. Ted came in from work about this time and asked, "Is she sick?" Jimmy quickly spoke up and said, "She was going to run away from home again and Mama was going to let her." Ted just laughed.

She feel asleep in my arms. To my knowledge, she never used that phrase again. It could have turned her into a very selfish, self-centered person.

A child is never too young to be taught the way of the Lord.

Ted, Alma, Jimmy and Nancy

Chapter 43

The Home Front (World War II)

I shall never forget the day the Japanese attacked Pearl Harbor and the United States entered World War II. It was Sunday morning about noon, December 7, 1941. We had gone to Ted's brother's house for dinner after church. We had just sat down to dinner and given thanks. Someone turned on the radio so we could hear the news. There had been fear that we would get into the war for quite a while, but no one ever dreamed it would begin as it did. Suddenly, there was an interruption in the broadcast and President Roosevelt's strong voice came on the air announcing the attack and the devastation of the U.S. Naval base in Pearl Harbor. Everyone sat looking horrified because we all knew what it meant. It wasn't long until the President came back on declaring war on Japan.

This was the president that had

Mother, Charles, Bill and Dad

led the country from the poverty and starvation of the depression days to jobs and happier times. Everyone loved him and trusted his wisdom and ability to save our country. Now we were at war! Even though it was anticipated the reality now set in. There was hardly a family that would not be affected. The registration and draft of all boys over 18 years old was already in effect and many boys had already enlisted or been drafted.

Two of my brothers, Bill and Charles, had already enlisted in the U.S. Navy. Hundreds of books have been written on the horrors and bravery exemplified during this war. I want to reminisce on the home front only, since this is a part of my remembrances.

It was heart warming to see a country band together as America did. Patriotism was exemplified in everything and everyone from the oldest to the youngest.

We, on the home front, did all we could to encourage our boys overseas. Everyone who had even a small plot of ground planted a Victory Garden and preserved every bit of food we could so that the farmers' products could be shipped to the fighting boys. Some foods were rationed; meats, sugar and coffee were among these. Other rationed things were gasoline and tires. People pooled their cars going to work, school or even grocery shopping. Emergency vehicles and war plant employees had priority on gas and tires. Everyone registered and were issued stamps which were used to purchase rationed items. Some did not need all the stamps issued to them for some items and would trade them to another person for stamps of a product they did need.

Ration Stamps

Anything that came from overseas was scarce; such as gas, coffee and rubber. Everyone saved every bit of scrap rubber they had so it could be recycled and made into tires. Even small children gave up their rubber toys. At that time all the small cars and trucks that little boys played with were made of rubber. It broke Jimmy's heart to give up some of his cars and trucks, but he (as he worded it) "had to help his Uncle Willie (Bill) whip the Japs." All the small toys the boys had were army or navy replicas. They dug trenches in the dirt and put up tiny American flags and had tiny soldiers, tanks, jeeps, and planes and played for hours wearing a helmet or army cap. Nancy had a little boy doll dressed in his Navy Blues, which Uncle Willie sent her.

I remember one winter during the war Jimmy had pneumonia. I could not get him to drink all the liquid he needed. One day I put a chart on the wall by his bed on which I drew a plane. I told him every time he emptied a glass of juice or water, he would sink a Japanese ship or plane and I would put a mark on the chart. Then we could write and tell Uncle Willie how he was helping him fight the Japs. I had no more trouble getting him to take fluids.

War bonds, much like our savings bonds today, were sold by the government. They issued stamps which could be purchased for ten cents and stuck in a book, which when filled was converted to a bond. Children participated in this also.

N⁹ 987404 ES

UNITED STATES OF AMERICA
OFFICE OF PRICE ADMINISTRATION

WAR RATION BOOK FOUR

Issued to *Ethridge J. Chaffin*
(Print first, middle, and last names)

Complete address _____

READ BEFORE SIGNING

In accepting this book, I recognize that it remains the property of the United States Government. I will use it only in the manner and for the purposes authorized by the Office of Price Administration.

Void if Altered _____
(Signature)

It is a criminal offense to violate rationing regulations.

OPA Form R-145   16—35570-1

We tried to keep the morale of the boys up by writing often. The mail was censored so great care was taken in what we wrote. We all listened carefully every day for any news from "our boys". That included every boy from our hometown. Any time news came, we made certain it was passed around. We shared all the happy news and rejoiced with our neighbors over it and were sorrowful and cried with them over every unfortunate bit of news.

Those were the times that tried men's souls and brought people together and back to God like I have never seen before or since.

Chapter 44

The Mail Must Go Through

One of the daily events we looked forward to was the postman's arrival. Mail was delivered twice a day—morning and afternoon. I suppose the reason for the mail being so special is the fact that there was little other way of communication. Very few people could afford a telephone. As I remember there were only two in our neighborhood. Those who had a phone were wonderful in sharing them with people who could not afford one. We were taught to respect the privilege by asking to use it only in business or emergency calls. The phones were installed in the hall near the front door for the convenience and privacy of all who used it. Few could subscribe to the newspaper and the time was before radio.

One could send a card anywhere for 1¢ and mail a letter for 3¢; therefore, much communication was done by mail. Whenever the postman stopped, you knew you had a message, not a box full of junk and advertisements.

The postman arrived in a little horse-drawn green buggy.

The Mail Wagon, my Uncle Jimmy Derryberry

The horse waited patiently for the postman to deliver the mail to two or three nearby houses. Then the postman gave a little whistle and the horse would move on up to where the postman was waiting. You could not fool that horse, he would not move to anyone's whistle but his master's.

My uncle was our postman. A truck carried the mail from the train station to the post office. Then the mail was loaded on the buggy for the postman to deliver.

Mail was one of the most enjoyable things to our service men during World War II. Sometimes it would be delayed in getting to them and their morale dropped low when they couldn't hear from home.

All mail was censored that went overseas or came from overseas. All was opened and read and sometimes parts were blacked out for fear of the enemy picking up on some planned movement of the troops.

The mail grew heavy and difficult to transport so the government came up with the idea of "V-Mail" (Victory Mail) stationery. This was one sheet that folded into an envelope. You couldn't write much on it but the idea was that the boys would get more mail, more often, and if a ship carrying mail was sunk, another ship had additional mail on the way to them. Service men who were overseas sent their mail home for free. Air mail stamps cost 8¢.

I've heard the boys say that at mail call, if someone received no mail, one of the other guys would share his mail with him. Of course it wasn't like receiving a letter from your own mother, sister, sweetheart or wife, but it helped for a lonely heart.

Mail truck

This is the actual size of the V-mail they received during the war

No. _____

Mr. W. A. Derryberry, y ¾,
U.S.S. Trever,
Pacific Fleet Post office,
San Francisco, California,

Mrs. J. B. Derryberry
1016 S. Garden Street
Columbia, Tennessee
Mar. 8 1942 -

My darling son.

Hello and how are you this Sunday morning here I am up early again. Just got daddy off to work. and waiting for mary to come in from work. she has been at the hospital 6 nights. she keeps busy most all the time. Ruth still in bed. she really is liking school this time. she is playing basket ball some enjoys it lot. in fact is liking everything she is doing. is grand with her short hand. every body is fine here. Clara Jimmie Haney stayed with us last night until Ted came from work which was 12 oclock then I had to get up at 4.30 you see I didn't get much sleep. but I must not and don't grumble at that to think how little some of the boys are getting. maybe you and Charlie to. haven't heard any more from him. only through papers. he was alright. Dean calles me every day said him and jimmie was going to get them some horns and drums and join the navy. that all he talks about. he really is patriotic he was by here to take about. he really would go places and do things write when you can. all my love to Mother.

Chapter 45

Let's Move To Florida!

It was the first snow of the season, early November and a severe winter was predicted. Ted came home a little early coughing and chilled to the bone. Jimmy had already come home from school in the same condition and I had put him to bed. "Let's move to Florida," Ted said, "I'm tired of this weather." "Okay," I said, thinking it was a joke. The next afternoon Ted told me to start packing for he had made arrangements and resigned his job. He had phoned his brother in Dade City to locate us a house.

Dade City is a beautiful little town near Lakeland and Tampa in the heart of the citrus belt. We couldn't have chosen a better place for us if we had worked at it for a year. It was quiet, peaceful and friendly, everyone knew their neighbors and it was warm; many advantages that large towns do not have. So we were all settled into our new home in short order. Our house was just a frame of a house, not finished completely on the inside, near a sawmill.

The climate was marvelous. We continued to write home and tell them of our beautiful weather. No heat—no heavy clothing, only a sweater at night. Evelyn and Clide and Mary and her boyfriend decided to come spend Christmas with us. The move had been difficult for all of us. The night they arrived the temperature began dropping and didn't stop. They took my advice and brought only light clothing—to their regret. We had only a little wood burning heater, so the men took turns sitting up throwing pine slabs from the sawmill into the stove so we could keep a little warm. It burned up so quickly it didn't have time to heat the house.

We laughed it off and at night planned a trip for the following day so we could be in the sun, which was warmer than staying indoors. I guess they didn't mind the cold and inconvenience because they continued to come every Christmas for years. We visited them in Tennessee in the summer and Nancy and Jimmy would stay with Evelyn and Clide for several weeks.

The children went to school in Dade City. Ted worked as a mechanic and eventually owned his own repair shop. He soon saw the need for a tractor and farm equipment business and changed his repair shop to that. It was the right area for such a business and he soon purchased a building of his own. I was working in retail sales at Williams' Department Store, now Williams' and Lunch on Limoges, a unique little restaurant well known throughout central Florida. It wasn't long until we knew everyone and they knew us.

Ted had a serious heart attack and died in July, 1959. Jimmy was out of college and Nancy had completed the junior year at Pasco High School. Jimmy had worked with his dad during vacations so he and I decided we would continue to operate Johnson Tractor Company. Things went well until we had two hard freezes in two successive years which destroyed so much of the citrus groves. This hurt the growers and the tractor business.

I met and married Harvey in 1962. He was manager for Central Truck Lines for twenty years. He later worked as school bus manager and warehouse supervisor for Pasco County School Board. Later he became a court deputy for the Pasco County Sheriff Department where he worked until 1983. Harvey died in 1984.

When my eyesight began to deteriorate I sold my home in Dade City and moved to Tallahassee in 1989 to be near my daughter, Nancy and Dub, her husband. But my heart is still in Dade City, a little country town with a big heart and some of the best people in the world. It holds many fond memories since this is where Ted and I reared our children and I spent most of my adult life. It is where my children spent their childhood, married and started their families and their own memories. I still love to go back and visit my son and his family and all my friends there.

Chapter 46

Twelve Red Roses

In 1953 I was very ill and in the hospital in Brooksville, Florida. One day I received a bouquet of twelve red roses from my sister, Evelyn, in Tennessee. As I looked at the roses from day to day, they became symbolic of my family. My mother and dad and my sisters and brothers—12 in all. So I gave each rose the name of each of my family, the two standing tallest being Mother and Dad. After that, twelve red roses were at every special function or get together my family had. They personified our love and devotion to one another and the beauty and happiness we shared as a struggling family who had finally grown up to become successful and content, still sharing with our fellow man the glory and blessings wrought by God. I wrote Evelyn a letter thanking them for the twelve red roses and telling how I had named them and they had become symbolic to me of our family. As they began to wither and die I asked the nurse to take them away, it saddened me to see them in this condition.

Back row: Sarah, Ruth, Evelyn, Charles, William, Frances, Alma, Cornelia. Front row: Mary, Dad, Mother, G.B.—60th. Wedding Anniversary

When Mother and Dad celebrated their 50th wedding anniversary on April 11, 1956, I was unable to attend and in my place sent a bouquet of twelve red roses. On each rose was a tag with a family member's name on it. Each one carried their rose home with them to press and preserve. Evelyn sent me her rose and she kept mine....so typical of us—the two inseparable still.

On April 11, 1966, Mother and Dad celebrated their 60th anniversary. An arrangement of twelve red roses decorated the mantel above the chairs they sat in. We were all together for the first time since World War II.

Shortly after that Dad became ill. Many of us took turns staying at the hospital with him. He was very ill but I had to return to Florida for a few days, intending to go back, for his chances for recovery were very small.

One morning as I looked out the window, I saw that my red rose bush had many blooms—eleven blooms. I glanced at the next bush. There, alone, was one beautiful white rose. I immediately thought of my family and said, "Dad is dead. The first white rose amidst the red." Just then I heard my phone ring—I ran to answer it. It was Evelyn. "Dad is dead.", she said. "No," I thought, "he has just begun to live." This was June 30, 1967. We placed a vase at the head of his casket with eleven red roses and one white rose in it.

Mother died on April 4, 1974 and at the head of her casket was a vase of ten red roses and two white roses. We continued with this tradition at the death of each brother or sister, replacing a red rose with a white rose. At the last death (until the time of this writing) there were six red roses and six white roses so there still remain six children to share our love and happiness. My children have promised they will continue our family tradition until all twelve red roses have turned to twelve white roses.

As roses wither and die, we too must wither and die; but may God give us the same beautiful magnetism He has given the red rose that one can look at each of us and truly see the work of our Maker and that, like the rose, we each may make someone happier each day by having come into their lives.

Chapter 47

The Old Oak Table

I have a table in my living room on which my T.V. sits. If this table could talk I am sure it could tell many more stories than I can tell. The table is handmade but I don't know who made it or if they were in my family. It is made of beautiful oak wood and has one drawer with a hand carved pull. It is very plain, has some split wood in the top and at one time has been repaired by putting nails in the top and the nail heads are exposed which does not leave a very nice looking finish.

I don't remember where it came from but it has found a use in our house as far back as I can remember. It never had any particular attention and protection from the wear, weather, or time.

I first remember the table on our back porch. On one end of the table sat an old oak bucket with a dipper in it for pouring and a wash pan sitting in front of it. This is where we

Harvey and Alma

washed our face and hands before meals. There was a saucer sitting there which held homemade lye soap (our cleansing product). On the other end of the table was a water cooler which contained our drinking water. In the summer Mother got an extra nickel's worth of ice to put in the cooler.

After we were grown and Mother got new furniture, I don't really know how the table was used.

The next remembrance that I have of the table was after I was married to Harvey and we went home one day and saw the table sitting in Mother's back yard with pots of flowers sitting on it. I don't know how long it was used for this.

In about 1984, our (Harvey's and mine) little house at the fishing camp burned. After we rebuilt it we were looking for used furniture to replace what burned. One day while visiting my sister in Tennessee, Harvey went to the basement and found the table leaning against a wall, all four legs laying beside it. Poor little table, all those years of use and now here it was, all in pieces! But all was not lost or useless! Mary gave it to us to repair and use it at our camp. I removed three layers of paint from it when I refinished it and Harvey put in back together.

When we sold the camp property, the table found a home in my living room. Together we've found many happy memories. It is very strong and sturdy and the wood is beautiful after its many years of wear and use. It continues to be very useful.

I have seen people who have been a Christian for a long time and been very useful in the Lord's church feel, when they get old, that they should retire and let someone else teach the classes and do all the work. They say, "I taught classes when my children were growing up—now let the younger people teach their children. They are actually willing to be "leaned against a wall in the cellar!" We can never retire in the Lord's work. The compensation may seem small but the fringe benefits are eternal. A Christian is never too old that he cannot speak a word of encouragement, write a letter, make a phone call or strive to keep a young person from going astray!

Moses was 120 years old when he led the children of Israel out of Egyptian bondage and he still gave years of service to God. Like my table gave years of service to a happy, caring family—so we can do the same for our caring and loving Christian family.

Remember, a piece of machinery will rust out from lack of use quicker than it will wear out with much use.

Chapter 48

A Boat Ride In The Storm

In studying the 27th chapter of Acts of Paul's fourteen days on a stormy sea, I remembered a storm we once endured on rough waters, but ours was only a part of a day...a very scary day.

We were fishing out in the Gulf, off the Florida coast. It was a beautiful day and we were drifting out a little farther than usual. We were having a good time and carelessly drifted too far from our markers. We had Cathy, our grand-daughter, with us, she was only about five at the time. She was in my Sunday school class and just the Sunday before I had told them the story of Jesus walking on the water.

Suddenly, the wind began to blow hard and it became dark overhead. We quickly reeled in our lines and aimed toward markers or land, but we could see neither. So we were strictly dependent on our compass and Harvey's knowledge of directions. He turned up the speed and we were banging into the waves. Harvey pointed toward the direction he knew the first marker was located and told me to watch for it. Our glasses were so misted with salt spray we could hardly see.

I took Cathy on my lap to soften her bumps a little (or perhaps it was to weigh me down some). Anyway, she was squeezing my arms tightly around her waist. Suddenly, she turned those big beautiful brown eyes up to me and said, "Granny, I don't blame Peter for being scared in the storm, do you?" I said, "No, but Jesus is out there watching over us just like He did Peter." She asked, "Where?" I said, "This way," and pointed into the direction of the channel markers. She kept watching and suddenly said, "There He is!" I looked and saw the black post sticking up out of the water. When we reached the marker, she looked all around and said, "Where did He go?" Harvey made a 35 degree angle right turn at this marker to the next one. I said, "He's showing us the way. Look in this direction now," and pointed toward the next marker, "and when you see

Jesus, keep your eyes on Him. He is showing us the way home."

Soon she spotted the next marker. She became so excited looking for Jesus that she just forgot about being afraid. At the next marker, we made another turn and I pointed for her to watch in that direction. And so it went from marker to marker until we safely reached shore.

She told the class about it the following Sunday and they too became excited. I explained to the class that we could not see Jesus in person but if we looked hard enough, we could see Him in every good thing God made and in every kind deed we do for others. So while we didn't actually see Jesus walking on the water, we could see the wonders of His great world and feel His closeness in keeping us safe in the storm. I told them when they were obedient and good, other people could see Jesus in them.

Perhaps we should become more excited about Jesus and tell our friends more about Him who walked on the water and died for our sins. Sometimes we get to having fun or become too busy or too involved with worldly things that we carelessly drift away. We take our eyes off Jesus and the rough winds or tides of life will cause us to drift too far away from safety. You may not have a little child to help you back. "A little child shall lead them." Isa. 11:6. It is hard to turn around in a storm and high winds. There are many rocks to hit when we get out of the channel. But if we stay focused on Jesus and keep our eyes on Him, He will lead us safely home to "that evergreen shore". Can others see Jesus in you?

If we miss heaven, we will miss it all!

Chapter 49

A God Walk

Did you ever take a God walk with a small boy? It can be very enlightening. My oldest grandson, Ted, came along at a very low ebb in my life. My husband, Ted, had died at age fifty. Ted was born about one year later and was named for his grandfather, so his presence turned a lot of lonely days into happy times. He loved spending time with me. Needless to say I loved it also.

When he was about five years old, he came almost every Friday to spend the day. This was the day his mother shopped. This was also the day I went to the church building to arrange my visual aid table for my Sunday class, I taught Ted's age group. He wanted to know what story I was going to tell Sunday and loved helping me fix the table. He wanted me to practice on him. If it held his interest, I knew it would do the same for the other children. He often made very useful suggestions.

One day when Ted came over to visit, he wanted me to make a picnic lunch and us to walk up on the hill in our orange grove and eat lunch. This we did. During our walk he asked, "Granny, did God make all these trees?" I answered, "Yes, He did." He said, "Tell me about it." So I told him about the creation.

On his next visit he wanted to picnic again. As we walked along he saw a dove. He asked what kind of bird it was. When I told him it was a dove, he asked, "Can you tell me a 'God story' about a dove?" I said, "Sure." So I told him about Noah sending a dove from the ark during the flood.

The following week Ted was startled by a covey of quail as they flew away. Again he wanted a 'God story' about the quail. Every week was something different; a snake, a pretty cloud, a rainbow, a big rock, the wind, etc., until I got the feeling he was trying to trap me. But so far I was able to remember a story from the Bible.

This was confirmed one day when he saw a big ant bed. He

very proudly said, "I bet you can't tell me a 'God story' about the ants." I said, "Well, I bet I can." So I told him about the lesson taught in Proverbs 6:6, "Go to the ant thou sluggard, consider her ways and be wise." We stood and watched how the ants worked together so diligently and I told him that this is the way God wants us to work for Him and for our family.

I'll have to admit, he finally got me when he noticed a big gopher hole, I never could find him a story about that. He began calling our walks through the orange grove a 'God walk' and he never ceased wanting to take one.

When his brother, David, was about four years old and began to spend the day, he shared our walks. Ted would ask me to tell David the various stories that I had told him. As David began to get interested, he too started to challenge me. He saw a big pile of rocks which had been stacked against the fence to prevent the disk or hoe machine from hitting them. Immediately David presented his challenge to me to tell a story about a pile of rocks. I told him the story of Joshua and the children of Israel crossing the Jordan River and the twelve stones, Joshua 4:1-24. I detected a bit of disbelief on his face, but he said nothing. When we got to the house he went straight to the table, picked up the Bible, handed it to me and said, "Here, Granny, read it to me." So I turned to Joshua 4 and read it. He took the Bible and said, "Yep, it's in there!", as he put the Bible back on the table.

We can be a David or a Ted. If in doubt, say as David did, "Here read it to me." Then accept it from God's Word as we learn in Acts 17:11 ....to receive the Word with all readiness of mind, and search the scriptures daily, whether those things were so." We can also be a Ted and desire a 'God walk' and a 'God story' every day to enlighten us and teach us how to live in this world. II John 6, "And this is love, that we walk after his commandments......" Do you seek a 'God story' daily to help you walk with God? I learned a lesson from these two small inquisitive boys and enjoyed every minute of our walks together, as challenging as they were.

Chapter 50

Big Men Do Cry

I recently witnessed a man, woman and little boy going across the street. The woman fell and her face and hand was bleeding. As the husband helped his wife up, the little boy was crying and trying to wipe the blood from his mother's face. He was crying uncontrollably at his mother's discomfort. She tried to comfort him and I heard his daddy say, "Quit crying. Big men don't cry!" I wanted to shout at him, "Big men do cry! Let the child cry, he is hurting, he sees his mother is hurt and he is showing great love and compassion for his mother." I wanted to take him in my arms and say, "Go ahead—cry. Show your mother your love."

Sure, big men cry! The shortest verse in the Bible tells us, "Jesus wept", John 11:35. Jesus loved Lazarus, Mary and Martha and he showed sorrow and compassion in His tears. In Luke 19:41, Jesus wept over Jerusalem. We can read in Hebrews 5:7-8 that Jesus wept on the night of His betrayal in the Garden of Gethsemane.

I can't help but believe that Jesus shed tears on the cross when He looked on the saddened and agonizing expression that must have been on His mother's face as He instructed John to care for her. One cannot see his mother cry without shedding a tear of his own.

Sure, men cry! Peter wept bitterly when he denied Christ three times. Jeremiah was called the weeping prophet. Most all the prophets and apostles shed tears over the sins of God's people.

I remember the night I obeyed my Lord in baptism. Dad was leading singing. As I walked down the aisle I glanced up at him and tears were rolling down his cheeks. I know now that these were tears of joy but when I saw his tears, mine fell also. Mine were tears of love for my dad and knowing he loved me. So we cry for different reasons but all are emotional releases.

Several years ago, after his parents moved to Tallahassee,

Brian stayed in Dade City with me to work and go to college.

In the summer he was working at a funeral home and cemetery. I remember one evening he came in from work very upset. He said, "Granny, they asked me to do something today and I just could not do it. We were burying a little baby. They laid the tiny casket in my arms and told me to put it in that hole. I couldn't! I just froze. I could not put that tiny baby in that black hole. Someone took it from me." There were tears on his cheeks. "I told them," he said, "from now on someone else had to bury the babies and the old people." Brian will always be special because of his show of love and affection toward the elderly. He seems to have a "soft spot" in his heart for them. Just a little pat on the back, a tap on the knee as he passes, an arm to lean on, a word of kindness, and a tear when you hurt are his special traits.

One night I was sick and having a chill. I remember Brian came into my room to check on me. I could feel him tucking the covers tighter around my feet and legs and patting them softly. The softness and tenderness showed his love and compassion and are qualities which make a good man - yes big man.

Our children need to be taught more kindness, love and compassion....... not the macho image that is so prevalent in today's society.

Yes! Big men cry! Strong men cry! Compassionate men cry! Joyful men cry! Godly men cry!

Chapter 51

"Read The Constructions, Grandpa!"

Ben was everywhere when he was growing up. He was the youngest of three boys, but he could do anything they could do—at least he was determined to try. The older boys were in Little League, but Ben was still in T-Ball. He attended all the games with his mom to watch the boys play and dream of days to come.

He was nicknamed "Tweetie Bird" because of his pudgy round cheeks and his quickness. He moved so fast when he ran his legs looked like little wheels going round and round.

In a small town like Dade City everybody knew everybody. Ben's dad and mom had gone through school with the man who was the radio announcer and he knew the boys.

Harvey and I stayed home one night and listened to one of Mark's games being broadcast. The announcer suddenly said, "There goes one over the fence—and there goes Tweetie Bird after it. He's got the ball, now he's gone to get a coke." The kids would carry the ball to the concession stand and receive a free coke for returning the ball.

It wasn't long until we heard, "Tweetie Bird after the ball again. Wonder what he does with all those cokes?" "Probably sells them," the other announcer replied. This continued through about four balls and four cokes. Then, POP!, another ball over the fence! The announcer said, "There goes about a dozen boys after that ball; but I don't see Tweetie Bird. I guess he's had enough." Only seconds passed, then we heard a big laugh and, "Look, there comes Tweetie Bird out from under that pile of boys, holding up the ball....and he looks like he's been ground in the dirt. How did he do that?" "I don't know," was the reply, "but the other boys are still looking!" That night we enjoyed the game at home more than being there in person.

Ben has a knack for getting right to the heart of things and getting them done. Sometimes when he would come to visit us Harvey would be trying to assemble or repair something. Harvey always thought he could just look at the picture and make it work without reading the instructions. Ben probably wanted to see if Grandpa could make it work. After several times of taking it apart and trying another way, with Ben watching in disgust, Ben would say, "Why don't you read the 'constructions', Grandpa?" Then sometimes Harvey would, but most of the time he wouldn't.

Ben has tackled his plans for his future with this same kind of determination; he knows what he wants and is working towards that goal.

Our goal is heaven. We need to strive to serve our Lord with this same determination and fervor. Then we can each come out from the bottom of the heap, holding the "ball" up high. And when doubt or fear arises, always—always, "Read the constructions"!

2 Timothy 3:16-17, All scripture is given by inspiration of God, and is profitable for doctrine, for reproof, for correction, for instruction in righteousness; That the man of God may be perfect, thoroughly furnished unto all good works.

Chapter 52

A Child's Love

Little Katie, who lives next door and calls me Great-Granny, brought over my Christmas present, a Nutcracker music box. She looked so proud and pleased as she showed me how to make it play and told me to be very careful with it and not break it. It was so pretty and much more beautiful after her mother told Nancy the story of why she gave it to me. Her mother had been on a trip to the mountains and brought the Nutcracker music box back to Katie. As they were wrapping presents, she handed Katie a sun-catcher for hanging in the window to wrap for me. Katie looked at the sun catcher and said, "Mama, I can't give Great-Granny this because she can't see it. I want to give her my Nutcracker music box because she can hear it." What an unselfish act of love and understanding for a five year old!

As I sat and pondered this, I remembered some other small children and their acts of love and kindness.

A little six year old girl named Connie, who lived across the street from my sister Mary, who was an invalid with Lou Gehrig's disease (A.L.S.), came to her door one day and said, "My Mama said the lady here was sick. Can I see her?" I said, "Sure, but she can't talk. She can smile and see you and hear you, but you will have to do the talking for her." So she came in and stood beside Mary's bed and never took her eyes off Mary. Mary smiled and looked from me to Connie as I told her Mary was trying to tell her she was glad that Connie had come and how pretty she was. The next afternoon, Connie came again to visit. She asked if she could hold Mary's hand and I said, "Yes." As she laid her little hand over Mary's twisted and gnarled hand, they smiled at each other, and I noticed a tear run down Mary's cheek. Connie noticed it also and asked for a kleenex. I handed her one and she wiped Mary's tear away and asked if she had hurt Mary. I said, "No, you've made her feel very good by coming to see her." (Then I needed a kleenex.) The next day,

Connie returned with a dead butterfly in her hand. She said, "I found this beautiful butterfly in the street, a car hit it. I saw Miss Mary had lots of butterfly pictures on her walls and I thought she might like to have it." I mounted it on a piece of bright construction paper and fastened it on the window curtain. Connie came often but never stayed long. What a bright spot in Mary's long lonesome days a small girl brought with her gentleness and compassion!

Then there was Sarah. Her grandmother and I were visiting in the nursing home. We carried Sarah and her new Rainbow Brite doll. She went to every person she saw, male and female, and asked, "Do you want to hold my Rainbow Brite doll?" They took her doll and smiled and talked to her as their eyes followed Sarah around the room. What joy, for a few moments of the day, Sarah gave as she shared her special doll with these people so confined from everything and everyone they loved.!

And a little four year old boy named Jimmy....he picked his mother a handful of dandelions, which had already turned white with seed. As he came in the door, a gust of wind blew the seed all over the room. Jimmy was in tears. "They were so pretty and I picked them for you," he cried. "They are still very beautiful," I said, "because this is the way God made them. Let's go outside and see what they looked like when they were little like you." So we went out and picked some of the little yellow flowers and some more of the white ones and put them in a little glass of water together. I told him, "God made people like flowers....bright and colorful when young, and white and bald when old. Both are beautiful. When they are young and colorful, they are like you and other children and when they are white and bald, they are like your grandmother and granddaddy. Don't you think they are beautiful?" And he did! That little boy has two grown sons today, and he can still find something beautiful in everything and everyone he meets.

Little children can spread so much joy and happiness, yet it takes so little to make them happy. No wonder Jesus said, "Verily I say unto you, except ye be converted, and become as little children, ye shall not enter into the kingdom of heaven." - Matthew 18:3

Chapter 53

Mark's Patience

Patience is a virtue we are not born with. When a baby cries to be fed, he doesn't cry one time and wait. He will cry continually and louder and louder until he gets what he wants.

As he gets older we begin to teach him patience by not rewarding him so quickly. It is interesting to watch a child as he gets older, learning to persevere and develop patience. It requires much patience on our part to hold out against his every request and childish reasoning.

We used to take the grandsons fishing with us a lot. This is one area in which much patience is required. We told them in the beginning taking care of their equipment and untangling their own line was their responsibility. We could readily see when they really needed help but would usually let them try a while before we asked if they wanted our help.

I remember one hot summer day, I saw Mark stooping down over his line trying to straighten it out. I asked if he needed help but he said, "No, Ma'am". As we continued to watch him struggle, every few minutes he would stop and wipe the perspiration from his face. I finally felt so sorry for him that I went out to help. I have never seen such a conglomerated mess of line, hook and bobber. He would never have got it untangled but he really persevered. I didn't tell him he couldn't do it, I just told him he was loosing precious time catching fish. So we just cut his line and put on a new hook and lead. He sat in the shade and had a coke while I fixed his line. He said it paid to be patient—he had a cold drink and a nice rest.

This Christmas I saw Mark portray that same patience and persistence with a vengeance. One evening while he was helping his dDad clean up and burn some limbs, he lost his Auburn class ring. He was out bright and early the next morning searching and looking, being assisted by his mom and dad. They searched the house, the yard, the shed—every place he had been. No ring to be found! He rented a metal detector and went over the area where he had been the night before. Still no ring! He went home and searched again there, even emptied the vacuum cleaner. Then he came back and went through the garbage because he remembered he had carried out the garbage for his mother. Still no ring! After work on Monday afternoon, here came Mark again, rake in hand to rake through the burned debris. He didn't rake long until his persistence rewarded him with his prized and hard earned Auburn ring! It was slightly scorched and discolored but restorable. We all rejoiced with him.

There is a lesson in this for us. There are many lost souls around us. So many children with no leadership, feeling lost and unloved who need someone to help them find the right way. These souls are as precious as Mark's ring is to him. If we work with the diligence and patience and persistence that Mark exemplified, who knows what wonders can be wrought. Oh, we won't save them all, but there is great rejoicing in Heaven over one lost soul that is saved, Luke 15:7   We are to "bear fruit with patience", Luke 8:15.

Chapter 54

Mary

She was a nurse, she knew she had A.L.S. (Lou Gehrigs Disease) before the doctor diagnosed it. She had never seen a case of it but she knew the devastating, slowly crippling characteristics of A.L.S., that the life expectancy was from two and a half to five years. She was my oldest sister, Mary. She was the one who was always there when sickness or trouble came to any one of us. She was the one who provided a home for Mother and Dad in their old age. The one we all went to for advice and help—and who was ready to help anyone, always with a smile.

Mary

We watched her slip slowly from a quad-cane to a walker to a wheel chair to the bed. We heard her speech slur to a gradual muteness, then she began communicating by writing notes until her crippled hands could no longer hold a pencil. She used a child's educational toy, a Speak and Spell, very successfully until she no longer had strength to push the buttons. By this time we almost knew what she wanted by her moving her eyes and a few guesses on our part. The weakness in her throat also affected her swallowing so all food was soft and thin and a suction machine was kept beside her bed for use when she became strangled. We saw the five and a half years she had been given to live extend to eighteen years. The disease did not affect her hearing, seeing or brain functions.

Here lay this once strong, independent lady, who shouldered everyone's problems; now totally dependent on others. More than once she begged us to put her in a nursing home but this was completely out of the question with all of us. With two hired girls to help us we divided our time together, four sisters and one brother. During the time of Mary's slow deterioration, she saw the deaths of Mother, two brothers (two weeks apart), one sister, and two brothers-in-law. In addition, one brother and one brother-in-law had major surgery. Each time of a death Mary wrote, "Why couldn't it have been me?" We never thought that, we just bonded a little closer with one another, rearranged our schedules, and prayed harder for strength and patience to endure, for all of us including Mary who always managed a smile no matter how bad a day she was having. We could never have lasted so long without the love, encouragement, and patience of our spouses. Everyone loved Mary.

I remember promising myself I would never enter her room without a cheerful word and a smile. I often had to stop outside her door and think of some silly greeting to get a smile on my face, which always brought one in return.

Mary exemplified kindness, unselfishness, and love for her fellow man; she spent her life giving to others. She was a gentle and loving lady. When the time came that she was in need, she received much love and care in return. This is a perfect example of the words of Christ in Luke 6:38, "Give, and it will be given to you; good measure, pressed down, shaken together, running over, they will pour into your lap. For by your standard of measure it will be measured to you in return."

I used to tell her when she worried about our health, that I would rather be on the giving end than on the receiving end. I realize the truth of this statement more than ever now. The caregiver becomes the most important person in our lives. Nancy, Dub, Jim, and Denise have been my shining stars, also the grandchildren. I don't deserve such loving care but I thank God daily for my blessings.

As Jesus hung on the cross He gave his Mother to John to care for. John 19:26-27, "When Jesus therefore saw His mother, and the disciple whom He loved standing nearby, He said to His mother, "Woman, behold your son!" (27) Then He said to the disciple, "Behold, your mother!" And from that hour the disciple took her into his own household." Even Jesus chose a very special person to care for someone so special to Him. I'm sure a very special blessing goes to every caregiver.

Chapter 55

Brothers-Sisters, What Happened To Them?

All of my family during the 1930s

My brothers, what nuisances! What pests! What an aggravation! And then years later...what a blessing!

How could seven sisters endure three such mischievous brothers? Whatever makes them act so strange when they are young makes them endearing to you as the years go by.

G.B. was the oldest brother. He became a preacher though one would never have dreamed it could possibly be when he was growing up. He was the devilish one. He could think up more mischief than Tom Sawyer, but he never carried it out. He would begin laughing and say, "Wouldn't it be funny if..........", and somehow get someone else to do the dirty work. My second brother, Bill, was the doer so when G.B. mentioned a prank it was as if he had pushed a button on a robot, Bill went into action and Bill got the blame. This process never changed until the day G.B. died. Bill was still the robot—it was such fun after we were grown and couldn't get in trouble.

Charles was the youngest and was always small for his age. Bill loved to aggravate him. Mother told Bill she hoped to live to see the day Charles was the biggest and could whip him. That day came during World War II. Both Bill and Charles joined the Navy. The first time they both came home at the same time Charles was bigger; however, now they were both fighting on the same side...for Uncle Sam. They never argued or fought one another any more. But G.B. never changed, he always loved to pull pranks.

One night, when Charles was small, he got lost while walking in his sleep. Evelyn and I were awakened by a noise. We sat up in bed and listened. We heard glass breaking, then we heard Charles crying and realized he was in the attic. Mother kept her empty fruit jars there and he had bumped into them. We went to rescue him and found him black with soot because the chimney went up through the attic. I carried him downstairs to the back porch and washed him. He was still scared so I put him in bed between Evelyn and me so he would feel safe and go back to sleep.

Charles was accidentally killed while cleaning his gun, not knowing it was loaded, when he was fifty-five. G.B. died of a cerebral hemorrhage one Wednesday night while at church services, he was sixty-five.

Bill is still around teasing, playing pranks, and always the "Rock of Gibraltar" for us all. He was so good to Mother, she was his best friend. As long as she lived, he made sure she got anything she wanted. She loved him coming by and just sitting and talking with her after his work hours every day. It was the highlight of her day after Dad died. He used to come to Florida every year during his vacation and he and I fished the entire two weeks.

There are five sisters against one brother now and we give him a hard time—teasing him as he used to tease us. We have lots of fun when we all are together. He is our buddy, our pal, and still a robot! Just push his button and stand back—anything can happen. He will do anything for us that we ask of him when we need help.

Peace and harmony within a family honors our father and

mother. Thus peace and harmony between brothers and sisters in the family of God honors our Father in heaven.

Those brothers and sisters who drive us crazy when we are children will one day be one of our greatest blessings and our "Rock of Gibraltar."

*****

What happened to all these poor children who were raised primarily during hard times and depression days? The question most asked is, "How in the world did your parents do it?" The best answer I have is, "They trusted God and kept His commandments. They loved their children and their neighbors. They never failed to show their love to us as they expected in return respect, honesty, cooperation, hard work and faithfulness to God."

The children whom you have been reading about, who had so little material things, grew up having the most important things to make them able to cope in life and be responsible adults.

Mary became a registered nurse (with the financial assistance of our family physician) and retired as an industrial nurse at DuPont Chemical Company. She never married. Mary died in 1991.

Cornelia became a telephone operator. She married and reared four fine sons. She died in 1986.

G.B., Jr. became a bookkeeper and later preached for many small churches of Christ throughout middle Tennessee. He married a local girl and had one daughter. He died in 1975, just two weeks after Charles.

Frances was a bookkeeper for many years. She and her husband had a small farm in Maury County and had three sons and one daughter. They later moved to Florida.

Evelyn became a payroll clerk in a laundry and dry cleaners. Her husband, Clide, a Maury County boy, served in the Army in World War II. They never had children but always "claimed" Nancy and Jimmy as their children too and doted on them. This was never a problem and Nancy and Jimmy delighted in having "another Mommy and Daddy". That special relationship continues to this day. Nancy is named for Evelyn. Clide died in 1989. One of Nancy's sons is named for him.

I began retail sales at F.W. Woolworth. I later became a sales clerk and buyer for two department stores in Florida. I was buyer and fashion coordinator of the women's department in a fashion store. Later, I also was bookkeeper and manager of the office for Ted's garage and farm machinery business. Ted and I had two children, Jimmy and Nancy.

William, better known as Bill to everyone, served our country in the Navy in World War Il. After the war he was a foreman at Union Carbide Co. until his retirement. He met his wife in the Navy, she was a Wave, they married and had a daughter and son. I named Jimmy for William.

Charles also served in the Navy during World War II, after which he was a foreman at a Nashville Electric Company. He and his wife had four children, three sons and a daughter. Charles died in 1975.

Sarah married and spent her life being busy as a wife and mother of two daughters and one son. She didn't work out of the home but has cared for many children other than her own in her home and she and her husband did some farming.

Ruth, the youngest, did office work at the telephone company and later at DuPont Chemical Company and her husband's business. She had four daughters, two of which were fraternal twins, named after Mother and Aunt Fannie, her twin sister.

Two of Mother and Dad's twelve children died in infancy.

All were happy and successful in their individual jobs although none of us, except Mary, had more than a high school education. Thanks to proper training when we were young by our parents, we all succeeded in finding a respectable place in life for ourselves.

How different from most poor and large families of today who seem to think the government owes them a living and blame their parents for their misfortune of being poor.

Instead of blaming our parents for us being born poor and unable to have things like other children, we thank God every day for the wonderful parents we had; for the love, guidance and knowledge of God's word they instilled in us.

Chapter 56

My Best Friend

I've talked a lot about my sister Evelyn. I was a year behind her in school, 20 months younger, and we had always done everything together. We walked to school together, had always slept together, told one another all our secrets and problems, and yes, we were best friends. When Evelyn was a junior in high school, she had a nervous breakdown. When she got sick Mother had to move her into a room by herself. No one could go in except Mother or Mary. I don't remember how long she remained in that room. She cried a lot and every time I heard her cry, I went off somewhere by myself and cried too. I knew she needed me and I needed her and neither of us could get through those walls. I missed her as much as if she were 10,000 miles away. I missed her laugh, her funny little remarks and I missed talking to her. I missed walking to school with her and I missed her

Evelyn and Alma

arms around me at night as we tried to keep each other warm. At times I could hear her cry in the night and I prayed, "Please, God, don't let Evelyn die. I love her so much." One day I heard her sobbing and I went and stood beside the door and cried with her. When Mother came out she asked me what was the matter. I told her, "I want to see Evelyn, I know I can make her get better." Mother put her arm around me and assured me that Evelyn would be well soon but she would have to ask the doctor if I could go in the room with Evelyn. I was elated when the doctor agreed to give it a try for a brief supervised visit. That meant Mother had to be in the room so I couldn't tell her my latest secrets. That was all right though—there would be a tomorrow. At least I was going to see if she was okay and if she remembered me. When I entered her room she smiled at me. I bent over to kiss her and I could hear the sobs begin. I whispered in her ear, "Please don't cry, Mother will make me leave and won't let me come back." So she laughed aloud. Mother told the doctor that was her first laugh since she had been sick. "A good laugh is the best medicine. A brief visit daily is fine and you won't have to stay in the room," he said to Mother. I was ecstatic. I picked flowers for her, got friends at school to write her notes and read them to her. We had fun reading those.

Her hands trembled violently at times. Once I asked her why they were shaking. She said she didn't know but she wished they would stop. I said, "Here, let me hold them and they will stop shaking." They did and after that she asked me to hold her hands every time I went in her room. Sometimes she would ask Mother to tell me to come in and hold her hands. We never told Mother this secret either. We were afraid she would send someone else in to hold Evelyn's hands instead of me. We were both convinced I was the only one holding the magic power between us.

Bill had a paper route so we got a free daily newspaper. I saved my daily visit until the paper came. Every day I sat on the steps and waited. Sometimes I met the paper boy at the curb. (Bill didn't deliver our paper.) As soon as I got the comic page out I headed for Evelyn's room. The paper published a continued story, one chapter daily, so I read that to her too. I would stop reading sometimes and we would just chat. Often Mother came to the door to see why it was taking so long. Evelyn always begged her to let me stay longer and she usually would. I always kissed her good-bye and we prolonged the visit with some silly little chit chat. Her room was downstairs right underneath my room. Every night I tapped the floor twice for "good-night" and three times for "I miss you and I love you". She made some kind of noise in response.

Our friendship has continued to grow stronger as the almost 80 years together are drawing near. The most recent episode of supporting each other came during a rainy season when we had no sunshine for a week. I phoned Evelyn and said, "Don't you want to put a little sunshine in my life? I'm tired of rain." She said, "Sure do." And she did—to the tune of a $15.00 phone bill, we talked that long. Money well spent!! Her sunshine brightened my day.

We've shared many happy and momentous times together — our childhood days, dating years, our weddings, the birth of my children, vacations, Christmas holidays, birthdays, important events in my children's lives, grandchildren and great-grandchildren, even the deaths of our husbands. Now we spend all the time together that we can arrange, in Florida and in Tennessee. She still stands beside me and I beside her in whatever way we are needed.

Sisters are wonderful. Friends are wonderful. And it's such a blessing to have both in one person. She is one of my richest blessings—my sister and my best friend, Evelyn, so dear to my heart.

When I read this poem, I think of Evelyn—

I'd like to be the kind of friend
that you have been to me;
I'd like to be the special help
that you've been glad to be.
I know I'm blessed, for only God
can make a friend like you;
You know just how to cheer me up
whenever I feel blue.
Could I but have one wish fulfilled,
this one would only be -
I'd like to be the kind of friend to you
you've always been to me.

(Author unknown)

Chapter 57

Seventy-two Years Later

I guess a girl never tires of playing dolls. Perhaps it's the natural mother instinct that's always with her. On Christmas, 1993, after the story of my first doll was printed in the church newsletter, I received my second little blonde haired doll in a pretty pink dress from Linda, my grand-daughter. With the doll was the following note:

Dear Granny,
Seeing you now and how the way things use to be, how it is so hard now for you to see—from baking cookies to Rook parties. You feel now that you can barely see, your life is where there is nothing you can do and what you need to feel is there are different things for you to do now. Mom told me that you said you were never going to go to another play or musical again because at the talent show you couldn't see my face. Well, look at it this way, you see things in a different light now. In music you don't have to see it to hear it. Actually, musicians teach their students about music and how it should flow by closing their eyes and listening to it. It gives you a feel of the music. So when you think you are going to be missing out on everything, just close your eyes and FEEL the music. On Christmas this year I want to give you some thing special. You told us a story once about you when you were a little girl and the blonde haired doll you got for Christmas. Your brother broke it and you always wished for another little blonde haired doll in a pink dress.
Well - Merry Christmas, Granny.

Love, Linda

It brought back memories and tears to my eyes, and I named my doll Faith. I always had faith that I would someday get another doll.

A day or two later, Doreen gave me my third doll, which I

named Hope because I hope everyone has such dear friends and family as I have.

Faith and Hope sit in my living room, keeping me company until my great grand-daughters, Cassady and Jessica, come to visit their Granny. Then the dolls come 'alive' I turn to my second childhood and we love playing dolls together. A part of my childhood that I missed returns to provide happy hours for me and start fond memories for another generation.

Someone said, "Now you have Faith and Hope, what about Charity?" My reply was, "With Faith, Hope, and these precious great grand-daughters, family and friends, my cup runneth over— have Charity."

"And now abideth faith, hope, charity, these three; but the greatest of these is charity." 1 Corinthians 13:13

Chapter 58

The Hills And Valleys

The terrain of Tennessee, going from east to west is as different as Florida going from north to south. It is much like passing through three different states. In the east we find high mountains and rocks; in middle Tennessee there are beautiful rolling hills and valleys, rich farm land and green pastures with white-faced Hereford and black Angus cattle grazing; while in west Tennessee we see the flatland and deltas of the Mississippi River. It is the middle part of the state that holds my fondest memories. Columbia, The Dimple of the Universe as it is called, is about forty miles south of Nashville, the state capitol. It is a quaint little city with lots of beautiful historical homes and buildings. It is in the heart of what is known as the Bible belt.

We used to love to climb up those hills and see how far we could see. When the grass was green and soft we played a game of rolling down the hillside to see who could reach the bottom first. Sometimes we would line up and roll one behind the other and end up in a big pile at the bottom. Whoever rolled down last was naturally on the top of the pile so he had to go first next time and be on the bottom. We always tried to roll fast and hit hard. We showed no mercy. Sometimes we hit a rock or stick, which often hurt or slowed us down considerably. But we kept going back and trying again because we knew we would eventually land on top.

Our lives are much like this game. Sometimes we are on top of the hill where everything is peaceful and beautiful. We feel like we can just reach up and touch God. The children are all well, the bills are paid, nothing is broken down in the house and we have received a raise. Life is so beautiful. We are on top of the hill and everything looks perfect.

And suddenly we begin to roll down hill. The car breaks down, two of the children need braces, taxes are due, the house needs a new roof, and our jobs may be in jeopardy. This is when we must remember the same God who gives us those joyous hilltop experiences is always present for our valley experiences. God is good everywhere, all the time, under all conditions. It is in the valley that we receive the greatest blessings which we profit from the most. It is here that we learn patience, love, understanding, faith, long-suffering, endurance, and perseverance. Every valley shall be exalted. Isaiah 40:4, "Let every valley be exalted, and every mountain and hill be made low..." It is important for us to remember this when we are on the top of the hill. We will come rolling down and sometimes land on the bottom of the stack and it may hurt. Or sometimes we may hit a 'rock' (hindrance or stumbling block) which will slow us down —but we can still make it back to the top of the hill. If our faith doesn't waver and if we get up and make an effort, we will climb back up where we can reach up and almost touch God. For every hill there are two valleys. Just remember—the greatest blessings are in the valleys. That's where we learn the most, grow in faith and are made stronger. In 2 Corinthians 12:9-10, Paul tells us, "And He has said to me, "My grace is sufficient for you, for power is perfected in weakness." Most gladly, therefore, I will rather boast about my weaknesses, that the power of Christ may dwell in me. Therefore I am well content with weaknesses, with insults, with distresses, with persecutions, with difficulties, for Christ's sake; for when I am weak, then I am strong."

I remember this poem from my childhood, I don't know the author but it speaks so well for what I learned from the time and circumstances in which I grew up. We all would do well to learn this lesson.

Thank you for the valley I walk through today.
The darker the valley, the more I learn to pray.
I find you where the lilies are blooming by the way.
I thank you for the valley I walk through today.

Life can't be all sunshine or the flowers would die.
The rivers would be desert, barren and dry.
Life can't be all blessings or there'd be no need to pray.
So I thank you for the valley I walk though today.

Thank you for every hill I climb.
For every time the sun doesn't shine.

Thank you for every lonely night
I prayed 'til everything was right.
I thank you for the valley I walk through today.

And so has been my life—the good times, the bad times; the happy times, the sad times; the easy times, the hard times; the hills, the valleys. I am so thankful for our devoted and loving mother and father who taught us children these many lessons, to be the "happy singing family" and to look to God to direct our ways.

Love,

Granny

KIDS ♥ LOVE MICHIGAN

A PARENT'S GUIDE TO EXPLORING FUN PLACES IN MICHIGAN WITH CHILDREN. . .YEAR ROUND!

Kids Love Publications
1985 Dina Court
Powell, OH 43065

Dedicated to the Families
of Michigan

© Copyright 2003, Kids Love Publications

For the latest major updates corresponding to the pages in this book visit our website:

www.kidslovepublications.com

❑ ***REMEMBER:*** *Museum exhibits change frequently. Check the site's website before you visit to note any changes. Also, HOURS and ADMISSIONS are subject to change at the owner's discretion. If you are tight on time or money, check the attraction's website or call before you visit.*

❑ ***INTERNET PRECAUTION:*** *All websites mentioned in KIDS LOVE MICHIGAN have been checked for appropriate content. However, due to the fast-changing nature of the Internet, we strongly urge parents to preview any recommended sites and to always supervise their children when on-line.*

ISBN# 0-9726854-0-5

KIDS ♥ MICHIGAN ™   Kids Love Publications

TABLE OF CONTENTS

General Information..Preface
(Here you'll find "How to Use This Book", maps, tour ideas, city listings, etc.)

(Amusements, Animals & Farms, Museums, Outdoors, State History, Tours, etc.)

State Map

With Major Routes & Cities Marked

Chapter Area Map

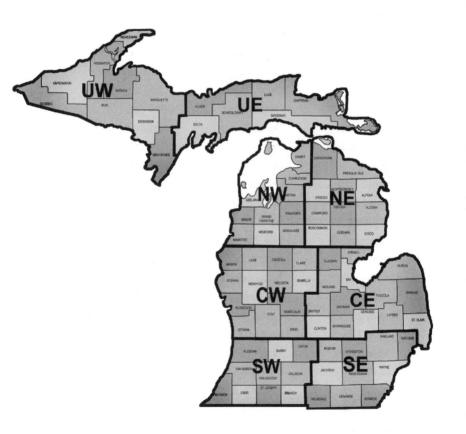

CITY INDEX (Listed by City & Area)

CITY INDEX (Listed by City & Area)

Acknowledgements

We are most thankful to be blessed with our parents, Barbara (Darrall) Callahan & George and Catherine Zavatsky who help us every way they can – researching, proofing and babysitting. More importantly, they are great sounding boards and offer unconditional support. So many places around Michigan remind us of family vacations years ago…

We also want to express our thanks to the many Convention & Visitor Bureaus' staff for providing the attention to detail that helps to complete a project. We felt very welcome during our travels in Michigan and would be proud to call it home!

Our own kids, Jenny and Daniel, were delightful and fun children during our trips across the state. What a joy it is to be their parents…we couldn't do it without them as our "kid-testers"!

We both sincerely thank each other – our partnership has created an even greater business/personal "marriage" with lots of exciting moments, laughs, and new adventures in life woven throughout. Above all, we praise the Lord for His so many blessings through the last few years. God does answer prayer…all prayer, *eventually*!

We think Michigan is a wonderful, friendly area of the country with more activities than you could imagine. Our sincere wish is that this book will help everyone "fall in love" with Michigan.

In a Hundred Years...

It will not matter, The size of my bank account...
The kind of house that I lived in, the kind of car that
I drove... But what will matter is...

That the world may be different
Because I was important in the life of a child.

- *author unknown*

HOW TO USE THIS BOOK

If you are excited about discovering Michigan, this is the book for you and your family! We've spent over a thousand hours doing all the scouting, collecting and compiling (*and most often visiting!*) so that you could spend less time searching and more time having fun.

Here are a few hints to make your adventures run smoothly:

❑ Consider the **child's age** before deciding to take a visit.

❑ Know **directions** and parking. Call ahead (or visit the company's website) if you have questions *and* bring this book. Also, don't forget your camera! *(please honor rules regarding use)*.

❑ **Estimate the duration** of the trip. Bring small surprises (favorite juice boxes) travel books, and toys.

❑ Call ahead for **reservations** or details, if necessary.

❑ Most listings are **closed major holidays** unless noted.

❑ Make a **family "treasure chest"**. Decorate a big box or use an old popcorn tin. Store memorabilia from a fun outing, journals, pictures, brochures and souvenirs. Once a year, look through the "treasure chest" and reminisce. "Kids Love Travel Memories!" is an excellent travel journal & scrapbook that your family can create. *(See the order form in back of this book)*.

❑ Plan **picnics** along the way. Many Historical Society sites and state parks are scattered throughout Michigan. Allow time for a rural/scenic route to take advantage of these free picnic facilities.

❑ Some activities, especially tours, require **groups** of 10 or more. To participate, you may either ask to be part of another tour group or get a group together yourself (neighbors, friends, organizations). If you arrange a group outing, most places offer discounts.

❑ For the latest **updates** corresponding to the pages in this book, visit our website: **www.kidslovepublications.com.**

❑ Each chapter represents an area of the state. Each listing is further identified by city, zip code, and place/event name. Our popular **Activity Index** in the back of the book **lists places by Activity Heading** (i.e. State History, Tours, Outdoors, Museums, etc.).

MISSION STATEMENT

At first glance, you may think that this is a book that just lists hundreds of places to travel. While it is true that we've invested thousands of hours of exhaustive research (*and drove nearly 3000 miles in Michigan*) to prepare this travel resource...just listing places to travel is not the mission statement of these projects.

As children, Michele and I were able to travel extensively throughout the United States. We consider these family times some of the greatest memories we cherish today. We, quite frankly, felt that most children had this opportunity to travel with their family as we did. However, as we became adults and started our own family, we found that this wasn't necessarily the case. We continually heard friends express several concerns when deciding how to spend "quality" and "quantity" family time. 1) What to do? 2) Where to do it? 3) How much will it cost? 4) How do I know that my kids will enjoy it?

Interestingly enough, as we compare our experiences with our families when we were kids, many of our fondest memories were not made at an expensive attraction, but rather when it was least expected.

It is our belief and mission statement that if you as a family will study and use the contained information to create family memories, these memories will grow a stronger, tighter family. Our ultimate mission statement is, that your children will develop a love and a passion for quality family experiences that they can pass to another generation of family travelers.

We thank you for purchasing this book, and we hope to see you on the road (*and hearing your travel stories!*) God bless your journeys and happy exploring!

George, Michele, Jenny and Daniel

GENERAL INFORMATION

Call *(or visit the websites)* for the services of interest. Request to be added to their mailing lists.

- ❑ DNR Parks & Recreation (517) 373-9900 or (800) 44-PARKS or **www.michigan.gov/dnr**
- ❑ Fisheries Division - Lansing (517) 373-1280
- ❑ Fishing Hotline - (800) 275-3474
- ❑ Skiing: **www.ultimateskiguide.com**
- ❑ Snowmobiling, Skiing and Cross-Country Skiing - (888) 78-GREAT, **www.michigan.org**
- ❑ Michigan Festivals and Events Association - **www.mfea.org**
- ❑ Michigan Association of Recreational Vehicles and Campgrounds, MARVAC - (800) 422-6478, **www.MARVAC.org**
- ❑ Michigan Association of Private Campground Owners (MAPCO) - **www.michcampgrounds.com**
- ❑ West Michigan Tourist Association - Grand Rapids (800) 442-2084 or **www.wmta.org**
- ❑ Travel Michigan - (888) 784-7328 or **http://travel.michigan.org**
- ❑ MSU Sports (517) 355-1610
- ❑ U of M Sports (734) 647-2583 or **www.umich.edu**
- ❑ **CE** - Genessee County Parks (810) 736-7100 or (800) 648-park.
- ❑ **CE** - Saginaw County Parks (989) 790-5280 or **www.saginawcounty.com/parks/**

General Information (cont.)

- ❏ **CW** - Muskegon County Parks (231) 744-3580
- ❏ **CW** - Newaygo County Parks, (269) 689-7383
- ❏ **NE** - Mackinaw Area Visitors Bureau (800) 666-0160 or **www.mackinawcity.com**
- ❏ **SE** - Detroit CVB (800) Detroit or **www.visitdetroit.com**
- ❏ **SE** - Greater Lansing CVB (888) 2-Lansing or **www.lansing.org**
- ❏ **SE** - Huron-Clinton Metroparks (800) 47-Parks or **www.metroparks.com**
- ❏ **SE** - Ingham County Parks (888) 517-1086
- ❏ **SE** - Oakland County Parks - (248) 858-0306
- ❏ **SE** - Washtenaw County Parks, (734) 426-8211
- ❏ **SW** - Kalamazoo Area county Parks (269) 383-8776
- ❏ **SW** - St. Joseph County Parks (269) 467-5519

Check out these businesses / services in your area for tour ideas:

AIRPORTS

All children love to visit the airport! Why not take a tour and understand all the jobs it takes to run an airport? Tour the terminal, baggage claim, gates and security / currency exchange. Maybe you'll even get to board a plane.

ANIMAL SHELTERS

Great for the would-be pet owner. Not only will you see many cats and dogs available for adoption, but a guide will show you the clinic and explain the needs of a pet. Be prepared to have the children "fall in love" with one of the animals while they are there!

BANKS

Take a "behind the scenes" look at automated teller machines, bank vaults and drive-thru window chutes. You may want to take this tour and then open a savings account for your child.

CITY HALLS

Halls of Fame, City Council Chambers & Meeting Room, Mayor's Office and famous statues.

ELECTRIC COMPANY / POWER PLANTS

Modern science has created many ways to generate electricity today, but what really goes on with the "flip of a switch". Because coal can be dirty, wear old, comfortable clothes. Coal furnaces heat water, which produces steam, that propels turbines, that drives generators, that make electricity.

FIRE STATIONS

Many Open Houses in October, Fire Prevention Month. Take a look into the life of the firefighters servicing your area and try on their gear. See where they hang out, sleep and eat. Hop aboard a real-life fire engine truck and learn fire safety too.

HOSPITALS

Some Children's Hospitals offer pre-surgery and general tours.

NEWSPAPERS

You'll be amazed at all the new technology. See monster printers and robotics. See samples in the layout department and maybe try to put together your own page. After seeing a newspaper made, most companies give you a free copy (dated that day) as your souvenir. National Newspaper Week is in October.

RESTAURANTS

PIZZA HUT & PAPA JOHN'S

❑   Participating locations

Telephone the store manager. Best days are Monday, Tuesday and Wednesday mid-afternoon. Minimum of 10 people. Small charge per person. All children love pizza – especially when they can create their own! As the children tour the kitchen, they learn how to make a pizza, bake it, and then eat it. The admission charge generally includes lots of creatively made pizzas, beverage and coloring book.

KRISPY KREME DONUTS

❑   Participating locations

Get an "inside look" and learn the techniques that make these donuts some of our favorites! Watch the dough being made in "giant" mixers, being formed into donuts and taking a "trip" through the fryer. Seeing them being iced and topped with colorful sprinkles is always a favorite of the kids. Contact your local store manager. They prefer Monday or Tuesday. Free.

SUPERMARKETS

Kids are fascinated to go behind the scenes of the same store where Mom and Dad shop. Usually you will see them grind meat, walk into large freezer rooms, watch cakes and bread bake and receive free samples along the way. Maybe you'll even get to pet a live lobster!

TV / RADIO STATIONS

Studios, newsrooms, Fox kids clubs. Why do weathermen never wear blue clothes on TV? What makes a "DJ's" voice sound so deep and smooth?

WATER TREATMENT PLANTS

A giant science experiment! You can watch seven stages of water treatment.   The favorite is usually the wall of bright buttons flashing as workers monitor the different processes.

U.S. MAIN POST OFFICES

Did you know Ben Franklin was the first Postmaster General (over 200 years ago)?   Most interesting is the high-speed automated mail processing equipment.   Learn how to address envelopes so they will be sent quicker (there are secrets). To make your tour more interesting, have your children write a letter to themselves and address it with colorful markers. Mail it earlier that day and they will stay interested trying to locate their letter in all the high-speed machinery.

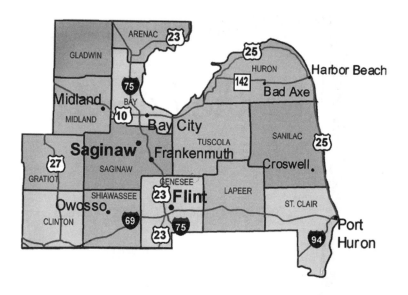

Chapter 1
Central East Area

Our Favorites...

Crossroads Village & Huckleberry Railroad

H.H. Dow Historical Museum

Huron Lightship Museum

Frankenmuth Shop Tours and Amusements

Huron Lightship Museum

SANILAC PETROGLYPHS HISTORIC STATE PARK

(M-53 to Bay City - Forestville Road Exit - East to Germania Road South), **Bad Axe** 48413

❑ Phone: (517) 373-3559

Web: www.sos.state.mi.us/history/museum/musesan/index.html

❑ Hours: Wednesday-Sunday 11:30am-4:30pm (Memorial Day-Labor Day).

❑ Admission: State Park entrance fee is $4.00 per vehicle.

❑ Tours: Guided tours (45 minutes)

Take a 1 mile, self-guided walking trail through the forest along the Cass River. Stop at the 19th Century logging camp or 100+ year old white pine tree. The main reason you probably came though is the petroglyphs. In the late 1800's, forest fires revealed chiseled sandstone etchings by Native Americans of an ancient woodland people dating back 300 - 1000 years ago. Look for figures like a hunter / archer or animals and birds.

BAY CITY STATE RECREATION AREA

3582 State Park Drive (I-75 exit 168 east to Euclid Avenue)

Bay City 48706

❑ Phone: (989) 684-3020

Web: www.michigandnr.com/parksandtrails/parklist.asp

❑ Admission: $4.00 per vehicle

Lots of camping (tent and cabins) plus a swimming beach free from sharp zebra mussels found in the area, make this an attraction. Also find boating, fishing, trails, winter sports. Another highlight is the Saginaw Bay Visitors Center which focuses on the importance of wetlands to the bay. It's open Tuesday - Sunday, Noon - 5:00pm. A great spot for birding, you'll also learn from the 15 minute video presentation, boardwalks and observation trails.

BAY COUNTY HISTORICAL MUSEUM

Bay City - *321 Washington Avenue (I-75, take exit 162A to Downtown), 48708. Web: www.bchsmuseum.org Phone: (989) 893-5733. Hours: Monday-Friday 10:00am-5:00pm, Saturday & Sunday Noon-4:00pm. Miscellaneous: Every Saturday at 2:00pm, a trolley leaves from the Museum for a 75-minute tour.* Visitors will experience maritime history from the geological formation of the Great Lakes and the Saginaw River to the completion of the area's first lighthouse. Exhibits focus on the shipbuilding and lumbering industries. Visitors will enter a re-creation of the tug wheelhouse, experience what the docks were like, and view an interactive shipwreck exhibit. A series of seven period rooms compares and contrasts life in the 1880s to the early 1930s. Visitors will see recreated rooms of the era and also see how consumerism helped to develop the "modern" home. You can also learn about Native Americans and the fur trade and early Bay County settlers. Many industries such as agriculture, lumbering and manufacturing will highlight the recent history section of the gallery.

DELTA COLLEGE PLANETARIUM & LEARNING CENTER

Bay City - *100 Center Avenue, 48708. Phone: (989) 667-2260 Web: www.delta.edu/planet/ Hours: Call or visit website for schedule. Admission: $3.00-$3.50 per person.* A wonderful place to teach children the fun of star-gazing. The planetarium is state-of-the-art and the rooftop observatory seats over 100 people. The audience actually gets to choose what to see in the solar system. Look for programs about sky pirates or cowboys or Garfield.

WILDERNESS TRAILS ANIMAL PARK

11721 Gera Road - M-83 (I-75 to Birch Run Exit)

Birch Run 48415

❑ Phone: (989) 624-6177
❑ Hours: Monday-Saturday 10:00am-6:00pm, Sunday 11:00am-6:00pm (April - October).

❑   Admission: $8.00 adult, $5.00 senior (60+), $5.00 child (3-15).

❑   Miscellaneous: Picnic area. Playground.

One of the most popular privately owned animal exhibits in the state, Wilderness Trails offers over 50 acres and 60 different types of animals. See lions, a Siberian tiger and bear, bison, elk, black bears, and deer just to name a few. Two gravel walking trails wind through park or a horse drawn covered wagon is available for a small charge. Kids can have fun touching and feeding the baby animals in the petting area.

JUNCTION VALLEY RAILROAD

7065 Dixie Highway (I-75, exit 144 south - Just before you turn to head into Frankenmuth), **Bridgeport** 48722

❑   Phone: (989) 777-3480
    Web: www.gtesupersite.com/jvrailroad/

❑   Hours: Monday-Saturday 10:00am-6:00pm, Sunday 1:00-
    6:00pm. (Memorial Day Weekend-Labor Day Weekend).
    Weekends Only (September & October & Special events).

❑   Admission: $4.25-$5.00 per person (age 2+).

❑   Miscellaneous: Picnic area and playground. You'll pull into a
    business parking lot, but the ride into the woods is cute,
    especially over the trestles.

See and ride the world's largest ¼ scale railroad. Voyage on rides through the woods, past miniature buildings, through a 100 foot long tunnel, and over 865 feet of trestles (one has diamonds underneath). Look for the roundhouse with a turntable and the 5-track switch yard.

FOR-MAR NATURE PRESERVE & ARBORETUM

Burton - *2142 North Genesee Road, 48509. Phone: (810) 789-8567 or (800) 648-7275.* ***Web: www.formar.org*** *Hours: Weekdays 8:00am-5:00pm. Trails 8:00am -Sunset. Special programs on Saturdays.* A 380 acre preserve with 7 miles of trails. Visitor Center with Gift Shop. Cross-country skiing in winter.

SLEEPER STATE PARK

Caseville - *6573 State Park Road (5 miles east of town on SR 25), 48725. Web:* **www.michigandnr.com/parksandtrails/parklist.asp** *Phone: (989) 856-4411   Admission: $4.00 per vehicle.* Hundreds of acres of woods and beachfront with camping make this a fun park. Also featured are hiking trails, winter sports, mini-cabins, fishing, and boating.

DURAND UNION STATION (MICHIGAN RAILROAD HISTORY MUSEUM)

Durand - *200 Railroad Street, 48429. Phone: (989) 288-3561.* **Web: http://durandstation.org/** *Hours: Tuesday-Sunday 1:00 - 5:00pm.* Visitors stop at the Durand Depot to study area history or maybe catch an Amtrak train roundtrip from Chesaning-to-Owosso. Learn about the Great Wallace Brothers Circus Wreck of 1903 or the Knights Templar Wreck of 1923. Do you know which presidents have made "whistle stops" here?

SILVER RIDGE SKI RESORT

Farwell - *1001 Mott Mountain (off Old US 10), 48622. Phone: (989) 588-7220.* 9 runs, ski lessons, rentals, and night skiing. Restaurant overlooks the slopes.

FLINT CULTURAL CENTER

1221 East Kearsley Street (I-475, exit 8A)

Flint 48503

❑ Phone: (810) 237-7330 or (888) 8CENTER (tickets)
  Web: www.visitflint.org
❑ Hours: Tuesday-Friday 10:00am-5:00pm, Saturday & Sunday Noon-5:00pm. Open Mondays in July & August (Closed Holidays).
❑ Admission: $5.00 adult, $4.00 senior, $3.00 child (4-11).
❑ Miscellaneous: Museum Store. Café.

The **SLOAN MUSEUM** (810-237-3450) highlights include:

❑ "**FLINT AND THE AMERICAN DREAM**" - 20th Century Flint beginning with the birth of General Motors, United Auto Workers, and then neon colorful advertising. Also 1950's - 70's typical household furnishings. Check out the 1950's station wagon (a Buick Super) that was available before today's vans and sport utility vehicles.

❑ "**HOMETOWN GALLERY**" - the area's early history with displays on fur trading, pioneer life, lumbering, and carriage making. Look for the 10,000 year old mastodon and Woodland Indian wigwam. Weekend hands-on history activities.

❑ "**SCIENCE DISCOVERY CENTER**" - hands-on science, weekends only.

Also in the same complex (recommended for grade school and up):

❑ **FLINT INSTITUTE OF ARTS** - 1120 East Kearsley. (810) 234-1695. FREE.

❑ **LONGWAY PLANETARIUM** - 1310 East Kearsley. (810) 237-3400 or www.longway.org. Monday - Friday 9:00 am - 4:00pm, Saturday & Sunday 1:00 - 4:30pm. Free displays. $3-6.00 for light and astronomy shows. 3D Digistar II projector in Sky Theater.

❑ **THE SHOWCASE SERIES** - Whiting Auditorium. Broadway, dance, classic theater and holiday shows.

FLINT GENERALS HOCKEY

Flint - *3501 Lapeer Road (IMA Sports Arena), 48503. Phone: (810) 742-9422. Web: www.flintgenerals.com Admission: General $6.00-11.00.* A UHL team plays mid-October thru March. Breakfast and post-game skates with players, occasionally. Seasonal characters and promos.

FLINT SYMPHONY ORCHESTRA

Flint - *1244 East Kearsley Street (Whiting Auditorium), 48503. Phone: (810) 237-7333 or (888) 8CENTER. Web: www.visitflint.net* Professional orchestra performs family concerts and a free summer parks concert series.

FLINT CHILDREN'S MUSEUM

1602 West 3rd Street (I-75 exit 118 - Corunna Rd. east. Left on
Ballenger Hwy., right on Sunset Drive, turns into 3rd), **Flint 48504**

❑   Phone: (810) 767-5437, **Web: www.flintchildrensmuseum.org**
❑   Hours: Monday-Saturday 10:00am-5:00pm, Sunday Noon-
      5:00pm. Closed major holidays.
❑   Admission: $3.50 general (age 1+), $3.00 senior (60+).
❑   Miscellaneous: Recommended for ages 3-10. Gift shop.

Over 100 exhibits focused on science, technology, and the arts.
Kids' favorites are the Crazy Mirrors and the Lego table. Be sure
to check out the different theme rooms: Grocery Room,
Transportation Room, Playhouse, News Room, and Health Room -
x rays, listen to heart, face masks and Stuffee.

CROSSROADS VILLAGE & HUCKLEBERRY RAILROAD

6140 Bray Road (I-475, exit 13 - follow signs),

Flint 48505

❑   Phone: (810) 736-7100 or (800) 648-PARK
      Web: www.geneseecountyparks.org/crossroadsvillage.htm
❑   Hours: Tuesday-Sunday, 10:00am-5:00pm (until 8:00pm on
      Wednesday) (mid-May – early September)
❑   Admission: $10.00 adult, $9.00 senior (60+), $7.00 child (3-12) -
      Village and Train Ride. Village only tickets discounted $2.00-$4.00.
❑   Miscellaneous: Mill Street Warehouse, Cross Roads Café,
      Concessions, Carousel, Venetian Swing, Ferris Wheel and
      Wagon Rides (pulled by ponies) - additional charge. Seasonal
      events keep the village open throughout the year - see Seasonal
      Chapter.

The 1860's era living village is a collection of 30 authentic
buildings that were relocated here to form a village. Friendly,
costumed villagers fill you in on the events of the day and answer
questions. For example, the barber shop (still operational) staff will
share their charges for a cut, shave or bath. We learned that they let
a dental patient (yes, they were the town dentist then) take a swig
of vanilla extract (full tilt variety!) before they extracted a tooth.

The fellas at the cider and sawmill will remind you of characters from "Little House on the Prairie" as they demonstrate their craft. Be sure to buy a cup of cider there - all natural with no added sugar. You'll also meet the town blacksmith, printer (try your hand printing a souvenir off the "kissing" press), doctor, storekeeper at the General Store (with cute, old-fashioned novelties for sale), and toymaker (try your hand walking on stilts - we have a video and George did it!). Before you leave, take a relaxing slow ride on the Huckleberry Railroad. The original line went so slow that passengers claimed they could get off - pick huckleberries along the tracks (still growing plentifully today) and catch the caboose a few minutes later. Watch out for the playful train robber skit - (don't worry...even pre-schoolers won't be scared!).

GENESEE RECREATION AREA

Flint - *(I-475 exit 13), 48506. Phone: (800) 648-7275. **Web:** www.geneseecountyparks.org Admission per activity.* This area includes Stepping Stone Falls on Mott Lake on Branch Road which are lit with color evenings between Memorial Day and Labor Day. The Genesee Belle sightseeing boat also docks here offering 45 minute cruises on the lake (Sunday evenings at 7:00pm) or lunch cruises (Wednesdays). You can also find Mott's Children's Farm, camping, hiking, boating, fishing, beach swimming, bicycle trails, and winter sports. Hours vary by activity (mostly dawn to dusk). (Memorial Day-October).

BAVARIAN BELLE RIVERBOAT TOURS

Frankenmuth - *South Main Street (RiverPlace), 48734. Phone: (866) 808-BOAT. Hours: Departures 11:00am until dusk (May - October). Admission: $6.00 adult, $3.00 child (3-12).* One hour sightseeing cruises narrated about the Cass River folklore and history. Open air canopied upper deck and enclosed lower salon (air-conditioned and heated). Snack bar and restrooms on board.

BAVARIAN INN

713 South Main Street, **Frankenmuth** 48734

❑   Phone: (800) BAVARIA. **Web: www.bavarianinn.com**

❑   Hours: Daily Lunch, Dinner or Overnight.

A famous Frankenmuth restaurant (established in 1888) offering family style dinners. An authentically dressed server (aren't their hats cute?) will help introduce your kids to all the menu offerings they will like such as potato pancakes, veal cutlets, baked chicken, etc. (except maybe the sauerkraut). None of the food is over-seasoned…all kid friendly…but the adults may want to use extra all purpose seasonings available at each table. Also see the Glockenspiel Clock Tower (with performances telling the Pied Piper of Hamelin story in music) and the Doll and Toy Factory (see dolls created before your eyes). The Lodge has five pools and overnight accommodations.

BRONNER'S CHRISTMAS WONDERLAND

25 Christmas Lane (I-75, northbound to exit 136, southbound to exit 144 - follow signs off Main Street M-83), **Frankenmuth** 48734

❑   Phone: (989) 652-9931 or (800) ALL-YEAR

       Web: www.bronners.com

❑   Hours: Monday-Saturday 9:00am-5:30pm, Sunday Noon-
       5:30pm, Open Friday until 9:00 pm (January-May). Monday-
       Saturday 9:00am-9:00pm, Sunday Noon-7:00pm (June-
       December). Closed Winter holidays including Easter and Good
       Friday.

❑   Admission: FREE

❑   Miscellaneous: "Season's Eatings" snack area.

A visit to Michigan wouldn't be complete without seeing the "World's Largest Christmas Store" that hosts over 2,000,000 visitors each year! View nativity scenes, 260 decorated trees, and 200 styles of nutcrackers. As dusk approaches drive through "Christmas Lane" that sparkles with over 40,000+ lights. While you're there be sure to check out the "World of Bronners" (an 18 minute multi-image slide show) that highlights the design and production of their selection of trains. Visit "Bronner's Silent

Night Memorial Chapel" - named after the famous song (the chapel was originally made in Austria). Kids seem to be most fascinated with the "It Feels Like Christmas" drive around the vast parking lot and the animated displays of seasonal bears, elves, and children playing around the upper perimeter of each theme room. Be sure to get at least one ornament to keep - but "oooh" - how to decide!

FRANKENMUTH CHEESE HAUS

561 South Main Street, Frankenmuth 48734

❑ Phone: (989) 652-672

   Web: http://frankenmuthcheesehaus.com

❑ Hours: Daily 9:30am-6:00pm. Open until 9:30pm (summer).

❑ Admission: FREE

Lots of tasting going on here! Ever tried "Chocolate" or "Strawberry" cheese? Not only will you sample some...you can also try cheese spreads (smooth, creamy and fresh tasting) or over 140 different kinds of cheese. Watch a video of the cheesemaking process, or if you time it right, actually see the ladies make it from scratch. They have giant photographs of each step of the process, so if the kids can't see it all they can still understand the process from the pictures. Yummy samples of cheese spreads in varieties from Garden Vegetable to Jalapeno! You will want some to take home (although this souvenir will soon be eaten with a box of crackers!)

FRANKENMUTH HISTORICAL MUSEUM

613 South Main Street (I-75 to Frankenmuth Exit - Next to the Visitor's Center, Fischer Hall), Frankenmuth 48734

❑ Phone: (989) 652-9701

   Web: http://frankenmuth.michigan.museum/museum.html

❑ Hours: Monday-Thursday 10:30am-5:00pm, Friday 10:30am-7:00pm, Saturday 10:00am-8:00pm, Sunday 11:00am-5:00pm. (April-December). Shorter hours (January-March). Closed winter holidays.

❑ Admission: $0.50-$1.00 per person.

❑ Miscellaneous: Museum Gift Shop with folk art and toy objects.

Exhibits depict the area's German ancestry and history from Indian mission days to a town called "Michigan's Little Bavaria". Begin with a scene from the immigrants' ship travel from Bavaria to the Saginaw Valley. They designed this museum along the trend of "hands-on" activities and there are a few interactive stations in realistic settings.

FRANKENMUTH WOOLEN MILL

570 South Main Street (I-75 to Frankenmuth Exit - Follow signs to downtown), Frankenmuth 48734

❑   Phone: (989) 652-8121 **Web: www.frankenmuthwoolenmill.com**
❑   Hours: Daily 9:00am-9:00pm (Summer). Daily 10:00am-6:00pm (Winter).
❑   Admission: FREE
❑   Miscellaneous: Video of wool processing plays continuously when workers aren't in, but the store is open.

We've all seen freshly shaven sheep and probably own wool clothing. But how is it processed? Here's your unique chance to see how it all happens. They began here in 1894 and the mill has produced over 250,000 hand-made, wool-filled comforters since then. See the mill in action where you can begin by looking through a window of the wash basins (great viewing for smaller children) where they clean wool brought in from farmers. Washed fleece is then air dried (it gets really fluffy that way) and then put through a "carding machine". The wool passes through wire-spiked rollers until it is untangled and meshed together to form a sheet. Comforters are assembled according to Bavarian tradition (hand-tied). Throughout the tour, your guide will let you handle samples of wool at different stages of the process. The kids will find "raw" wool disgusting, but love the way that it turns out. This "hands-on" activity keeps their interest throughout the demonstration.

MEMORY LANE ARCADE

Frankenmuth - *626 South Main Street (downtown), 48734. Phone: (989) 652-8881,* **Web: http://memorylanearcade.com** *Hours: Daily open at Noon (June-December). Open weekends*

(Spring). Closed Winter Holidays. Pay 25 cents per game as you step back in time... for a good time. The collection spans 100 years of penny arcades including 3D movies, baseball, kissing machines, modern games and computer games.

RIVERPLACE

925 South Main Street, **Frankenmuth** 48734

❑ Phone: (800) 600-0105
  Web: www.frankenmuth-riverplace.com
❑ Hours: Sunday-Thursday 10:00am-8:00pm, Friday-Saturday 10:00am-9:00pm (September-December, May). Slightly more limited hours (January-April). Daily 10:00am-9:00pm (June-August).
❑ Admission: Varies with activity.

A-MAZE-N-MIRRORS - life size maze of mirrors and glass.

A MAGICAL TOWN - theatrical sculptured art with sights, sounds and stories.

BAVARIAN BELLE - see separate listing

BEEBEE'S FUN PLACE AND EATERY - Foam Factory, video games, food.

LIGHTS FANTASTIC - nightly laser-light shows in amphitheater. FREE.

APPLE MOUNTAIN SKI AREA

Freeland - *4519 North River Road, 48623. Phone: (989) 781-6789 or (888) 781-6789. Web: www.applemountain.com Hours: Daily 10:00am-10:00pm (mid-December to mid-March).* 12 runs. Night skiing, snow boarding, equipment rental, and instructions are available.

HURON CITY MUSEUM

7930 Huron City Road (8 miles east of Port Austin on M-25)

Huron City 48467

❑ Phone: (989) 428-4123
  Web: www.tour-michigan.com/~hcmus/tours.htm

❑   Hours: Thursday-Monday 10:00am-5:00pm (July 1 - Labor Day).
❑   Admission: $6.00-10.00 adult, $5.00-8.00 senior (55+), $3.00-
     5.00 child (10-15). Children 9 and under are FREE. (Prices vary
     depending on tours chosen)

Show your kids Michigan's agricultural early days at this restored
19th century lumbering town. See a village inn, log cabin (that
survived 2 fires and a family with 17 children!), town church
(known for its passionate, spirit-filled sermons), carriage shed,
general store and the Pointe Auxe Barques lifesaving station (was a
predecessor of today's Coast Guard).

LAKEPORT STATE PARK

Lakeport - *7605 Lakeshore Road SR 25 north, 48059.* **Web:**
www.michigandnr.com/parksandtrails/parklist.asp *Phone: (810)*
327-6224. Admission: $4.00 per vehicle. Located along the shore
of Lake Huron, the park has two distinct units separated by the
village of Lakeport. Camping/cabins, hiking trails, boating, and
fishing.

METAMORA-HADLEY STATE RECREATION AREA

Metamora - *3871 Hurd Road (off SR 24 south), 48455.* **Web:**
www.michigandnr.com/parksandtrails/parklist.asp *Phone: (810)*
797-4439. Admission: $4.00 per vehicle. The park consists of 723
acres with 80-acre Lake Minnewanna in the center. Camping,
hiking trails, boating, fishing and swimming.

CHIPPEWA NATURE CENTER

Midland - *400 South Badour Road, 48640. Phone: (989) 631-*
0830. **Web: www.chippewanaturecenter.com** *Hours: Monday-*
Friday 8:00am-5:00pm, Saturday 9:00am-5:00pm. Sunday and
most Holidays 1:00-5:00pm. Admission: Donation. Site includes a
modern visitor center with indoor exhibits. Outdoors, there's a
wildlife viewing area, wildflower walkway, scenic river overlook,
1870 Homestead Farm (cabin, schoolhouse, heirloom/herb garden,
farm animals) and The Arboretum of Michigan Trees and Shrubs.
1000 acres of trails run through the forest, meadows, ponds, and
rivers. The Archeological District is the site of a territorial Indian
battle.

DOW GARDENS

1018 West Main Street (corner of Eastman Ave. and West St.
Andrew Street, next to the Midland Center for the Arts),
Midland 48640

- ❑ Phone: (800) 362-4874. **Web: www.dowgardens.org**
- ❑ Hours: 10:00am - sunset, daily except Winter holidays.
- ❑ Admission: $5.00 adult, $1.00 student (6-17)

These gardens were started in 1899 as landscaping around Dow's
home. Now there are 100 acres of gardens featuring flowers, trees,
rocks and water. Seasonal tulips and wildflowers are pretty to look
at. The Barnyard Garden is home to the hog sculpture, ponytail
grass, lambs ears and an array of other plants with farm animal
names. The Children's Garden has a treehouse and fountains. No
food or pets allowed.

H.H. DOW HISTORICAL MUSEUM

3100 Cook Road (US Business 10 into town. Head NW on Main
Street from downtown to Cook Road south), **Midland 48640**

- ❑ Phone: (989) 832-5319, **Web: www.mcfta.org**
- ❑ Hours: Wednesday-Saturday 10:00am-4:00pm, Sunday 1:00-
    5:00pm.
- ❑ Admission: $4.00 adult, $2.00 child.

First of all, please purchase the Children's Guidebook and use it as
you go through the museum. It's sure to keep the kids attention
because each page has an activity for them to do. You'll want to
start at the replica of Evens Flour Mill Complex - the original
Midland Chemical Company. This is where young Dow pioneered
experiments of separation of bromine from brine using electrolysis.
See a prototype of his first lab. Wood scraps were used to build
electrolysis boxes that feed onto "spread beds" that feed into a
wood tower full of scrap metal. The metal catches the bromine
liquid vapor. The museum has many clever interactive (holograms,
manual, conversation) displays conveying why Midland, Michigan
was an ideal spot to experiment, how Dow's parents felt about his
work (proud Dad, worried Mom), and his supportive wife. See a
scene where Herbert is running his business yet trying not to be a

workaholic. We feel the exhibits will inspire cleverness, tenacity, association with other great wise minds, hard work, and, in some, a zest for making money with science.

HALL OF IDEAS (MIDLAND CENTER FOR THE ARTS)

1801 West Saint Andrews Road, **Midland** 48640

❑   Phone: (989) 631-5930 **Web: www.mcfta.org**
❑   Hours: Daily 10:00am-6:00pm except Holidays.
❑   Admission: $5.00 adult, $2.00 child (12 and under).
❑   Miscellaneous: Art Gallery, Peanut Gallery (Theatre Guild's family division).

What's 10 feet tall, 10,000 years old, hairy and wears size 80 sneakers? See, touch, hear, explore the world's natural wonders of science, history, and art. "Captain" a Great Lakes fishing boat or set off a mine blast! Ride a John Deere combine (cab of one with panoramic view of field in front of you). Create computer music, visit an old-time theater and say "hi" to an American mastodon skeleton with size 80 feet!

DEER ACRES

2346 M-13 (I-75 to exit 164, go north on M-13), **Pinconning** 48650

❑   Phone: (989) 879-2849 **Web: www.deeracres.com**
❑   Hours: Daily 10:00am-6:00pm, Weekends until 7:00pm (early May-Labor Day). Weekends Only 10:00am-7:00pm (after Labor Day to mid-October).
❑   Admission: $7.00-$9.00 (age 3+). Additional fee for rides.

Watching your children's eyes light up as they see a deer eating out of their hand is something that you'll never forget. At Deer Acres, the deer are so tame that they even know to come toward you when they hear the food dispensers clicking! Additional fun attractions (small additional fee) include several amusement rides (antique cars, Ferris wheel, carousel, moonwalk) and a narrated safari trip (don't miss the monkeys). Story Book Village brings all of your child's fantasy characters to life like "The Three Little Pigs", "Old Woman In a Shoe", "Old Mother Hubbard" and many others.

MISS PORT AUSTIN

Port Austin - *(at M-53 in downtown), 48467. Phone: (989) 738-5271. Web: www.thumbtravels.com/missptaustin.htm Admission: $30.00 per person. 20% discount for families and weekday trips. Tours: Leaves dock at 7:30 am and 2:30 pm (starting in July). Call for other times and types of trips. Trips last 4 1/2 hours.* A home town fishing expedition is what the summer is all about. Join Captain Fred Davis (and up to 20 guests) on a quest for perch. Once the captain finds you a school of fish, you'll "bait up" using the minnows that he provides and then it's all up to you! A great, casual way to introduce your kids to fishing (and how to tell a fish story…).

PORT CRESCENT STATE PARK

Port Austin - *1775 Port Austin Road (along M-25, 5 miles southwest of town), 48467. Phone: (989) 738-8663. Web: www.michigandnr.com/parksandtrails/parklist.asp Admission: $4.00 per vehicle.* Port Crescent State Park is located at the tip of Michigan's "thumb" along three miles of sandy shoreline of the Saginaw Bay. Some of the modern campsites offer a waterfront view, either of Lake Huron or the Pinnebog River. A 900-foot boardwalk and five picnic decks offer scenic vistas from the top of sand dunes in the day-use area. A unique feature is their undeveloped beaches and sand dunes contrasted with many forest hiking trails. Camping and mini-cabins plus these activities are available: fishing, swimming, winter sports.

BLUE WATER AREA

(Off I-94, I-69 to Military to the Black River), **Port Huron** 48060

❑   Phone: (810) 987-8687 or (800) 852-4242, **Web: www.bluewater.org**

To navigate through this area of the state you might want to tour via one of the following services:

❑   THE BLUE WATER TROLLEY offers a nostalgic, narrated tour of historic sites including the THOMAS EDISON DEPOT on the St. Clair River (under the Blue Water Bridge). Young Tom moved here at the age of seven and began his road to self-education here. Admission: 10 cents. Season: June-September.

❑   THE HURON LADY is an international sightseeing tour boat.
       Seating up to 100 people, it cruises along the St. Clair River
       viewing large freighters, bridges, FORT GRATIOT LIGHTHOUSE
       (FREE tours May-September 810-982-3659) and the Canada
       coastline. Admission charged. Season: Daily in the summer. (888)
       873-6726 or **www.huronlady.com**. Reservations recommended.

EDISON DEPOT MUSEUM

Thomas Edison Parkway (under the Blue Water Bridge)
Port Huron 48060

❑   Phone: (810) 982-0891, **Web: www.phmuseum.org**
❑   Hours: Wednesday-Sunday 1:00-4:30pm. Daily 1:00-4:30pm
       (summer).
❑   Admission: $3.00 adult, $2.00 senior (55+), student (7-17).
       Discount combo pricing with Lightship & Port Huron Museum.
❑   Miscellaneous: Edison movie in theater, live science demos.

The Museum is housed inside the historic Fort Gratiot depot and
the exhibits portray Edison's boyhood story of creativity, family
support, adversity, perseverance, and ultimate triumph as the
greatest inventor of our times. Re-created period environments and
hands-on activities invite visitors to become participants and
encourages them to apply their own creativity and ingenuity as
they learn about Edison's life and his inventions. The story traces
the Edison family's relocation from Ohio to Port Huron, young
Tom's boyhood and school experiences, his avid curiosity and
scientific study fostered by his mother, adolescent entrepreneurial
efforts and his work on trains - and in this very depot. Outside the
depot, a restored baggage car rests on a spur of railroad track.
Inside this baggage car, visitors discover a re-creation of young
Edison's mobile chemistry lab and printing shop.

HURON LIGHTSHIP MUSEUM

(End of I-94 east - Moored at Pine Grove Park along the St. Clair
River), Port Huron 48060

❑   Phone: (810) 982-0891, **Web: www.phmuseum.org**
❑   Hours: Wednesday-Sunday 1:00-4:30pm. Daily 1:00-4:30pm
       (Summer).

For updates visit our website: www.kidslovepublications.com

❑   Admission: $3.00 adult, $2.00 senior (55+), $2.00 student (7+).
      Discount combo pricing with 2 other Port Huron museums.
❑   Miscellaneous: Nearby is the PORT HURON MUSEUM - 1115
      Sixth Street, that traces 300 years of local history, especially
      American Indian & marine history (step into a real ship's pilot house).

Your entire family will really enjoy the brief tour of this unique lighthouse. It is the last "floating lighthouse" to sail the Great Lakes (decommissioned in 1970) called the "Huron". Used where it wasn't practical to build a lighthouse, it was built in 1920 and was operated by a crew of 11 who took 3 week turns (16 days out, 5 days in). Board the boat that bobbed through thick fog and rode out heavy storms to warn passing freighters of treacherous shoals ahead in the channel. Listen to the fog horn's "heeeee....ooohhhh" deep sound that bellows that sound of the ship's heart. What has replaced the Huron? Find out with self-guided tours of the interior hull, mess hall, captain's quarters, and then experience a panoramic view of the Blue Water Bridge from the pilothouse on top of the boat. It was most interesting to hear stories of freighters like the famous "Edmund Fitzgerald" and to know the dangers of being in a smaller boat that is calling giant ships right to you!

SANILAC COUNTY HISTORICAL MUSEUM & VILLAGE

228 South Ridge Road - (SR25), **Port Sanilac** 48469

❑   Phone: (810) 622-9946
❑   Hours: Tuesday-Friday 11:00am-4:30pm, Weekends Noon-
      4:30pm (mid-June - Early September).
❑   Admission: $2.00-$5.00.

Start at the 1875 Victorian Home with original home furnishings, period medical instruments, original post office cancellation stamps, and an "American" sewing machine (later they changed their name to "Singer"). The Dairy Museum features cheesemaking equipment and you can wander through the Log Cabin where they used some charred logs from the tragic Thumb Area fire of 1881. See an old schoolhouse and stop at the General Store (really cute - try a bottle of old-fashioned "body splash" or some penny candy - lots of licorice!)

JAPANESE CULTURAL CENTER AND HOUSE

Saginaw - *527 Ezra Rust Drive (Celebration Square), 48601. Phone: (989) 759-1648. Hours: Tuesday-Saturday Noon-4:00pm (Memorial Day-September). Gardens are open Spring thru Fall. Admission: Gardens are FREE. Tea House Tour $2.00-$3.00 (students+). Full tea ceremony is $6.00 per person.* Study the ritual and ceremony of Japanese culture by participating in a tea service. Following a tour of the garden's many bridges and stones (from Japan), tea and sweets are served. Traditional full teas are offered every second Saturday at 2:00pm.

SAGINAW CHILDREN'S ZOO

1730 South Washington (I-675 to 5th/6th Exit to Celebration Square), **Saginaw** 48601

- ❏ Phone: (989) 759-4200
- ❏ Hours: Monday-Saturday 10:00am-5:00pm, Sunday & Holidays 11:00am-6:00pm. (Mother's Day weekend - Labor Day).
- ❏ Admission: Average $3.00 per person (age 3+).

This "kid-sized" zoo features all the fun animals including: monkeys, bald eagles, alligators, and farm animals. Take a miniature train or pony ride rides and then a chance to see and ride a unique, locally built carousel. After choosing your mount (from horses, rabbits, ponies or sea horses), enjoy the views of hand-painted panels depicting scenes of Saginaw's history.

SHIAWASSEE NATIONAL WILDLIFE REFUGE

Saginaw - *Green Point Environmental Learning Center is at 3010 Maple Street in town. (Refuge is 6 miles south of town, west of SR13), 48601. Phone: (989) 777-5930 or (989) 759-1669 (Learning Center)* **Web: http://midwest.fws.gov/Shiawassee/** *Hours: Dawn to Dusk.* The 9000 acre Refuge provides food and rest for a variety of birds and other wildlife. This includes 250 species of birds, 10 miles of observation trails to walk, two observation decks with scopes, and The Green Point Environmental Learning Center. The Center offers 2.5 miles of hiking trails, indoor exhibits and many displays. For Shiawassee

Flats "Michigan Everglades" Boat Trips, call Johnny Panther Quests (listed below).

SAGINAW ART MUSEUM

Saginaw - *1126 North Michigan Avenue, 48602. Phone: (989) 754-2491. Web: www.saginawartmuseum.org Hours: Tuesday-Saturday 10:00am-5:00pm, Sunday 1:00-5:00pm. Closed holidays. Admission: Donations.* Housed in an early 1900's mansion, you'll find 19th and 20th century American art mostly. The Visionary Hands-On Room is the best place to spend time with kids (global art jewelry or Celebrating Diversity pictographs).

CASTLE MUSEUM OF SAGINAW COUNTY HISTORY

Saginaw - *500 Federal Avenue, 48607. Phone: (989) 752-2861. Web: http://saghistcastle.org Hours: Tuesday-Saturday 10:00am-4:30pm, Sunday 1:00-4:30pm. Closed holidays. Admission: $0.50 to $1.00.* View the winding spiral staircase as you enter the old post office that now traces the industrial development of Saginaw County. GM exhibit, Postal exhibit (Find out how the mail sorters were kept under secret watch), USS Saginaw, and clothing styles thru time.

JOHNNY PANTHER QUESTS

Saginaw - *(meet near the Shiawassee National Wildlife Refuge), 48607. Phone: (810) 653-3859 (Voice Phone). Admission: $80.00 to $120.00 per couple. $30.00 to $40.00 per additional person depending on trip scheduled. Tours: Boat tours last 3-4 hours.* The Everglades in Michigan? Just a few short moments from downtown Saginaw is one of the greatest examples of wildlife and wetlands that you and your kids will ever see. Take a private boat tour that is personalized for your family. A quiet day with nature...floating along...with a chance to see deer, beaver and maybe even a bald eagle. As owner says, "Eliminate the stress...get out of the mainstream and go on a Quest!"

SAGINAW BAY SYMPHONY ORCHESTRA
YOUTH THEATRE

Saginaw - *Saginaw County Event Center (Heritage Theatre), 48607.* **Web:** *www.saginawbayorchestra.com* *Phone: (989) 755-6471.* *Admission: $5.00 per person.* Family-and-kid-friendly productions like Amelia Bedelia and favorite fairy tales.

SAGINAW SPIRIT HOCKEY

Saginaw - *Wendler Arena, Saginaw County Event Center, 48607. Phone: (989) 497-7747.* **Web:** *www.saginawspirit.com* Experience the excitement of OHL hockey and the Saginaw Spirit when they play at home. Season tickets are available. Individual tickets range from $10.00-14.00. Season: September-March.

MARSHALL M. FREDERICKS SCULPTURE GALLERY

7400 Bay Road (SR84) (Arbury Fine Arts Center on Saginaw Valley State University), **Saginaw (University Center)** 48710

- ❏ Phone: (989) 790-5667. **Web: www.svsu.edu/mfsm**
- ❏ Hours: Tuesday-Sunday 1:00-5:00pm. Closed university holidays.
- ❏ Admission: FREE.

Home to more than 200 sculptures by the same artist. He is known nationally and internationally for his impressive monumental figurative sculpture, public memorials and fountains, portraits, medals, and animal sculptures. Free-standing sculptures, drawings and portraits, and photos of bronze pieces are displayed. There's a sculpture garden and fountain, too.

Chapter 2
Central West Area

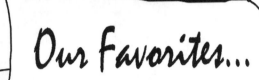

Our Favorites...

Dune Rides & Gillette Dune Center

Fish Ladder Sculpture

Gerald Ford & Van Andel Museums

Musical Fountain

Windmill Island

Wooden Shoe Factory / DeKlomp Dancing

Dressup at Windmill Island

SHRINE OF THE PINES

M-37, **Baldwin** 49304

❑   Phone: (231) 745-7892

     Web: http://baldwin.localis.com/shrineopine

❑   Hours: Monday-Saturday 10:00am-6:00pm, Sunday 1:30-6:00pm
     (May 15-October 15).

❑   Admission: $1.00-$3.50 (age 6+).

It was Raymond W. Overholzer's (a hunting and fishing guide)
vision to create a shrine to the white pine trees that once covered
Michigan. He began hand-carving and hand-polishing stumps,
roots, and trunks (using the simplest of tools). Over 30 years of
"works of art" are shown here including candlesticks, chairs,
chandeliers, and beds. There is even a 700 lb. table with drawers
carved from a single stump!

CANNONSBURG SKI AREA

Cannonsburg - *6800 Cannonsburg Road NE (10 miles east of US-
131 on West River Dr), 49317.* **Web: www.cannonsburg.com**
Phone: (616) 874-6711. Day and night skiing with 10 runs.
Lessons and equipment rental are available. Cannonsburg offers
the highest vertical in Southwest Michigan.

COOPERSVILLE & MARNE RAILWAY

Train Departs from Downtown (I-96 to Exit 16 or 19)

Coopersville 49404

❑   Phone: (616) 997-7000

     Web: www.coopersville.com/train/index.html

❑   Admission: $10.00 adult, $9.00 senior, $6.00 child (3-14).

❑   Tours: Saturday 11:00am & 1:00pm (July - September).

A great way to introduce your children to rail travel at a relaxed
pace. The summer rides offer a 5 mile tour though rural Michigan
to the town of Marne and then returns on the same line. There are
special theme rides that include The Great Train Robbery with
Chuck Wagon Barbecue, The Pumpkin Train (in October), and
The Santa Train (in December).

GRAND HAVEN STATE PARK

Grand Haven - *1001 Harbor Avenue (Take US-31 into Grand Haven and follow the "waterfront" signs. Go south at the waterfront to the park entrance), 49417.* **Web: www.michigandnr.com/parksandtrails/parklist.asp** *Phone: (616) 847-1309. Admission: $4.00 per vehicle.* 48 acre park with the beautiful sandy shore of Lake Michigan along the west side of the park and the Grand River along the north side of the park. The park consists entirely of beach sand and provides scenic views of Lake Michigan and the Grand Haven pier and lighthouse. There's also boating, fishing and swimming.

HARBOR STEAMER

Grand Haven - *301 North Harbor Drive (off US 31 - head West), 49417. Phone: (616) 842-8950.* **Web: www.harborsteamer.com** *Hours: Daily cruises afternoons and evenings (Memorial Day-Labor Day). Admission: $5.00-$10.00 (age 5+).* This cute replica paddlewheel boat offers tours of Spring Lake and the lower Grand River. Choose from a 45 minute waterfront or 90 minute scenic narrated lunchtime (or brown-bag lunch) tour. The lower deck is enclosed, snack items are available, and there are restrooms on board.

HARBOR TROLLEY

Grand Haven - *440 North Ferry (departures at Chinock Pier & points around town and in Spring Lake), 49417. Phone: (616) 842-3200.* **Web: www.grandhaven.com/harbortransit/trolley.htm** *Hours: Daily 11:00am-10:00pm (Memorial Day-Labor Day). Admission: $1.00-$2.00 (age 3+).* A reproduction trolley that connects the towns of Ferrysburg, Spring Lake, & Grand Haven. See the sights or use it as a convenient means of transport.

MUSICAL FOUNTAIN

(Downtown Riverfront. Viewing best at Grandstand at Harbor and Washington Streets), **Grand Haven** 49417

❑   Phone: (616) 842-2550
     Web: www.grandhaven.com/fountain.shtml

- ❏ Hours: Summers at dusk-approximately 9:30pm. Weekends only in September and May.
- ❏ Admission: Donations.
- ❏ Miscellaneous: Tri-Cities Museum is in front of the grandstand and is open most evenings until the concert begins. It contains displays on railroading, shipping, pioneers, the lumber industry, Coast Guard and Maritime vessels in a former railroad depot.

The world's largest synchronized light, water and music show. For 30 years now, jets of water up to 125 feet high go through a series of pipes to create displays that change color to the beat of music. We thought some looked like angel wings and sunrises. The show lasts approximately 20 minutes.

FISH LADDER SCULPTURE

Grand Rapids - *(US131 East to exit 87 - turn right onto Front Street - On Grand River at junction of 4th and Front Streets), 49503. Phone: (800) 678-9859. Hours: Daily, daylight hours. Admission: FREE.* A concrete, 5 step ladder (actually a series of steps) was built by a local artist to assist salmon in jumping up a 6 foot dam to reach their popular spawning grounds further upstream. Leaping fish can be seen anytime, but the best time is late September to late October. If you spend about 20 minutes there you will witness at least one fish make it up all five steps! We sure are glad that Grand Rapids decided to help these pretty "fishies" out!

GRAND RAPIDS ART MUSEUM

Grand Rapids - *155 Division Street (US 131 to Pearl Street Exit), 49503. Phone: (616) 831-1000.* **Web: *www.gramonline.org*** *Hours: Tuesday-Sunday 11:00am-6:00pm. Friday 11:00am-9:00pm. Admission: $5.00 adult, $2.00 senior (62+), $1.00 child (ages 6-17).* A nationally recognized art museum featuring work by local, state, and national artists. The museum collection spans Renaissance to Modern art, with particular strength in 19th and 20th century paintings, prints and drawings. Call or visit website for current exhibitions.

GRAND RAPIDS CHILDREN'S MUSEUM

22 Sheldon Avenue NE (Division to Library Street)

Grand Rapids 49503

- ❑ Phone: (616) 235-4726 **Web: www.grcm.org**
- ❑ Hours: Tuesday-Saturday 9:30am-5:00pm, Sunday Noon-5:00pm. Also Family Night on Thursday from 5:00-8:00pm.
- ❑ General Admission: $4.00 (ages 2+). Family Night: $1.00

A well supported hands-on museum focuses on learning. The Lego Building Station leaves kids wanting to come back to make new creations (you never have that many Legos at home) and build cities with new friends. Dress up in all kinds of clothes, choose an array of backgrounds and watch as your image is transformed from in front of a green screen to in front of a weather map or city scapes and more. Bubbles, Bees and a Farm Market, too.

GRAND RAPIDS CIVIC THEATRE

Grand Rapids - *30 North Division Street, 49503. Phone: (616) 222-6650. Web: www.grct.org* Children's Theatre with productions like Annie or the Velveteen Rabbit. The second largest community theatre in the U.S. Season runs September-June.

GRAND RAPIDS GRIFFINS HOCKEY

Grand Rapids - *130 West Fulton (Van Andel Arena), 49503. Phone: (616) 774-4585. Web: www.grgriffins.com Admission: $5.00 - $25.00.* This IHL team plays in March and April. Affiliate of Detroit Red Wings.

GRAND RAPIDS HOOPS BASKETBALL

Grand Rapids - *130 West Fulton (Van Andel Arena), 49503. Phone: (616) 559-7936. Web: www.grandrapidshoops.com* This Continental Basketball Association team plays late November - early March. $5.00-$20.00 tickets. Look for the green HOOPIE mascot.

GRAND RAPIDS RAMPAGE FOOTBALL

Grand Rapids - *130 West Fulton (Van Andel Arena), 49503. Phone: (616) 222-4000.* **Web: *www.grrampage.com*** *Tickets* $10.00-$30.00. This Arena Football League plays mid-February through mid-May.

GRAND RAPIDS SYMPHONY / YOUTH SYMPHONY

Grand Rapids - *169 Louis Campau Promenade, Suite One (DeVos Hall), 49503. Phone: (616) 454-9451.* **Web: *www.grsymphony.org*** Family and Lollipop Series available September-May. Picnic Pops at Cannonsburg Ski Area. Holiday Pops. Youth Symphony concerts feature the 100 + member ensemble (ages 12-21) performing classical favorites. Admission charged.

BLANDFORD NATURE CENTER

1715 Hillburn Avenue NW (US 131 to Leonard Street exit west to Hillburn), **Grand Rapids** 49504.

- ❏ Phone: (616) 453-6192. **Web: www.grmuseum.org/bnc/index.htm**
- ❏ Hours: Monday-Friday 9:00am-5:00pm. Weekends 1:00-5:00pm. Closed major holidays. Trails are open from dawn to dusk.
- ❏ Admission: FREE

The visitor center is probably where you'll start. Learn about their wildlife care program and then go out on the grounds along self-guided trails to see wildlife. A total of 140 or so acres of fields, forests, ponds and streams can be leisurely explored. Other trails pass the Carriage Barn, Sugar House, Blacksmith, General Store, Barn & Log Cabin (most open summertime). The trails turn into cross-country ski areas in the winter.

GERALD FORD MUSEUM

303 Pearl Street NW (I-196 to US131 to Pearl Street Exit - East - on the West bank of the Grand River), **Grand Rapids** 49504

- ❏ Phone: (616) 451-9263 **Web: www.ford.utexas.edu**
- ❏ Hours: Daily, 9:00am-4:45pm. Closed New Year's Day, Thanksgiving Day, and Christmas Day.
- ❏ Admission: $4.00 adult, $3.00 senior (62+), Children Free (under 16)

This display of history through artifacts is outstanding to parents, but kids will gravitate to only a handful of displays. As you may have to race through some interesting exhibits, be sure to help your kids look for these (hey…tell them it's a scavenger hunt!): See Elvis' suit, James Dean's motorcycle, Bert and Ernie, A pole sitter, the first video game, Mr. Roger's sweater, and those "groovy" platform tennis shoes (since they are now back in style they may be wearing something similar!). The best areas for kids:

❑   OVAL OFFICE REPLICA - See the room that very few people ever see and listen as you eavesdrop on a typical day in the Ford Presidency.

❑   HOLOGRAPHIC WHITE HOUSE TOUR - Tour (using photographs taken by the Fords) up to 11 rooms usually off limits to the public. Attend a White House State Dinner or play in the Solarium.

❑   CAMPAIGNS - Deliver a speech like the President using a teleprompter or stand on the floor of a political convention. We have a great video of this memory!

JOHN BALL PARK ZOO

1300 West Fulton Street, **Grand Rapids** 49504

❑   Phone: (616) 336-4300
    Web: www.co.kent.mi.us/visiting/zoo/zoo_index.htm
❑   Hours: Daily 10:00am-6:00pm (mid-May to Labor Day). Daily 10:00am-4:00pm (rest of the year). Closed Christmas Day only.
❑   Admission: $4.00 adult (14-62), $2.50 (63+), $2.50 child (5-13). No admission is charged in December - February.

See more than 1000 specimens (you know…animals, fish, amphibians, etc.) from around the world at the state's second largest zoo. In addition to the usual lions, tigers, and bears there is a special exhibit on Nocturnal Animals and a petting zoo with farm animals for the young kids. Newer additions include the Spider Monkeys, Bongo, Penguins, and a sassy Hornbill.

VAN ANDEL MUSEUM CENTER

272 Pearl Street NW (US131 to Pearl Street, exit 85B)

Grand Rapids 49504

❑   Phone: (616) 456-3977
     Web: www.grmuseum.org/vamc/museum.htm
❑   Hours: Monday–Saturday 9:00am-5:00pm, Sunday Noon–
     5:00pm
❑   Admission: $6.00 adult, $5.00 senior, $2.50 child (3-17).
❑   Miscellaneous: Planetarium and laser shows (additional charge).
     Museum Café. Curiosity Shop. Carousel rides for small fee.

Exhibits that depict heritage and manufacturers of the region. Best picks for children might be:

❑   FURNITURE CITY - a partially operational reconstruction of an early
     1900's furniture factory and displays of artistic and funky chairs.
❑   THE 1890'S DOWNTOWN - a recreated street with a theater
     and shops plus the sights and sounds of transportation and
     people's conversations as you wait with them at the train station.
❑   AMERICAN INDIANS - Anishinabe people were the first
     inhabitants of the area. Why do they re-tell the stories of their
     ancestry so much?

Be on the lookout for the 76 foot finback whale skeleton which greets you at the entrance in the main hallway. Also, you'll feel like you're in the movie "Back to the Future" when you see the Giant Clock taken from Old City Hall (it's transparent so you can see the mechanisms - and it's still keeping time).

FREDERIK MEIJER GARDENS &
SCULPTURE PARK

1000 East Beltline NE (I-96 to East Beltline exit - go north)

Grand Rapids 49525

❑   Phone: (616) 957-1580 **Web: www.meijergardens.org**
❑   Hours: Monday-Saturday 9:00am-5:00pm. Sunday Noon-
     5:00pm. Closed only Christmas and New Years.

❑   Admission: $7.00 adult, $6.00 senior (65+), $5.00 student, $3.50
      child (5-13). Outdoor tram rides for about $1.00 each - weekends
      only.

A 125-acre complex featuring indoor (5 stories tall) and outdoor
gardens. See tropical and various plants from five continents on
nature trails. The sculpture park offers 25 works by renowned
artists. The collection is subdivided into two categories: the
Sculpture Park and Gallery Collection focuses on work from the
era of Auguste Rodin to the present, while the Garden Trails and
Conservatory Collection focuses primarily on representational,
animal imagery displayed in natural surroundings (change color
with the seasons). Gift shop and café. Current special events are
available on their website.

WEST MICHIGAN WHITECAPS BASEBALL

Grand Rapids - *US 131 & West River Drive (Fifth/Third Ballpark
- Old Kent Park), 49544. Phone: (616) 784-4131 or in Michigan
(800) CAPS-WIN. **Web: www.whitecaps-baseball.com** Admission:
$4.00-$8.00.* A baseball stadium with lawn seats? Show your kids
the way that baseball used to be watched in the early days.
Bleacher and box seats are also available too. The Whitecaps are
the Class "A" farm team for the Detroit Tigers and always offer a
great family fun value. Playland. (April - September).

GRAND LADY RIVERBOAT CRUISES

Grandville - *4243 Indian Mounds Drive SW, 49418. Phone: (616)
457-4837. **Web: www.river-boat.com** Admission: $10.00 adult
(for sightseeing tours). Children ages 3 - 11 are 1/2 price except
on weekends.* Their 1 1/2 hour sightseeing cruise tells the story of
sites you view and riverboat landings you pass between Grand
Rapids & Grand Haven. One of the main features of early riverboats
was the giant paddlewheel. The Grand Lady has two identical
sternwheels, which may be operated independently. This allows her
to be easily maneuvered in the narrow channels and sandbars of the
river. The paddle wheels also allow her to operate in very shallow
water (as little as 2 ½ feet), where a modern vessel would be
grounded. Call or visit website for seasonal schedule of events.
Sightseeing tours Daily, subject to prior charters (May - October).

WILSON STATE PARK

Harrison - *910 North First Street (BR-27 one mile north of Harrison), 48625. Phone: (989) 539-3021. Admission: $4.00 per vehicle. Web: www.michigandnr.com/parksandtrails/parklist.asp* Situated on 36 beautifully wooded acres with a sandy beach, Wilson State Park is located on the north end of Budd Lake in Clare County. Camping/cabins, boating and boat rental, fishing and swimming.

HOLLAND MUSEUM

Holland - *31 West 10th Street, 49423. Phone: (888) 200-9123. Web: www.wowcom.net/commerce/museum Hours: Monday, Wednesday, Friday, Saturday 10:00am-5:00pm, Thursday 10:00am-8:00pm, Sunday 2:00-5:00pm. Admission: $3.00 general, $7.00 family.* As you enter, you'll be mesmerized by the collection of miniature glass churches built by Dutch immigrants for a World's Fair. Most all the displays are "no touch" but kids take an interest in the Dutch Fisherman's Cottage (kids sleep in bunks in the walls) and the carousel made by a Dutch sailor for his kids.

WINDMILL ISLAND

7th Street and Lincoln Avenue (US 31 to 8th Street)

Holland 49423

❑   Phone: (616) 355-1030 **Web: www.windmillisland.org**

❑   Hours: Monday-Saturday 9:00am-6:00pm, Sunday 11:30am-6:00pm. (April, May, July, August). Monday-Saturday 10:00am-5:00pm, Sunday 11:30am-5:00pm. (June, September, early October).

❑   Admission: $6.00 adult, $3.00 child (5-12).

❑   Miscellaneous: Candle, sweets, and gift shop. Every windmill product you could imagine is in there. Some activities are for summer only.

"DeZwann" (Dutch for the swan) is a 230+ year old, 12 story high, working, authentic Dutch windmill. It's the only one operating in the United States…they produce graham flour almost daily and sell it at the complex. Take a tour of all of the floors, learn how they change the direction of the windmill, see the mechanical wood gears turn (if there's at least a 15 MPH wind) and learn how the miller worked upstairs and sold product on the first floor at the same time. After your tour, Klompen (wooden shoe) dancers perform to organ music as those wooden shoes "klomp" to the beat. The Posthouse museum is an exact architectural replica of a 14th century wayside Inn and features a 12 minute slide presentation of Windmills, The Netherlands and our "De Zwaan". See a display of the Netherlands in miniature. The kids won't believe how many water canals are used as streets.

DEKLOMP WOODEN SHOE AND DELFTWARE FACTORY

12755 Quincy Street - US31

Holland 49424

- ❑   Phone: (616) 399-1900 **Web: www.veldheertulip.com**
- ❑   Hours: Daily 9:00am-5:00pm.
- ❑   Admission: FREE
- ❑   Miscellaneous: Veldheer Tulip Gardens. Colorful tulips, peonies, daylilies, iris, Dutch lilies, daffodils. Admission charged for gardens (when in season).

The Dutch began making wooden shoes as a replacement for leather which was too expensive and deteriorated quickly because of all the exposure to water in the Netherlands. Watch local craftsmen carve "Klompen" (wooden shoes) on machines brought over from the Netherlands. Sizes from Barbie (they really fit!) to Men's size 13. Plain or hand decorated they are great for gardening or decoration. Lots of sawdust! Delftware began being made by potters in the city of Delft in the 13th Century. It is known for its delicately hand-painted blue and white porcelain. This is the only U.S. factory that is producing replica Chinese porcelain and it's just beautiful! While you're having your wooden shoes or small souvenir magnet burned with a special personalization, be sure to take the time to watch the artist use Delft colored paints to decorate plain pieces.

DUTCH VILLAGE

12350 James Street (US 31 and James Street)

Holland 49424

- ❑ Phone: (616) 396-1475 **Web: www.dutchvillage.com**
- ❑ Hours: Daily 9:00am-5:00pm. (late April - Mid-October)
- ❑ Admission: $8.00 adult, $5.00 child (3-11).
- ❑ Miscellaneous: Café. Ice cream shop. Specialty shops.

You'll feel like you're in Europe (Netherlands) as you see the quaint Dutch Style buildings, canals and flower gardens. Klompen Dancers perform to the music of the Amsterdam Street Organ and wooden shoe crafters are working in their shops with old tools that shape logs into shoes. Demonstration every 15 minutes! In the museum, you can learn how the famous Dutch cheeses of Gouda and Edam are made. There are museums and historical displays (w/ 20 minute movie about the Netherlands) plus the kids favorite spot (and Michele's when she was little)...STREET CARNIVAL - Wooden Shoe Slides, Dutch Chair Swing, and antique Dutch pictured carousel. There's also a farmhouse with "pet and feed" animals.

HOLLAND STATE PARK

Holland - *2215 Ottawa Beach Road (west off US 31 on Lakewood Road), 49424. Phone: (616) 399-9390. Admission: $4.00 per vehicle. Web: www.michigandnr.com/parksandtrails/parklist.asp* Drawn to the beaches and swimming along with the beautifully well-kept, bright red, lighthouse is the reason most come. The park is divided into two separate units; one along Lake Michigan and the other along Lake Macatawa. Almost 150 campsites, boating, fishing, swimming, and bicycle trails are also available.

SAUGATUCK DUNES STATE PARK

Holland - *2215 Ottawa Beach Road (Off US 31 north), 49424. Web: www.michigandnr.com/parksandtrails/parklist.asp Phone: (269) 637-2788 Admission: $4.00 per vehicle.* Over 2 miles of secluded shoreline along Lake Michigan. In addition, the park has fresh water coastal dunes that are over 200' tall. The park's terrain varies from steep slopes to rolling hills. Hiking trails, swimming, winter sports, and dunes, of course.

HOMESTEAD ACRES FARM

6720 Ainsworth Road (I-96 to Ionia exit, north to Grand River, turn left, turn right on Ainsworth), **Ionia** 48846

❑ Phone: (616) 527-5910
  Web: http://home.ionia.com/~homesteada/index.html
❑ Hours: Saturday 11:00am-5:00pm. Weekdays by appointment. (May-October).
❑ Admission: Farm tour $2.00-$3.00.

A working farm with rare and exotic animals, farm tours and retail store with fiber, yarns and sweaters. Please call ahead to schedule tours. Most of the animals at Homestead Acres are fiber producing, giving us a product without harm to the animal. They shear the majority of them once a year, the sheep for their beautiful wool, the llamas and alpacas for their luxurious fiber and the angora goats for mohair. Angora rabbits are not sheared but rather their fiber is combed or plucked and collected over a period of time.

IONIA STATE RECREATION AREA

Ionia - *2880 West David Highway (I-96, Exit 64), 48846. **Web:** www.michigandnr.com/parksandtrails/parklist.asp Phone: (616) 527-3750. Admission: $4.00 per vehicle.* Rolling hills, babbling brooks, open meadows, forested ridges, a lake nestled in the hills and a river winding its way through woods and fields. Camping/cabins, hiking, boating, fishing, swimming, bicycle trails and winter sports.

LUDINGTON CITY BEACH

Ludington - *North Lakeshore Drive, 49431. Phone: (231) 845-0324. Hours: Daylight (Memorial Day-Labor Day). FREE admission.* A great summer place to cool off featuring swimming and miniature golf.

LUDINGTON STATE PARK

Ludington - *M-116, 49431. Phone: (231) 843-8671 or (231) 843-2193 (boat rental). Admission: $4.00 per vehicle. **Web:** www.michigandnr.com/parksandtrails/parklist.asp* Over 300 campsites or cabins, plenty of beaches (one with surfing waves), and extensive hiking trails are big hits here. Lots of dunes here and a great canoe trail, boating, swimming, and fishing. Many love the cross-country skiing and the nature center. Big Sable Point Lighthouse on M116 (2 miles north of the State Park entrance - 231-845-7343 or **www.bigsablelighthouse.org**).

SS BADGER

701 Maritime Drive, **Ludington** 49431

- ❑ Phone: (888) 337-7948 **Web: www.ssbadger.com**
- ❑ Hours: Depart times vary (usually morning departure from MI, afternoon departure from WI). Call for details (early May - early October).
- ❑ Admission: $78.00 adult, $72.00 senior (65+), Approx. half price, child (5-15), Ages 4 and under are FREE. Vehicle transport fee $98.00. (All rates are per person, round trip and subject to change). Shorter cruises are available in Mid-May and special select dates. One way rates available, too.
- ❑ Miscellaneous: Cafeteria, movie room, bingo, children's activities.

The 410-foot "SS Badger" is the only Great Lakes car ferry boat running today and can carry over 600 passengers and 180 vehicles. The current voyage is a 4-hour tour that travels from Ludington to Manitowoc, Wisconsin. Kids will be fascinated at the thought of this all day cruise with plenty of activities to keep their attention. Be sure to call or visit their website for information on travel packages.

WHITE PINE VILLAGE

1687 South Lakeshore Drive

Ludington 49431

- ❑ Phone: (231) 843-4808 **Web: www.historicwhitepinevillage.org**
- ❑ Hours: Tuesday-Saturday 11:00am-4:00pm (Early May to mid-October).
- ❑ Admission: $4.00-$5.00. Slightly higher admissions for special events (i.e. Brunches, pioneer dinners)

A reconstructed 1800's village that features over 20 buildings including a courthouse, hardware store, fire hall, schoolhouse, chapel, and logging and maritime museums. The Exhibit Building has numerous antique transportation vehicles. They have an old-fashioned ice cream parlor, too. Outside are two more wooden boats and railroad carts used for moving heavy rail freight. Along with the automobiles are various tools from the era of the corner garage during the early days of the automobile repair business.

HART-MONTAGUE TRAIL STATE PARK

Mears - *9679 West State Park Road (along US31), 49436. Phone: (231) 873-3083.* A paved, 22-mile trail passing through rural forested lands. It showcases the beauty of Oceana county - from patchwork fields of asparagus, cherries, apples to marshlands...all with no motor vehicles. Picnic areas and scenic overlook areas are available along the trail.

MAC WOOD'S DUNE RIDES

West Silver Lake Drive (off US 31)

Mears 49436

❑   Phone: (231) 873-2817 **Web: www.macwoodsdunerides.com**
❑   Hours: Daily rides 9:30am-Dusk (Memorial Day-Labor Day).
      Daily rides 10:00am-5:00pm (mid-May - Sunday before
      Memorial Day & Labor Day - early October).
❑   Admission: $13.50 adult, $9.00 child (3-11).

A "Model A Ford" with big tires, a big engine, and 2000 acres of rolling sand...a man's dream! Nearly 70 years ago Malcolm "Mac" Woods created the thrill of dune buggying with this vehicle. Today, your vehicle is a multi-passenger, modified, convertible truck "dune scooter". Hang on as you begin a fun and educational 40 minute, 8-mile ride that helps you understand the dunes and why people have come to love this sport. You even get to race along the hard-packed sand beach...just...not too close to the waves!

SANDY KORNERS JEEP RENTALS

1762 North 24th Avenue (US 31 Hart/Mears exit, follow signs to Lake), **Mears** 49436

❑   Phone: (231) 873-5048 **Web: www.sandykorners.com**
❑   Hours: Daily 10:00am-5:00pm (May-October). Extended sunset tours in the summer.
❑   Admission: 4-5 passenger jeeps rent $75.00-$100.00 per hour on guided tours.

Enjoy the thrill of driving your very own Jeep up and over the sand dune mountains at Silver Lake. It is 60 minutes of fun driving over the great sweeps of sand ridges and valleys near the shores of beautiful Lake Michigan. An experienced guide will make sure you get the most fun and see all of the remarkable sights in this unique area. Make a stop or two to take pictures and if desired, change drivers. They also have Fall Color Tours thru dunes and forest. Car seats are welcome.

SILVER LAKE STATE PARK

Mears - *9679 West State Park Road (US 31 exit Shelby Road west), 49436.   Web: www.michigandnr.com/parksandtrails/parklist.asp Phone: (231) 873-3083. Admission: $4.00 per vehicle.* Lots of campsites along the dunes is one draw but dune buggy riding is considered the best here. The dune ridges and valleys are mostly windblown sand and lack trees, scrub brush, and dune grass. The dune area is sometimes compared to a desert. Silver Lake State Park contains more than four miles of Lake Michigan shoreline and boasts a large sandy beach. Look for the Little Sable Point Lighthouse (great for pictures at sunset or dawn) and participate in swimming, boating, fishing, and hiking trails on and off dunes.

WEST MICHIGAN SAND DRAGWAY

Mears - *7186 W. Deer Road (north of Silver Lake),   49436. Phone: (231) 873-3345.   Web: www.sanddragway.com/slsd/* Sand Drag Race programs include top fuel dragsters, funny cars, 4 X 4's ATV's dune buggies, Jr. Dragsters, Jr. ATV's and Mighty Midgets.

HACKLEY HOSE COMPANY NO. 2

Muskegon - *510 West Clay Avenue (Muskegon County Museum), 49440. Phone: (231) 722-0278. Hours: Wednesday-Sunday Noon-4:00pm (May-October). FREE admission.* Tour a replica Fire Barn, complete with firefighting equipment artifacts, horses stalls, firemen's living room. Youngsters can sit up in an old pumper.

MUSKEGON COUNTY MUSEUM

Muskegon - *430 West Clay Avenue, 49440. Phone: (231) 728-4119.* **Web: www.muskegonmuseum.org** *Hours: Monday - Friday 9:30am-4:30pm, Saturday - Sunday 12:30-4:30pm. FREE admission.* History of Muskegon County with features of Lumbering, Industry and Wildlife, Native Americans, and a favorite kid spot - Hands on Science Galleries with Body Works. The Coming to the Lakes exhibit examines why various groups of people have migrated to this region for the last 10,000 years. Educational Gift Shop.

MUSKEGON FURY HOCKEY

Muskegon - *955 Fourth Street (L.C. Walker Arena), 49440. Phone: (231) 726-3879.* **Web: www.furyhockey.com** *Admission: $7.00-$11.00.* United Hockey League professional team plays here October - April. The Muskegon Sports Hall of Fame is located in the Arena. Meet Furious Fred, the team's mascot.

HOFFMASTER STATE PARK / GILLETTE DUNE CENTER

6585 Lake Harbor Road (I-96, exit 4 west - Pontalune Road)

Muskegon 49441

- ❑ Phone: (231) 798-3711 or (231) 799-8900 center
  Web: www.michigandnr.com/parksandtrails/parklist.asp
- ❑ Hours: Daily 10:00am-5:00pm (Summer). Tuesday-Friday 1:00-5:00pm, Saturday & Sunday 10:00am-5:00pm (Rest of year). Park open 8:00am - Dusk.
- ❑ Admission: $4.00 per vehicle
- ❑ Miscellaneous: Winter hosts cross country skiing, sledding, and snowshoing. Campsites on shaded dunes. Fishing, boating, & swimming.

For updates visit our website: www.kidslovepublications.com

P.J. Hoffmaster State Park features forest covered dunes along nearly 3 miles of Lake Michigan shore. Its sandy beach is one of the finest anywhere. A focal point of the park is the Gillette Visitor Center. The Center has exhibits and hands-on displays. See a multi-media presentation that illustrates and explains both dormant and living dunes. Nature trails to observation decks (one is handicap and stroller accessible). Towering dunes with a dune climbing stairway to the top overlook (it's a workout). The Center has lots of live turtles and frogs, similar to ones that live in dune environments. The favorite for our kids was the giant crystal of sand and the samples of different types and color of sand found around America. Do you know what 3 things are needed to form dunes?

PORT CITY PRINCESS CRUISES

Muskegon - *1133 West Western Ave (off US-31 - Downtown), 49441.* **Web:** *www.portcityprincesscruises.com* *Phone: (231) 728-8387 or (800) 853-6311. Admission: General $15.00. Tours: Daily at 2:00pm. 90 minutes. (Memorial Day - Labor Day).* A sightseeing tour of Muskegon Lake and if the weather is good a brief look at Lake Michigan.

USS SILVERSIDES

1346 Bluff at Pere Marquette Park (Southside of Channel Way)

Muskegon 49443

- ❑ Phone: (231) 755-1230 **Web: www.silversides.org**
- ❑ Hours: Daily 10:00am-5:30pm (June-August). Monday-Friday 1:00-5:30pm, Saturday & Sunday 10:00am-5:30pm (May & September). Saturday & Sunday 10:00am-5:30pm (April & October).
- ❑ Admission: $3.50-$5.50 (age 5+).
- ❑ Miscellaneous: Watch out if you're claustrophobic. Difficult to take pre-schoolers around on poor footing, cramped quarters.

A restored, famous WW II submarine that was once used for sinking ships. At Great Lakes Naval Memorial & Museum, you can open up to the thrill of going back to WW II and taking part in an authentic submarine experience. Go through the sub's compartments and see how sailors work and live in such cramped quarters (for up to 2 months). Explore decks, engine rooms, and battle stations. Also, a Camp Aboard program is available for a real fun time!

MICHIGAN'S ADVENTURE AMUSEMENT PARK & WILDWATER ADVENTURE

4750 Whitehall Road (I-96 to US-31)

Muskegon 49445

- ❑ Phone: (231) 766-3377 **Web: www.miadventure.com**
- ❑ Hours: Daily 11:00am-9:00pm. (Memorial Day weekend - Labor Day weekend). Hours vary slightly throughout the season. Call or visit website for complete schedule.
- ❑ Admission: General $23.00 (under 2 FREE). Admission is good for both parks. Season passes available. Parking $6.00.

Summer…thrill rides, waterparks and food…right? Michigan's largest amusement park awaits your family for a day (or 2) of summer's best. With over 40 rides with names like Mad Moose, Big Dipper, Wolverine Wildcat, and Shivering Timbers (the 3rd largest wooden roller coaster in the country), you can be sure that your day will be fun-filled! Don't worry there are also some "calmer" rides (7 are made just for younger children) including the Zachary Zoomer, a special scaled down coaster just for younger children. A tree house and play areas are also included for younger children. Wildwater Adventure admission is also included (the state's largest waterpark) with the Lazy River water tube ride, a wave pool, and Michigan's longest waterslide.

MUSKEGON WINTER SPORTS COMPLEX

Muskegon - *(Inside Muskegon State Park), 49445. Phone: (231) 744-9629. Web: www.msports.org Hours: Friday night, Saturday, Sunday. Admission: All day passes $20.00 - 30.00. Skating $2.00-$3.00.* Are Mom and Dad ready to re-live their glory days of winter fun? Of course there is the normal winter fun of ice skating and cross-country skiing trails, but that's only where the fun begins. Two luge tracks (ice covered with banked turns) allow beginners and advanced sledders to go at their own pace (starting at different ascents on the tracks). Speeds range from 25 - 45 MPH! Hang on!

For updates visit our website: www.kidslovepublications.com

NEWAYGO STATE PARK

Newaygo - *2793 Beech Street (US131, exit 125 West), 49337.*
Web: www.michigandnr.com/parksandtrails/parklist.asp Phone:
(231) 856-4452. Wooded rustic campsites, boating, and swimming
access to Hardy Dam Pond.

DUCK LAKE STATE PARK

North Muskegon - *3560 Memorial Drive (US-31, take the*
Whitelake Drive (Duck Lake State Park) exit, west and
go a half-mile to Whitehall Road). 49445. Web:
www.michigandnr.com/parksandtrails/parklist.asp Phone: (231)
744-3480. (Day use park only). Admission: $4.00 per vehicle.
Duck Lake State Park is a 728 acre day use park, located in
Muskegon County. Featuring a towering sand dune, the park
stretches from the northern shore of Duck Lake to Lake Michigan.
A public beach with swimming and boating; fishing and hiking.

MUSKEGON STATE PARK

North Muskegon - *3560 Memorial Drive (US-31 to M-120 exit),*
49445. Web: www.michigandnr.com/parksandtrails/parklist.asp
Phone: (231) 744-3480. Admission: $4.00 per vehicle. Features
over 2 miles of shoreline on Lake Michigan and over 1 mile on
Muskegon Lake. The vast expanse of Great Lakes sand beach
ranks among the most beautiful in the world. Forested dunes that
join miles of Great Lakes shoreline. Check out their four luge runs.
Camping, hiking trails, boating, fishing, swimming, and winter
sports.

MEARS STATE PARK

Pentwater - *West Lowell Street (US-31, take the Pentwater exit and*
go west on Lowell Street), 49449. Phone: (248) 869-2051. Web:
www.michigandnr.com/parksandtrails/parklist.asp Admission:
$4.00 per vehicle. Located on Lake Michigan with several hundred
yards of white sandy beach. Camping, hiking, fishing and
swimming.

DOUBLE JJ RESORT

5900 South Water Road (US 31 to Exit 136 - East)

Rothbury 49452

❑   Phone: (800) DOUBLEJJ or (231) 894-4444
Web: www.doublejj.com

❑   Admission: Prices are all inclusive for a week stay and are subject to change. $400.00-$600.00 (age 5+), 4 and under FREE. Meals are included in rates. Call or visit website for weekend and 3-day rates. Family cabins, tent camping, RVs, covered wagons or teepees, too.

Did you know that Michigan has "Dude Ranches"? Well...Double JJ is actually more than a dude ranch. Daily rides are offered and staffed by experienced "cowpokes" who will teach you all the skills along the way. There is even a rodeo at the end of the week where you can test your newly acquired talent. There is something for all ages. Adults and children (with supervision) can learn separately at there own pace. Some of the attractions and fun include a swimming hole with 145-foot waterslide, a petting farm, riding center, Wild West Shows for the adults in the dance hall (kids have their own shows), fishing, hot tubs, pools, and an award-winning 18-hole golf course "Thoroughbred". Aaahhh...the life of a cowboy!

SHELBY MAN-MADE GEMSTONES

Shelby - *1330 Industrial Drive (off US 31), 49455. Phone: (231) 861-2165. **Web: www.megalogs.com** Hours: Showroom: Monday - Friday 9:00am-5:30pm. Saturday Noon-4:00pm. Admission: FREE. Miscellaneous: Look for new Megalogs in the showroom - it's a toy wood building set made right here. (the pieces fit and stay together). Stimulates creativity and imagination.* In a 50 seat theatre you can learn the fascinating manufacturing process of how man can actually create gemstones such as diamonds, rubies, and sapphires. They are the largest manufacturer in the world of simulated and synthetic gemstones in the world. See how they can process smaller gems into larger ones at a much lesser cost. If your kids are into rocks (especially pretty colored ones, like our daughter) they'll love this place!

WHITE RIVER LIGHT STATION MUSEUM

Whitehall - *6199 Murray Road (US-31 to White Lake Dr. exit (west) to South Shore Dr., turn left and follow Museum signs), 49461.* **Web: www.whiteriverlightstation.org** *Phone: (231) 894-8265. Hours: Tuesday-Friday 11:00pm-5:00pm. Saturday-Sunday Noon-6:00pm (Summer). Weekends only in September. Small admission fee.* At one time, the Muskegon/White Lake area was known as "The Lumber Queen of the World". Shipping over the Great Lakes was the primary means of transporting this lumber. This historic lighthouse was built in 1875 and your family can still climb the old spiral stairs to the top for a view of White Lake and Lake Michigan. Made of Michigan limestone and brick, it features photographs, paintings, artifacts and maritime stories.

Chapter 3
North East Area

Our Favorites...

Hartwick Pines State Park

Mackinac Bridge & Museum

Mackinac Island Carriage & Bike Tours

Mackinac State & Historic Parks

Mackinaw Trolley Tours

Presque Isle Lighthouses

Biking on Mackinac Island

JESSE BESSER MUSEUM

491 Johnson Street (Off US 23 near Alpena General Hospital)

Alpena 49707

❑ Phone: (989) 356-2202, **Web: www.oweb.com/upnorth/museum**

❑ Hours: Tuesday-Saturday 10:00am-5:00pm, Sunday Noon-4:00pm.

❑ Admission: $3.00 adult, $2.00 senior and child (5-17).

❑ Miscellaneous: Planetarium $1.00 extra. Planetarium programs are Sunday at 2:00pm (Under age 5 not admitted to Planetarium).

Mostly local history with a re-created 1800's street of shops and cabins. If you come during a festival or special event weekend, make sure you see the display on the role of concrete in the area. The concrete block-making machine was perfected here in a land rich with limestone. Other permanent exhibits include: Gallery of Man, Lumbering and Farming, a Focult Pendulum, Area Fossils and Restored Historic Buildings.

CLEAR LAKE STATE PARK

Atlanta - *20500 M-33 (M-33 nine miles north of Atlanta), 49709. Web: www.michigandnr.com/parksandtrails/parklist.asp Phone: (989) 785-4388. Admission: $4.00 per vehicle.* Located in elk country, Clear Lake State Park is a quiet, secluded retreat offering a sandy beach and a shallow swimming area that is ideal for children. Camping, hiking, boating, fishing, and winter sports.

WILDERNESS STATE PARK

Carp Lake - *898 Wilderness Park Drive (west of Mackinaw City by CR 81), 49718. Phone: (231) 436-5381. Admission: $4.00 per vehicle. Web: www.michigandnr.com/parksandtrails/parklist.asp* Rough campsites and cabins. Hiking, boating, fishing, swimming, and bicycle trails.

ALOHA STATE PARK

Cheboygan - *4347 Third Street (M-33 South), 49721. Web: www.michigandnr.com/parksandtrails/parklist.asp Phone: (231) 625-2522. Admission: $4.00 per vehicle.* The largest freshwater lake in Michigan (Mullett Lake) is here along with activities such as camping/cabins, boating, fishing, and swimming.

CHEBOYGAN COUNTY HISTORICAL MUSEUM

Cheboygan - *404 South Huron Street, 49721. Phone: (231) 627-9597. Hours: Monday-Friday 1:00-4:00pm. Admission: $2.00 adult (18+).* The county sheriff used to call this place home from 1882 - 1969 - it even was the area jail complete with 8 cells. Today, these cells have become exhibit areas featuring local history including: lumbering, farming, and lifestyle. See a recreated late 1800's "parlor room", bedrooms, and even a schoolroom.

CHEBOYGAN STATE PARK

Cheboygan - *4490 Beach Road, 49721. Phone: (231) 627-2811. Web: www.michigandnr.com/parksandtrails/parklist.asp Admission: $4.00 per vehicle.* One of the main highlights of the park is the Cheboygan Point Light or the Duncan Bay Beach. Camping/cabins, fishing, hiking, swimming and winter sports.

COAST GUARD "MACKINAW" TOURS

Cheboygan - *Coast Guard Drive (SR 27 to US 23 South, across bridge), 49721. Web: www.continuouswave.com/boats/mackinaw Phone: (231) 627-7183. FREE admission.* Home port of Mackinaw along the Cheboygan River. The boat is not always in port (it visits around the Great Lakes). When commissioned, Mackinaw was the most powerful and capable icebreaker in the world. She is still the standard by which other icebreakers are measured. If in port, hop aboard and take a look around.

CORSAIR SKI AREA

East Tawas - *218 West Bay Street, 48730. Phone: (989) 362-2001 or (800) 55-TAWAS. Web: www.skinordic.org/corsairski Admission: Donation to pay for trail grooming.* A cross country ski area with over 35 miles of groomed trails. All skill levels. Rentals are available in town. Great picnic area and hiking in summer and fall. Help your kids try their luck at trout fishing in the Silver Creek.

TAWAS POINT STATE PARK

East Tawas - *686 Tawas Beach Road (3 miles east of town off US 23), 48730. Web: www.michigandnr.com/parksandtrails/parklist.asp Phone: (989) 362-5041. Admission: $4.00 per vehicle.* Check out the 1876, 70 foot lighthouse, Tawas Point Lighthouse. The lighthouse is open to the public for viewing by appointment or on special occasions. The lighthouse stands 70 feet above Lake Huron and the walls at the base are 6 feet thick. The Coast Guard station adjacent to the park on Lakeview Drive was also built in 1876 and is the only surviving example of the First Series Life Saving Stations built on the Great Lakes. The park overall has been referred to as the "Cape Cod of the Midwest". Mini-Cabins and campsites, beach, birding (best in May), nature trails, boating and fishing are there, too.

MICHIGAN AUSABLE VALLEY RAILROAD

230 South Abbe Road (off SR33, 3.5 miles south of the blinker light in town), **Fairview 48621**

❑   Phone: (989) 848-2229
    Web: www.michiganausablevalleyrailroad.com
❑   Hours: Weekends and Holidays 10:00am-5:00pm. (Memorial Day - Labor Day)
❑   Admission: $3.00 (ages over 2).
❑   Tour: 1 and 1/2 mile trip is approximately 18 minutes long. Perfect for smaller kids.
❑   Miscellaneous: Quaint depot and gift shop where you can purchase tickets and fresh, hot popcorn.

This ¼ scale train offers visitors a calm, scenic tour which travels through a jackpine forest (Huron National Forest) and overlooks the Comins Creek Valley. You'll get to pass through a 115 foot wooden tunnel and over two wooden trestles (one of them is 220 feet long). Some passengers get a glimpse of wildlife such as deer, hawks, heron, beaver and maybe even elk or bear!

BOTTLE CAP MUSEUM

Gaylord - *4977 Sparr Road (5 miles east of Gaylord on F-44, next to Sparr Mall), 49735. Phone: (989) 732-1931. Hours: Wednesday-Saturday 11:00am-5:00pm (May-October). Otherwise, by appointment. Admission: $1.50-$2.50 (ages 6+).* Plus you receive a free Coke and a season pass to the Museum. Bill Hicks personal huge collection of Coca-Cola memorabilia including hundreds of novelty items, 1930-1970 dispensers and coolers, signs and posters and vintage bottles. Be sure to peek in the Coca-Cola Christmas Room and Bathroom.

CALL OF THE WILD MUSEUM

Gaylord - *850 South Wisconsin Avenue (east on Main Street, then south on Wisconsin), 49735. Phone: (989) 732-4336 or (800) 835-4347. Hours: Daily 8:30am-9:00pm. (mid-June-Labor Day), Daily 9:30am-6:00pm. (Rest of year). Admission: $3.00-$5.00. Miscellaneous: Also at location are Bavarian Falls Adventure Golf, Go Carts, Krazy Kars Tot Ride, and Gift Shop.* The museum is full of dioramas of over 60 North American Animals in natural settings. As you look over displays of elk, moose, black bear, timber wolves, etc., you'll learn about their behavior and habitat and sounds. The Michigan History area has stories recounted by an early fur trapper named Joseph. The Four Seasons Display of Michigan changes as you watch. They have an observation beehive there, too.

OSTEGO LAKE STATE PARK

Gaylord - *7136 Old 27 South (off I-75 south, Take I-75 to the village of Waters, Exit 270, and go west to Old 27. Go north on Old 27 five miles to park), 49735. Phone: (989) 732-5485.* **Web: www.michigandnr.com/parksandtrails/parklist.asp** *Admission: $4.00 per vehicle.* "The Alpine Village." The park is shaded with large oak, maple and pine. The park encompasses 62 acres and provides more than a half mile of sandy beach and large sites near or within sight of the lake. Camping/mini cabin, boating, fishing, swimming (mid-April to early November).

CRAWFORD COUNTY HISTORIC MUSEUM

Grayling - *97 Michigan Avenue (west end), 49738. Phone: (989) 348-4461.   Web: www.grayling-mi.com/history.html   Hours: Monday-Saturday 10:00am-4:00pm (Summer). Admission: $1.50 per person.* Located in the former Michigan Central Depot, the museum details local history from Camp Grayling military history to lumbering and fire fighting. The museum also has a railroad caboose, a farm shed, a trapper's cabin and a display dedicated to the greatest archer of all time - Fred Bear. Audio visual tapes of some of the area's old-timers telling family histories and stories of the early days.

GRAYLING FISH HATCHERY

North Down River Road (I-75 to exit 254)

Grayling 49738

- ❑   Phone: (989) 348-9266, **Web: www.hansonhills.org/hhfish.html**
- ❑   Hours: Daily 10:00am-6:00pm (Memorial Day-Labor Day).
- ❑   Admission: $1.50 adult, $1.00 child (6-17), $6.00 family.

It's always fun to watch kid's eyes light up at a "fish farm". See 11 ponds that contain more than 40,000 trout. See fish ranging from tiny aquarium size (2 inches long) to several pounds (28 inches long), and yes, you can even buy some to take home (priced by the inch). Fish food is available from dispensers for a nominal fee and is a great way to really bring the fish to life. Entertainment and demos every Sunday at 2:00pm.

HARTWICK PINES STATE PARK

4216 Ranger Road (I-75 exit 259 - on M-93)

Grayling 49738

- ❑   Phone: (989) 348-2537 center or (989) 348-7068 park
  Web: www.michigandnr.com/parksandtrails/parklist.asp
- ❑   Hours: Park open 8:00am-10:00pm. Museum buildings 9:00am-7:00pm (Summer). Open until only 4:00pm and closed Mondays the rest of the year. Generally only open weekends (Winter). Logging Museum is closed November - April.
- ❑   Admission: $4.00 per vehicle

❑   Miscellaneous: Bike trails, Braille trails, hiking, camping, fishing, picnic areas, winter sports, small gift shop. Summers-living history programs along the Forest Trail.

Some call it an "outdoor cathedral of nature", walking along the Old Growth Forest Foot Trail as it winds through the forest behind the Visitor Center. Along the 1¼ mile long trail, you can stop (¼ mile from Visitor Center) at the Logging Museum (open May-October only). Depending on the event, you'll see logging wheels and other logging equipment, a steam sawmill, plus logger's quarters in use. Be sure to stop in the Michigan Forest Visitor Center before your walk out into the pines. See the history of logging - both past cut and run phases - and modern conservation forestry. The nine slide projector audiovisual show gives you a great overview. Did you know, today, there is more paper recycled than trees cut down? Find hands-on exhibits on computer (Forest Management Simulation), dioramas (Reading the Rings, Sounds of Birds), and the talking "Living Tree"... or talking Loggers and Rivermen displays.

SKYLINE SKI AREA

Grayling - *4020 Skyline Road (I-75 to exit 251), 49738. Phone: (989) 275-5445. Hours: Thursday evenings, Friday-Sunday & Holidays 10:00am-9:00pm.* 14 runs. Rentals, lessons and ski shop.

HARRISVILLE STATE PARK

Harrisville - *248 State Park Road (US-23 South of M-72), 48740.* **Web: www.michigandnr.com/parksandtrails/Parklist.asp** *Phone: (989) 724-5126. Admission: $4.00 per vehicle.* Harrisville State Park features a campground/mini-cabins and day-use area nestled in a stand of pine and cedar trees along the sandy shores of Lake Huron. The park is within walking distance of the resort town of Harrisville. Over 1/2 mile of Lake Huron frontage with Cedar Run Nature Trail, boating, fishing, swimming, bicycle trails, and winter sports.

NEGWEGON STATE PARK

Harrisville - *248 State Park Road, 48740. Phone: (989) 724-5126.* **Web: www.michigandnr.com/parksandtrails/parklist.asp** A rustic, undeveloped area for hiking. No camping, no services.

STURGEON POINT LIGHTHOUSE

Sturgeon Point Road (5 miles north of Harrisville State Park
entrance, off US 23, Lakeshore Drive, follow signs)

Harrisville 48740

- ❑   Phone: (989) 724-5107
- ❑   Hours: Daily 10:00am-4:00pm (Memorial Day-September).
- ❑   Miscellaneous: Small gift shop.

An 1869 lighthouse. Tour the restored lighthouse keeper's house,
but not the tower (it's still in use). The stark contrast of the white
painted bricks against the bright red trim makes the building very
photogenic. Sitting on the shore end of a long and rocky
submerged finger of land that juts into Lake Huron, it is plain to
see why a lighthouse was needed here.

BURT LAKE STATE PARK

Indian River - *6635 State Park Drive (I-75 exit 310 west to SR 68
to Old US 27), 49749. Phone: (231) 238-9392. Admission: $4.00
per vehicle. Web: www.michigandnr.com/parksandtrails/parklist.asp*
Burt Lake State Park is open from April to November (depending
on the snowfall). It is located on the southeast corner of Burt Lake
with 2,000 feet of sandy shoreline. Great beaches on the state's
third largest lake, the park has numerous campsites and cabins,
boating and rentals, fishing, swimming, and winter sports.

ROMANIK'S RANCH

Levering - *10941 Weadock Road (I-75 exit 326, 13 miles south of
Mackinaw), 49755. Web: www.romaniksranch.com Phone: (231)
627-6106. Hours: Daily 10:00am-8:00pm (June-August). Friday-
Sunday 10:00am-6:00pm (September-October). Admission: $8.00
adult, $7.00 senior, $5.00 child (5-12).* See donkeys, cows, goats,
peacocks, ponies, sheep, pigs, horses, Koi fish ponds, chickens,
prairie dogs and rabbits. Now touch and feed farm animals or take
a hayride on the mile-long trail to see buffalo and elk herds in
Michigan woodlands. There's also a playground, rustic barn,
chuckwagon, and gift shop. Maybe try a buffalo burger or buffalo
chip cookies?

BUTTERFLY HOUSE

Mackinac Island - *1308 McGulpin Street (Huron Street north to Church Street west to McGulpin), 49757. Phone: (906) 847-3972. Web: www.mackinac.com/butterflyhouse Hours: 10:00am-7:00pm (Summer), 10:00am-6:00pm (Labor Day-early October). Admission: $5.00 adult, $2.00 child (6-12).* See several hundred live butterflies from Asia, Central and South America and the United States in free flight. A great setting of tropical gardens. One of America's first butterfly houses featured in popular magazines.

FORT MACKINAC STATE HISTORIC PARK

(on the bluff above downtown Mackinac Island)

Mackinac Island 49757

- ❑   Phone: (906) 847-3328
     Web: www.mackinacparks.com/fortmackinac/
- ❑   Hours: Daily 9:30am-6:00pm (mid-June to mid August). Daily until 4:30pm (early May to mid-June and mid-August to mid-October).
- ❑   Admission: $9.00 adult, $5.75 child (6-17). Combo admission with Colonial Mackinac and Mill Creek sites available for discount.
- ❑   Miscellaneous: Food available at Tea Room (lunch). Summers-guided tours w/ costumed interpreters. Beaumont Memorial (dedicated to the studies of human digestion), Blacksmith, Biddle House (crafts), McGulpin House, Indian Dorm are off premises but part of package fee in the summer.

Your carriage is greeted by a period dressed soldier inviting strangers to visit. Children and families will want to see the short audio visual presentation in the Post Commissary Theater. It's quick and simple but enough to "pull you in". Next, if it's close to the top of the hour, be sure to check out the kid-friendly, wonderfully   amusing,   cannon   firing   and   rifle   firing demonstrations. Maybe volunteer to help the soldiers (check out the funny, pointed hats). The Post Hospital and Officer's Quarters (costumes/hands-on or "Hanging with Harold") and Blockhouses (short narrative by an animatronic figure) will intrigue the kids. On your way in or out of the complex, be sure to visit the Soldier's Barracks exhibits featuring Mackinac: An Island Famous in These Regions". Mackinac island history from Furs (touch some) to Fish (step on a dock and listen to the fishermen come into port) to No Cars (1898 law) to Fudge! Oh yea, check and see if your ancestor was a Victorian soldier at Fort Mackinac.

GRAND HOTEL

Mackinac Island - *49757, Phone: (906) 847-3331 or (800) 33-GRAND Web: www.grandhotel.com Season: First weekend in May through the end of October.* At 660 feet, Grand Hotel's Front Porch (full of white rockers) is the world's largest. Self-guided grounds tours are $10.00 per person if not a hotel guest. The kitchen staff of 100 serves as many as 4,000 meals per day. Their gourmet food is unforgettable! Ask to take a Kitchen Tour to see how they do it! Kids won't believe the large number of plates, pies and potatoes they use! *(Kitchen tours by pre-arrangement only or at special events).* Recreational activities include: golf, tennis, croquet, bocci ball, swimming (outdoor pool), bicycling, saddle horses, carriage tours, duck pin bowling and a game room. Children's Programs (day or evening-3 hours) include "kids-style" lunches or dinners and fun group games, arts and crafts or a hike or tour. Rebecca's Playroom is open daily for families to enjoy games, crafts, videos and play when they are not conducting a paid program. Off-peak or special family rates begin at around $400.00 per night (includes full breakfast and five-course dinner and gratuities). Great family weeks are planned for: Old Fashioned Mackinac Fourth of July Celebration and the Grand's Summer Children's Programs. Watch the movies "Somewhere in Time" (Christopher Reeve/Jane Seymour) or "This Time for Keeps" (Esther Williams) before your visit to get the feel for the place. If you forget, they have a TV/VCR in every room and a copy of "Somewhere in Time" ready to watch. Remnants of these movies are found throughout the grounds (i.e.. Esther Williams pool or "Is it you?" twin trees). Believe it or not, this place is not stuffy...just casually elegant...best for a special treat or occasion.

MACKINAC ISLAND HORSE-DRAWN CARRIAGE TOURS

(Across from Arnold Ferry Dock), Mackinac Island 49757

- ❑ Phone: (906) 847-3307 **Web: www.mict.com**
- ❑ Hours: Daily 8:30am-5:00pm (mid - June - Labor Day). Daily 8:30am-4:00pm (mid-May to mid-June and Labor Day to October).
- ❑ Admission: $16.50 adult, $7.50 child (4-11)
- ❑ Tours: 1 hour & 45 minutes. You also have on/off privileges at several "hot spots".
- ❑ Miscellaneous: Since Motor vehicles aren't permitted on the Island, this is one fun way to leisurely see the sites. It keeps the island quaint to have the clip-clop sound of carriages - we think you'll agree!

It's guaranteed you'll hear amusing stories of the history (past & present) of the island. The multi-seated carriages stop at all of these highlights: Arch Rock (which story of formation do you believe?), Skull Cave, the Governor's Mansion, Grand Hotel, Fort Mackinac, Surrey Hill shops and snacks (including Wings of Mackinac Butterfly House), and the horse's stable area. Look for several "parking lots" full of bikes and carriages! We recommend this tour on your first trip to the island.

MACKINAC ISLAND STATE PARK

Mackinac Island 49757

- ❑ Phone: (906) 847-3328
  Web: www.mackinacparks.com/statepark/
- ❑ Admission: FREE
- ❑ Miscellaneous: Visitors Center located downtown on waterfront. Maps of numerous different trails to bike and/or walk (and easy-reading history of places you'll see) is available on many ferries or at the Visitors Center.

Most of Mackinac Island is preserved as a state park. Stretching eight miles around the island's perimeter, M-185 is a scenic shoreline road and the nation's only state highway without motor vehicle traffic. There are 70 miles of roads and trails within

Mackinac Island State Park, most of which are wooded inland trails for hikers, bikers and horseback riders in spring, summer and fall. There are 1,800 acres under canopies of cedars, birches and crossings of creatures like butterflies. The prehistoric geological formations, Arch Rock and Sugar Loaf, are natural limestone wonders that tower over the Straits. These can be viewed from below on biking trails or from a walking overview. Fort Holmes features a panoramic view of the Fort Mackinac and the Straits of Mackinac at the island's highest point - 320 feet above Lake Level. Look for historic caves and nature trails around most every turn.

MISSION POINT RESORT

Mackinac Island - *One Lakefront Drive (from the ferry docks, head east one-half mile), 49757. Phone: (906) 847-3312 or (800) 833-7711* **Web: www.missionpoint.com** *Rates: Start at ~ $149.00 per night.* This is truly a "family-friendly" resort and with the features they keep adding...it's a destination to stay at for a few days. You can just hang out around the grounds with amenities like: outdoor heated pool, tennis, croquet, horseshoes, video arcade/game room and lawn bowling. Or, sign up for a one hour Island sail or Ferry tour. Now, rent bikes or in-line skates and explore the 8 mile Island trail. They have four eateries and kids 12 & under eat FREE (most restaurants). They have hayrides, picnic games, poolside bingo and Sundae parties, too. Probably the best feature is their children's programs: Little Ones (2-4), Discovery Club (4-10) and Tweeners (11-15). The clubs have themes like "Space Day", "Nature Day", "Under the Sea", or "Wild West Day".

WINGS OF MACKINAC

Mackinac Island - *(Surrey Hill Shops, just past Grand Hotel), 49757.* **Web: www.wingsofmackinac.com** *Phone: (906) 847-WING. Admission: $2.00-$5.00 (age 4+). Hours: Open daily (May-October).* Free-flying butterflies in a lush garden paradise setting. See exotic butterflies from around the world including: White Peacocks, Long-Tailed Skippers, Painted Ladies, Spice Bush Swallowtails, Graphium Decolors, Ruddy Daggerwings, Blue Morphos, Tiger Swallowtails and Monarchs. Curators available to answer questions.

CENTER STAGE THEATRE

Mackinaw City - *248 South Huron Avenue (Mackinaw Crossings entertainment/shop complex), 49701. Phone: (231) 436-2200 or (877) 43-STAGE.* **Web: www.mackinawcrossings.com** *Showtimes: Tuesday-Sunday Mid-afternoon and early evening shows (May - mid-October). Admission: Avg. $23.00-$28.00 adult. Children half price.* With each note, travel back to the "I remember when" places of your heart through two hours of tempos and tunes celebrating the impact of all forms of music on the memorable moments of our lives. It is the kind of show that makes you feel better about life and love. Kids like the silly sounds of songs and cool dance moves.

COLONIAL MICHILIMACKINAC STATE HISTORIC PARK

102 Straits Ave (Downtown under the south side of Mackinac Bridge - Exit 339 off I-75), **Mackinaw City** 49701

❑ Phone: (231) 436-5563

   Web: www.mackinacparks.com/michilimackinac/

❑ Hours: Daily 9:00am - 4:00pm (May to mid-October). Extended hours until 6:00pm (mid-June to mid-August).

❑ Admission: $9.00 adult, $5.75 youth (6-17). Combo tickets for Fort Mac, Colonial Michi and Mill Creek are available at great discounts.

❑ Miscellaneous: Many festivals are held here including encampments and Colonial weddings.

"Join the Redcoats (if you promise to grow). Watch a Dig. Dance a Jig". In the Summer, costumed docents (in character) demonstrate musket /cannon firing, cooking, blacksmithing, barracks living, church life, and trading. Pies cook near fireplaces, chickens roam free, and an amusing soldier leads you on a tour of the village. Originally occupied by the French, then the British, even the Indians - an audiovisual program will explain the details. Archeological digs are held in the summer to look for ongoing significant finds. Be sure to check out the updated "Treasure From the Sand" exhibit as it takes you to a unique underground tunnel display of subterranean artifacts recovered. In the Soldiers

Barracks hands-on building: Dress up, stir the pot, lie in a bunk, try on coats, play a game or go into the "Black Hole" - a dark "time-out". Many areas of this park engage the kids interest - how cool to play (and learn) in a real fort!

HISTORIC MILL CREEK

South US 23 (5 minutes southeast of town)

Mackinaw City 49701

❑   Phone: (231) 436-7301

   Web: www.mackinacparks.com/millcreek/

❑   Hours: Daily 9:00am-5:00pm (mid-June to mid-August). Daily 9:00am-4:00pm (mid-May to mid-June) & (mid-August to mid-October).

❑   Admission: $7.50 adult, $4.50 youth (6-17). Good combo rates when add Fort Michilimackinac and Fort Mackinac.

❑   Miscellaneous: Cook house Snack Pavilion. Museum Store. Forest trails with working beaver dam.

As you walk along wooden planked paths, notice the different tree names - Thistleberry, Ironwood, etc. You'll have an opportunity to see a replica 18th century industrial complex - the oldest sawmill yard to provide finished lumber - in the Great Lakes Region. Water-powered sawmill and sawpit demos are given daily (Summers -lumberjack demos). Participants can help demo old & "newer", easier techniques to saw wood (which would you rather do?). There's also a reconstructed millwrights' house on site along with a museum. The audiovisual orientation is only 12 minutes long and is a great way to understand Michigan lumber history. Did you know a local amateur historian discovered this site, accidentally, in 1972? Creatures of the Forest is a naturalist outdoor "forest" talk - dress up as a beaver (why the raincoat?) and learn how creatures and trees co-exist.

MACKINAC BRIDGE MUSEUM AND "MIGHTY MAC" BRIDGE

231 East Central Avenue (Downtown within view of bridge)

Mackinaw City 49701

- ❑   Phone: (231) 436-5534 **Web: www.mackinacbridge.org**
- ❑   Hours: Daily 10:00am-9:00pm (May-October). Bridge open 24 hours.

Go to the upstairs museum at Mama Mia's Pizza (donations only). Watch the all new digitally re-mastered movie covering the history and construction of the Mackinac Bridge back in the mid-1950's. Why build the longest bridge ever - the "bridge that couldn't be built"? When you see the black & white photos of the long lines, staging cars to get on ferry boats to cross over the lake to the Upper Peninsula, you'll see the reason. On display, are the original spinning wheels that spun and ran cable (41,000 miles of it!) across the bridge; the original wrench (9-10 feet long) used to tighten anchor bolts on the towers; and most interesting, the hard hats of the numerous iron workers. Now, pay the $1.50 toll and cross the 5 mile long steel super-structure! P.S. On a windy day the bridge bows or swings out to the east or west as much as 20 feet!

MACKINAC ISLAND FERRIES

(Stops/Dock Pickups are clearly marked)

Mackinaw City 49701

Call for season schedules. Rain or shine. (early May - mid to late October). * Budget $7.00+ for kids (age 5-12). $14.00+ for adults. (RT)

- ❑   <u>ARNOLD LINE FERRY</u>. (800) 542-8528. Smooth trips, large ships, comfortable seats and cabins. Restrooms.
- ❑   <u>SHEPLER'S FERRY</u>. (800) 828-6157 or **www.sheplerswww.com**. Fast trips with very courteous and efficient staff. Restrooms. Narrative on the way over.
- ❑   <u>STAR LINE FERRY</u>. (800) 638-9892. Newest fleet. Most scheduled daily departures. Restrooms.

MACKINAW TROLLEY TOURS

(pickup at hotels), **Mackinaw City** 49701

❏   Phone: (231) 436-7812 **Web: www.mackinawtrolley.com**

❏   Miscellaneous: Kids of all ages get to ring the trolley bell (and
get a sticker, too). If you climb Castle Rock, you get a sticker for
that, too! This is a wonderfully organized tour with amusing
stories and enough stops along the way to keep the kids attention
from wandering. Try a different trip each visit!

HISTORICAL TOUR OVER THE BRIDGE: Ride through
history on the Mackinaw Trolley as they narrate happenings and
events along the way. Fort Michilimackinac area, Old Mackinac
Point Lighthouse, Train and Car Ferry Docks, The Mackinac
Bridge, Father Marquette's Mission and Grave Site at St. Ignace,
Indian lore at Ojibwa Museum and the magnificent view from
Castle Rock. 2 1/2 hours. Departs 10:00am daily (mid-May to mid-
October). Additional departure at 1:30pm during summer. Rates
$6.00-$16.00 (age 3+).

LIGHTHOUSES, SHIPS & SHIPWRECKS: Visit the Great
Lakes Shipwreck Museum at Whitefish Point on Lake Superior to
see artifacts and exhibits of shipwrecks, including the famous
Edmond Fitzgerald, and many other ships that went down in the
cold waters of Lake Superior. Tour the original Whitefish Point
Lighthouse, and then venture along the Lake Superior shore line
and through the Hiawatha Forest to climb and explore the famous
Point Iroquois Lighthouse and tower. Enjoy the freighter watching
from both lighthouses as 'the shipping lanes are just off shore.
Lunch included. 5 1/2 hours. Departs Wednesday & Saturday
9:30am (late June-late September). Rates $20.00-$36.00.

MACKINAW TROLLEY TRAIL: Ride along the desolate shores
of sparkling Lake Michigan, walk the Wild Sand Dunes and
through Forests in the faded footsteps of moccasins. View fields of
rare wildflowers. Visit the McCormick Mansion overlooking
historic Cecil Bay on Mackinac Headlands. Enjoy a delightful
Polish-American lunch at the unique Legs Inn overlooking Lake
Michigan. 3 1/2 hours. Departs Wednesday & Saturday 9:30am
(mid-May-mid-June). Rates $10.00-$21.00.

Mackinaw Trolley Tours (cont.)

FALL COLOR TOUR: See Northern Michigan's brilliant fall colors and visit a scenic working farm producing 100 acres of pumpkins, gourds, Indian corn, and vegetables. Pick a pumpkin or a bucket of gourds right out of the field. Ride down back roads to Lakeshore Drive's famous tunnel of trees and view Michigan in all of her glory. Stop at a very special farm and store with garden fresh herbs, spices, vegetables, homemade preserves and canned goods, cut and dried flowers and other fall specialties. Finally, enjoy a delicious lunch on Paradise Lake from Goldie's Cafe Patio. 4 hours. Departs Tuesday, Thursday, Saturday & Sunday 9:30am (mid-September to mid-October). Rates $18.00-$21.00.

ONAWAY STATE PARK

Onaway - *3622 North M-211 (M-211 six miles north from the City of Onaway), 49765. Phone: (989) 733-8279. Admission: $4.00 per vehicle. Web: www.michigandnr.com/parksandtrails/parklist.asp* One of the oldest State Parks in Michigan is located on the southeast shore of Black Lake. The park covers 158 acres of rugged land, including sand cobblestone beaches, large unique rock outcroppings and a diversity of trees including a stand of virgin white pines. Known for game fishing, they also have camping, hiking trails, boating, and swimming. Just 10 miles east of the park is the picturesque Ocqueoc Falls, the largest waterfall in Michigan's Lower Peninsula.

AU SABLE RIVER QUEEN

Oscoda - *West River Road (6 Miles West Of Oscoda), 48750. Phone: (989) 739-7351 or (989) 728-3775. Admission: $5.00-$10.00 (age 5+). Prices can be slightly higher for fall color tours. Tours: 2 hour tours depart once or twice daily. Call ahead for times. (Memorial Day weekend - 3rd weekend in October).* An authentic paddle wheel boat that has been touring this section of the river for over 40 years hosts you for a relaxing and narrated 19 mile trip. "Captain Bill" teaches about the area's history and wildlife along the journey. Glass enclosed decks and a snack bar are also available.

IARGO SPRINGS

Oscoda - *(Au Sable River Road Scenic Byway), 48750. Phone: (800) 235-4625. Hours: Daily, year-round. FREE admission.* What once was a spot for tribal ceremonies (the Chippewas believed that the spring had medicinal qualities), today is a great place to take the family into nature. Be sure to tell your kids not use up too much energy as you descend the 294 steps down the banks to the spring (don't worry, there are benches to rest on the way back up!). A new nature boardwalk (with a 30' tall observation deck) and interpretive center are worth a look, too.

DINOSAUR GARDENS PREHISTORIC ZOO
11160 US 23 South, **Ossineke** 49766

- ❑ Phone: (989) 471-5477 or (877) 823-2408
- ❑ Hours: Daily 9:00am-6:00pm (mid-May to mid-October).
- ❑ Admission: $3.00-$5.00 per person.
- ❑ Miscellaneous: Miniature golf. Snack bar. Neat gift shop full of dinosaur souvenirs.

An 80 foot long, 60,000 pound Brontosaurus is one of the many thrills that awaits your kids at this unique family tradition. A mixture of dinosaurs and cavemen with Christianity, as you're greeted by a Christ statue holding the world in his hand. Original owner Paul Domke spent some 38 years creating and sculpting 26 full scale dinosaurs that are "exploring" the forest of trees inside this attraction. A monstrous T-Rex in one exhibit is battling a Triceratops. Several scenes show cavepeople locked in mortal combat with giant snakes and Mastodons. A big-headed Aptosaurus is entered via a staircase. Inside the belly you'll find a heart-shaped Jesus — "The Greatest Heart." Storyboards and sound effects accompany each exhibit to help bring them to life. This is a great way to see the size and scale of the creatures that once walked the earth.

PRESQUE ISLE LIGHTHOUSE MUSEUMS

East Grand Lake Road (US 23 to CR638)

Presque Isle 49777

❑   Phone: (989) 595-2787

❑   Hours: Daily 9:00am-5:00pm. (Mid-May to Mid-October).

❑   Admission: $1.50-$2.50 (age 6+).

❑   Miscellaneous: Gifts shops at both locations.

OLD LIGHTHOUSE: Supposedly haunted old lighthouse and keepers' house full of artifacts. Built in 1840, you can visit with the "lightkeeper lady" inside the keeper's cottage (so-o cute!). Kids can make noise blowing a foghorn or ringing a giant bell (or as George called it when he visited with his family when he was 2 years old...the Bongy Bell!). Any age can climb the minimal 33 stairs to the top of the lighthouse for a great view.

NEW LIGHTHOUSE: An 1871 lightkeepers' quarters and a larger, more classical lighthouse. At 113' high, New Presque Isle is one of the tallest lighthouses that shines on the Great Lakes. It has a Third Order Fresnel lens and a focal plane of light that is 123 feet above lake Huron. It's a challenge to climb the some odd 193 steps - but what a rush!

HOEFT STATE PARK

Rogers City - *US-23 North, 49779. Phone: (989) 734-2543.* **Web: www.michigandnr.com/parksandtrails/parklist.asp** *Admission: $4.00 per vehicle.* Contains 300 heavily wooded acres with a mile of sandy Lake Huron shoreline in the 654 total acres of park. The park features 4 1/2 miles of trails that run through the forest and along the shoreline that is perfect for hiking or cross-country skiing. The park also has mini-cabins available that sleep four people. Visitors can also enjoy swimming in Lake Huron, a picnic area and shelter, a playground, and boating and fishing.

PRESQUE ISLE COUNTY HISTORICAL MUSEUM

Rogers City - *176 Michigan Street, 49779. Phone: (989) 734-2141. Hours: Weekdays Noon-4:00pm. (June-October). Also Saturdays (July-August). Admission: Donations.* The restored

Bradley House contains exhibits based on local history. In various theme rooms on three floors, see a re-created general store or Victorian parlor. Displays include marine, lumbering and American Indian artifacts.

THOMPSON'S HARBOR STATE PARK

Rogers City - *US23 North, 49779. Phone: (989) 734-2543. Web: www.michigandnr.com/parksandtrails/parklist.asp* For the rugged outdoorsman in the family, explore over 6 miles of trails in an area that is located on the Lake Huron shoreline. Adjacent to the Presque Isle harbor. Park roads are undeveloped. Call ahead for driving conditions. No camping. No services.

NORTH HIGGINS LAKE STATE PARK

11252 North Higgins Lake Drive (I-75 or US 27 exits - 7 miles west of town via US 27 and Military Road), **Roscommon** 48653

- ❑ Phone: (989) 821-6125 or (989) 373-3559 (CCC Museum)
  Web: www.michigandnr.com/parksandtrails/parklist.asp
- ❑ Hours: Park open dawn to dusk. Museum open summers 11:00am-4:00pm.
- ❑ Admission: $4.00 per vehicle

Over 400 acres available for camping/cabins, picnicking, hiking, boating, fishing, swimming, and winter sports. Most people find the Civilian Conservation Corps Museum is the reason for their trip here. During the Great Depression, many men without work were enrolled to perform conservation and reforestation projects throughout Michigan. CCC planted trees, taught and practiced fire fighting, constructed trails, built bridges and even built buildings (some are still standing). Housed in replica barracks, the museum has displays of highlights and techniques of their work. Interpretive, outside walks are available too.

SOUTH HIGGINS LAKE STATE PARK

Roscommon - *106 State Park Drive (I-75 at Roscommon Road south), 48653. Web: www.michigandnr.com/parksandtrails/parklist.asp Phone: (989) 821-6374. Admission: $4.00 per vehicle.* Voted some of the most beautiful lakes in the world, this park caters to families.

The beaches are family-friendly and there's plenty of camping sites. Hiking trails, fishing, and winter sports are there too. For information on canoe and boat rentals call (989) 821-5930.

RIFLE RIVER RECREATION AREA

Rose City - *(off M-33 southeast), 48654. Phone: (989) 473-2258.   Web: www.michigandnr.com/parksandtrails/parklist.asp Admission: $4.00 per vehicle.* Rifle River Recreation Area is a wilderness located within the AuSable State Forest. Includes Devoe Lake and Grousehaven Lake, Lupton. Camping/cabins, hiking trails, boating, fishing, swimming and winter sports.

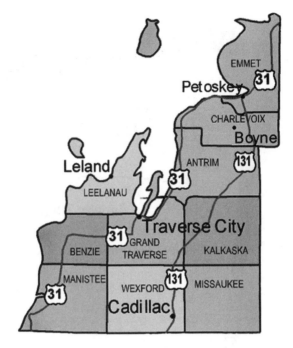

Chapter 4
North West Area

Our Favorites...

Beaver Island

Huron-Manistee National Forest

Kilwin's Candy Kitchens

Petosky State Park

Sleeping Bear Dunes

Climbing Sleeping Bear Dunes

MUSIC HOUSE MUSEUM

Acme - *7377 US 31 North, 49610. Phone: (231) 938-9300. **Web:** www.musichouse.org Hours: Monday-Saturday 10:00am-4:00pm, Sunday Noon-4:00pm (May-October).* Plus Holiday hours Friday-Sunday (mid-November thru December). Guided tours feature major instruments being played and explained. Rare antique musical phonographs and music boxes.

SHANTY CREEK RESORT

Bellaire - *One Shanty Creek Road (off M-88), 49615. Phone: (231) 533-8621 or (800) 678-4111. **Web:** www.shantycreek.com Resort is open year-round. Summer is golf, Winter is skiing.* A resort that features 41 runs, ski lessons, and equipment rentals. Accommodations include a new slopeside hotel. An Arnold Palmer designed golf course awaits your golfing skills in the summer. Great children's ski school. Babysitting is available.

PLATTE RIVER STATE FISH HATCHERY

Beulah - *15120 US-31, 49617. Phone: (231) 325-4611. **Web:** www.michigan.gov/dnr Hours: Monday-Friday 8:00am - 4:00pm (year-round). FREE self-guided tours.* Fish hatcheries are always a family favorite. The new information center, hatchery building, lower weir harvest facility and the upper weir egg-take station are the best places to learn. Best time to visit is in the fall when thousands of salmon can be seen.

BOYNE MOUNTAIN

Boyne Falls - *(off US 131), 49713. Phone: (231) 549-6001 or (800) GO-BOYNE. **Web:** www.boynemountain.com/bm_fr_ss.htm Hours: Resort is open year-round. Summer is golf, Winter is skiing.* One of the Lower Peninsula's finest resorts, Boyne Mountain 40+ runs, many new trails, rentals, ski lessons, outdoor pool and slopeside lodging/cabins. A children's ski program and baby sitting are also available.

HURON-MANISTEE NATIONAL FORESTS

1755 South Mitchell Street (over 960,000 acres in the northern part
of the Lower Peninsula), **Cadillac** 49601

❑   Phone: (800) 821-6263
    Web: www.fs.fed.us/r9/hmnf/hmindex.htm
❑   Hours: Open 24 hours daily.
❑   Admission: $3.00 per carload per day.

Popular activities here are swimming in Lakes Huron and
Michigan, cross-country skiing, snowmobiling, trout fishing,
modern and rough camping, boating and bicycle trails. Popular
spots within the forests are:

❑   THE NORDHOUSE DUNES - one mile of undeveloped
    shoreline along Lake Michigan.
❑   THE LODA LAKE WILDFLOWER SANCTUARY - one mile
    trail through marsh, forest and orchards. Over 40 miles of trails
    for hiking along the Manistee River.
❑   THE RIVER ROAD SCENIC BYWAY - runs 22 miles along
    the south bank of the Au Sable River. View reservoirs, bald
    eagles, salmon, the Canoeists Memorial and the Lumberman's
    Memorial and Visitors Center of logging.
❑   TUTTLE MARSH WILDLIFE AREA - Managed 5000 acres of
    fox, deer, coyote, muskrat, beaver, otter and weasel.

MITCHELL STATE PARK

6093 East M-115

Cadillac 49601

❑   Phone: (231) 775-7911
    Web: www.michigandnr.com/parksandtrails/parklist.asp
❑   Admission: $4.00 per vehicle
❑   Miscellaneous: Camping and cabins, boating and rentals, fishing,
    swimming, and winter sports.

The park is 245 acres and is situated between Lake Mitchell and
Lake Cadillac and provides an excellent opportunity to view a
variety of wildlife on the outskirts of Cadillac. A historic canal
connects the two lakes and runs directly through the park. The

Visitor's Center is also called the Carl T. Johnson Hunting & Fishing Center. A full size Michigan elk mount is on display in the exhibit hall, as well as other wildlife species which have been "brought back" by the efforts of sportsperson's organizations. With the push of a button, visitors can hear the call of the elk or other species featured in the wildlife exhibit. Exhibits include a wall-length aquarium and trapping and conservation efforts. Many come here for the birding too. You may see great blue heron, yellow finches and mallards. Center open Tuesday - Sunday 10:00am - 5:00pm (May-November). Weekends only the rest of the year.

SUGAR LOAF RESORT

Cedar - *4500 Sugar Loaf Mountain Road (off M-72), 49621. Phone: (231) 228-1553 or (800) 952-6390. Hours: Resort is open year-round, but skiing is usually from December-March. Golf in summer.* 20 runs, an excellent kids' ski schools (toddlers and up), rentals, lessons, outdoor and indoor pools, and a restaurant.

BEAVER ISLAND BOAT COMPANY

Charlevoix - *103 Bridge Park Drive, 49720. Phone: (231) 547-2311 or (888) 446-4095.* **Web:** *www.bibco.com* *Admission: $33.00 adult, Basically Half Price-child (5-12). Rates are roundtrip. Vehicle transport also available.* Passenger and Car Ferry service from Charlevoix to Beaver Island, the Great Lakes' most remote inhabited island. Tour drivers will guide you through Beaver Island's beautiful scenery & intriguing history, while giving you an idea of why island life is so unique. Beaver Island is home to two lighthouses. Packages include round trip cruises and possible escorted island tours of museums and island lunches. Call for schedule and information (April-December).

FISHERMAN'S ISLAND STATE PARK

Charlevoix - *Bells Bay Road (off US-31 southwest), 49720.* **Web:** *www.michigandnr.com/parksandtrails/parklist.asp* *Phone: (231) 547-6641. Admission: $4.00 per vehicle.* A 2,678-acre park in Charlevoix County that features a park road that travels for two and one-half miles along the Lake Michigan shoreline. Away from the shoreline, the park's terrain consists of rolling dunes, covered with maple, birch, and aspen, broken up by bogs of cedar and black spruce. Camping, hiking, fishing, swimming and bicycle trails.

YOUNG STATE PARK

Charlevoix - *2280 Boyne City Road (US-131, west on M-75), 49720. Web: www.michigandnr.com/parksandtrails/parklist.asp Phone: (231) 582-7523. Admission: $4.00 per vehicle.* Young State Park is located at the east end of beautiful Lake Charlevoix. The park spans over 560 acres in Charlevoix County and is a mix of gently rolling terrain, lowlands, and cedar swamp. Camping, hiking, boating and rentals, fishing, swimming and winter sports.

LEGS INN

Cross Village - *M-119 (US 31 to Carp Lake Village to Gill Road west through Bliss Township to Cross Village), 49723. Phone: (231) 526-2281. Web: www.legsinn.com Hours: Daily, Lunch and Dinner. (mid-May to mid-October).* Included on the State Historic Register, this restaurant's roof line is ornamented with inverted cast-iron stove legs. The fantasy-like atmosphere of this medieval looking stone, timber and driftwood landmark was created by one man, Polish immigrant, Stanley Smolak. The original Polish owner was also inducted into the Ottawa Indians tribe locally. His sculptures and whimsy decorating using tree trunks will intrigue you. The authentic Polish cuisine is the specialty, but delicious American dishes are also served. Indoor/Outdoor dining but no A/C. Casual dress. Moderate prices. Children's Menu.

SLEEPING BEAR DUNES NATIONAL LAKESHORE

9922 Front Street (SR 72) (35 miles along northwest Lower Peninsula shores), **Empire** 49630

- ❑ Phone: (231) 326-5134 **Web: www.nps.gov/slbe**
- ❑ Hours: (Visitor's Center) Daily 9:00am-6:00pm (Summer). Daily 9:00am-4:00pm (rest of year).
- ❑ Admission: $7.00 per week.

For updates visit our website: www.kidslovepublications.com

❏   Miscellaneous: Visitor's Center in Empire has nice slide show to understand area better.

The name of the shore comes from Chippewa Indian stories of a mom and her two bear cubs separated by a forest fire. The cubs now stand for the North and South Manitou Islands - still stranded. Among the dunes are rugged bluffs, ghost forests, and exposed bleached trees. Mid-May to Mid-October take the Pierce Stocking Scenic Drive route to view the dunes. On South Manitou Island, climb the 100 foot lighthouse or view the wreck of a freighter or the Valley of Giants (white cedar trees). The islands are accessible by ferry from Leland. The Maritime Museum at the Coast Guard Station in Glen Haven displays maritime area history and is open summers only. A daily re-enactment of a Life-Saving Service rescue is the highlight of every afternoon (specifically directed toward kids!). The ever-popular Dune Climb is a challenge, but so worth it! (Remember, climbing down is much easier than climbing up!). Be sure to take pictures once you arrive on a high summit. Ranger-led walks, campfire programs and other activities are available in July and August. Fishing, canoeing, hiking and cross-country skiing are favorite activities here.

BOYNE HIGHLANDS

Harbor Springs - *600 Highlands Drive, 49740. Phone: (800) GO-BOYNE or (231) 526-3000. Web: www.boynehighlands.com* Besides great family skiing (on your choice of 44 slopes), this resort offers a large heated outdoor pool that is warm even when the outside temperature is below zero. Babysitting, rentals, slopeside lodging (inn and cottages), children's activities and lessons are also available.

NUB'S NOB

Harbor Springs - *500 Nub's Nob Road, 49740. Phone: (800) SKI-NUBS or (231) 526-2131. Web: www.nubsnob.com* Across the street from Boyne Highlands (see listing), Nub's Nob offers 41 runs, rentals, instructions, and children's activities. Also, for the beginners, be sure to check out the Midwest's only Free LEARN-TO-SKI & SNOWBOARD AREA (all ages) complete with its own chairlift.

FUN COUNTRY WATER PARK
9320 US-31 South (US 31 & M-137)
Interlochen 49643

❑   Phone: (231) 276-6360

❑   Hours: Daily 11:00am-11:00pm. Water slide closes at 6:30pm
      (Memorial Day - Labor Day).

❑   Admission: Begins at ~$12.00 (age 4+). Toddlers are half price.

Two water slides over 300 feet long assures a day of summer fun.
Also bumper boats, a carousel, go-carts, and miniature golf.

INTERLOCHEN STATE PARK

Interlochen - *M-137 (South of US 31), 49643. Phone: (231) 276-
9511.   Web: www.michigandnr.com/parksandtrails/parklist.asp
Admission: $4.00 per vehicle.* Camping on the beach of the lake
with bathhouses and boat rentals is popular especially in the
summer. Summer Music Camp Shows. Hiking trails, fishing,
boating, bicycle trails, and winter sports are available.

BOTTLE HOUSE MUSEUM

Kaleva - *14451 Wuoksi (next to Bethany Lutheran Church),
49645. Phone: (231) 362-3793. Hours: Saturday Noon-4:00pm
(Memorial Day weekend-Labor Day weekend). Other times by
appointment.* Over 1500 articles of historical interest housed in the
beautiful and unique building well known as the "Bottle House."
The home was built with over 60,000 soft drink bottles in 1941. It
is listed on the Michigan Register of Historical Sites, Ripley's
Believe it or Not and the National Register of Historic Sites.

ORCHARD BEACH STATE PARK

Manistee - *2064 Lakeshore Road, 49660. Phone: (231) 723-
7422. Web: www.michigandnr.com/parksandtrails/parklist.asp
Admission: $4.00 per vehicle.* Lots of reasonable camp site rentals
on the dunes, great beaches with swimming, hiking trails.

WATER BUG, THE

Manistee - *Manistee River Walk, South River Bank (west of Maple/Washington St. off River St, behind Department Store), 49660. Phone: (231) 398-0919. Tours: Historical (1:00 & 3:00pm) or Lighthouse (sunset). Closed Mondays and Tuesdays except holidays. Memorial Day weekend-Labor Day. $10.00 adult, $5.00 child.* View the Historical Victorian Port City of Manistee from the water. Trip includes view of Historic Downtown, Wetlands and the beautiful Lighthouse from a 22 passenger riverboat.

LEELANAU STATE PARK

Northport - *15310 North Lighthouse Point Road (north of Traverse City on M-22 through Northport and take M-201 eight miles north), 49670. Phone: (231) 386-5422. Admission: $4.00 per vehicle. Web: www.michigandnr.com/parksandtrails/parklist.asp* The word Leelanau is the Indian word for "A Land of Delight" and could not better describe the area. Grand Traverse Lighthouse tours along coastal dunes are a big draw (**www.grandtraverselighthouse.com**). Along the shorelines, Petoskey stones can be found. Camping/cabins, hiking trails, fishing, swimming and winter sports.

KILWIN'S CANDY KITCHENS

355 North Division Street

Petoskey 49770

- ❑ Phone: (231) 347-3800 **Web: www.kilwins.com**
- ❑ Hours: Monday-Friday 9:00am-4:30pm.
- ❑ Admission: FREE
- ❑ Tours: Monday - Thursday 10:30am, 11:00am, 2:00pm, 2:30 pm. 20 minutes (June - August). Group tours (10+) by reservation during non-peak candy-making (after holidays).
- ❑ Miscellaneous: Retail store sells over 300 types of mouth-watering candy.

When first arriving, you'll probably park your car where the sign reads, "Chocolate Lovers Parking - All Others Will Be Towed". This is just the right kind of invitation to let you (and the kids) know that you are in for a real treat. Northern Michigan seems to have a real taste for fudge and candy and Kilwan's is one of the area's most respected candy-makers. Get "close to the action" on this tour and see all of the various production processes. The kids will love watching 2 workers stretching 3 foot slabs of peanut brittle!

LITTLE TRAVERSE HISTORICAL MUSEUM

Petoskey - *100 Depot Court (Waterfront at Bayfront Park), 49770. Phone: (616) 347-2620.* **Web: *www.petoskeymuseum.org*** *Hours: Thursday - Saturday 1:00-4:00pm (May - late December). Admission: $1.00 adult (over 18). FREE for children.* Housed in an old railroad depot, you'll find information about the area's Okawa Indians and pioneer times. Exhibits about Ernest Hemingway (Much of the exhibit revolves around the time when Hemingway lived in the Petoskey area as a young man) and Civil War author Bruce Catton. Display of Petoskey stones, too.

PETOSKEY STATE PARK

2475 M-119 (north of US 31)

Petoskey 49770

❑   Phone: (231) 347-2311

   Web: www.michigandnr.com/parksandtrails/parklist.asp

❑   Admission: $4.00 per vehicle

Old Baldy Trail includes a stairway that leads up Old Baldy, a stable dune that is one of the attractions in the park. After climbing the dune, the view that is available of the bay is breathtaking. The Portage Trail winds through very diverse terrain where a nature lover may find different species of plants and wildlife. Campsites along Little Traverse Bay with a great beach and trails in and out of wooded dunes. There's well developed nature trails and in Spring, sort through Winter's debris for Petoskey stones (designated Michigan state stone). Look for the coral fossils in the stones and you've probably found one. Boating and winter sports are also available.

CRYSTAL MOUNTAIN SKI AREA

Thompsonville - *12500 Crystal Mountain Drive (off M-115), 49683. Phone: (231) 378-2000 or (800) 968-4676.* **Web:** *www.crystalmtn.com Hours: Resort is open year-round. Skiing usually December-March. Golf in summer.* Crystal Mountain is a "family- friendly" resort that offers 34 runs with a children's "learn to ski" program, indoor and outdoor pools, restaurant, and slopeside rooms.

TALL SHIPS "WESTWIND" & "MANITOU"

13390 SW Bay Shore Drive (Grand Traverse Bay - West arm)

Traverse City 46984

❑   Phone: (231) 941-2000 or (800) 678-0383
      Web: www.tallshipsailing.com
❑   Admission: Varies by length of "get-away". 2 hour sails range
      from $32.00-40.00 adult/ Half price child. Call or visit website
      for sailing schedules and rates. (Memorial Day – September)

The Westwind (66') and Manitou (114') ships offer tours and accommodations during the summer months. The Westwind calls Traverse City her home port. From there, she offers fun-filled 2-hour outings, three to four times a day throughout the sailing season. Her bright white sails and hull are a most popular sight on the sparkling waters of West Grand Traverse Bay. The sunset cruises can be breath-taking. "Manitou" is one of the largest sailing ships on the Great Lakes, similar in design to vessels that sailed one hundred years ago. She was built specifically for passenger service, making her one of the most comfortable windjammers afloat. Up to twenty-four passengers can enjoy the pleasure and thrill of sailing aboard "Manitou."

CLINCH PARK ZOO

Union & Grandview Parkway (Next to the beach)

Traverse City 49684

❑   Phone: (231) 922-4904
      Web: www.ci.traverse-city.mi.us/services/zoo.htm

- ❑ Hours: Daily 9:30am-5:30pm (Memorial Day-Labor Day). Daily 10:00am-4:00pm (mid-April - Memorial Day & day after Labor Day - October).
- ❑ Admission: $3.00 adult, $1.50 child (5-12). Free admission mid-April until Saturday of Memorial Day weekend.

A smaller zoo in the heart of the downtown resort/shopping area that features wildlife that is native to Michigan. Picnic area and small train rides (Memorial Day - Labor Day).

GREAT LAKES CHILDREN'S MUSEUM

336 West Front Street (downtown), **Traverse City** 49684

- ❑ Phone: (231) 932-GLCM **Web: www.glcm.org**
- ❑ Hours: Tuesday-Saturday 10:00am-5:00pm, Sunday 1:00-5:00pm. (September-May). Open Mondays, 10:00am-5:00pm (June-August)
- ❑ Admission: $4.00 per person (age 2+).

A hands-on interactive children's museum focused on the Great Lakes and water. Exhibits include kid-sized lighthouse, a sailboat, and a periscope. A child can pilot a Great Lakes freighter, operate the locks in the water table, or navigate the Lakes on the navigation wall. In the Water Cycle children can go up the sunshine climb as they evaporate, condense in the cloud chamber, slide down as precipitation, and then go into the groundwater tunnel. There are over 30 exhibits and activities awaiting.

PIRATE'S COVE ADVENTURE PARK

Traverse City - *1710 US-31 North, 49684. Phone: (231) 938-9599. Web: www.piratescove.net Hours: Daily 10:00am-11:00pm (late April-late October). Admission: $6.00-$9.50 adult, $5.50-$8.00 child (4-12). Rides use tokens can be purchased.* Adventure Miniature golf in a fun-filled setting of lavish landscaping and delightful pirate themes. Putt your way over footbridges, under waterfalls, and through mountain caves. Sharpen your putting skills on Blackbeard's Challenge Course, Captain Kidd's Adventure or The Original Course. A fun park for kids of all ages. Electric cars entertain the youngest kids while go-carts and waterslides (must be 42" tall to use) help keep the older kids entertained. Maybe try a bumper boat pond with squirt gun-equipped boats.

DENNOS MUSEUM CENTER

Traverse City - *1701 East Front Street (On campus of Northwestern Michigan College), 49686. Phone: (231) 995-1055.* **Web: www.dennosmuseum.org** *Hours: Monday-Saturday 10:00am-5:00pm, Sunday 1:00-5:00pm. Closed on major holidays. Admission: $4.00 adult, $2.00 child (under 18).* A regional hub for arts and culture, this dramatic building features three rotating exhibition galleries, a sculpture court, a "hands-on" Discovery Gallery (hands-on art, science and high tech), a gallery of Inuit Eskimo art from the museum's permanent collection as well as the 367-seat Milliken Auditorium, a 32-seat video theater, and a museum store.

OLD MISSION PENINSULA LIGHTHOUSE

Traverse City - *(along M-37). 49686.* View this 19th Century lighthouse and step back in time as your kids stand at the geographical point that is exactly halfway between the Equator and the North Pole.

SAND LAKES QUIET AREA

Traverse City - *(M-72 to Broomhead Road - South), 49686. Phone: (231) 922-5280. Hours: Always open (year-round). FREE admission.* This adventurous place is so "quiet" (as the name implies) because all motor vehicles are banned from the 10 miles of trails that feature fishing and camping. Make your plans to hike in and camp and see how Michigan must have looked to the early pioneers and Native Americans. (Note: Trails are not stroller accessible).

TRAVERSE CITY STATE PARK

Traverse City - *1132 US-31 east, 49686. Phone: (231) 922-5270.* **Web: www.michigandnr.com/parksandtrails/parklist.asp** *Admission: $4.00 per vehicle.* Almost 350 campsites opposite Grand Traverse Bay with bridge to beach and close to attractions. Hiking trails, boating, fishing, swimming, and winter sports, too.

GREAT WOLF LODGE

Traverse City - *3575 North US 31 South, 49684. Phone: (231) 941-3600. **Web: www.greatwolflodge.com**.* A Northwoods themed year-round resort with family-sized suite lodging; a huge indoor waterpark (waterslides, a family boat ride, indoor/outdoor pool, children's pool, lazy river, whirlpools and interactive water fort); an arcade and restaurant.

Chapter 5
South East Area

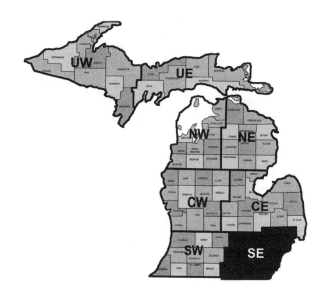

Our Favorites...

Diamond Jack's River Tours

Henry Ford Museum & Greenfield Village

Impression 5 Science Center

Jiffy Mix Tour

Marvin's Marvelous Mechanical Museum

Michigan Historical Center

MSU's Children's Garden & Dairy Plant

Rainforest Cafe Educational Tours

Stagecoach Stop USA

"Mold-O-Rama" fun

WILD SWAN THEATER

Ann Arbor - *416 West Huron Street (performances at Towsley Auditorium), 48103. Web: http://comnet.org/wildswan Phone: (734) 995-0530. Admission: $6.00-$8.00 for single tickets.* A professional theater company that performs for family audiences using dance, masks, puppets and music. Productions like "Winnie the Pooh" or "Peter Rabbit" and other famous storybook tales come to life for the kids. Mostly matinees.

ANN ARBOR HANDS-ON MUSEUM

220 East Ann Street (between 4th & 5th Avenue - Downtown)

Ann Arbor 48104

❑   Phone: (734) 995-5439 **Web: www.aahom.org**

❑   Hours: Monday-Saturday 10:00am-5:00pm, Sunday Noon-
        5:00pm.

❑   Admission: $7.00 adult, $5.00 senior, student, child (age 3+).

❑   Miscellaneous: Explore Store.

Your kid's eyes will light up with amazement as you explore over 250 exhibits on 4 floors in this old firehouse. Watch your skeleton ride a bicycle as you explore human movement, play a song on a walk-on piano, "be one" with a green screen, touch fossils, have bubble fun, climb walls, and whisper across the room to a friend (and they can hear you) are just a few of offerings. Learn "How Things Work" with gears, pulleys and air movement or play a laser harp in "Light & Optics". Become the exhibit in "Recollections" and let the little ones find their own space in the "Preschool Gallery". (Remember Mom & Dad...you came for the children...but learning sure is fun!).

ANN ARBOR YOUTH CHORALE

Ann Arbor - *1110 North Main Street, Suite 117, 48104. Phone: (734) 996-4404. Web: http://comnet.org/aayc/ Admission.* A children's (ages 9-16) choir comprised of 80 members from around the area. The kids come from different racial, economic, and religious backgrounds and perform various culturally diverse music. Local concerts are in the winter and spring.

DOMINO'S FARMS

24 Frank Lloyd Wright / Earhart Road (East of US22, exit 41)

Ann Arbor 48106

- ❑ Phone: (734) 998-0182 **Web: www.pettingfarm.com**
- ❑ Hours: Monday-Friday 9:30am-4:00pm, Saturday & Sunday 10:30am-5:00pm.
- ❑ Admission: $3.00-$3.50 per person (age 2+).
- ❑ Miscellaneous: Picnic area. Domino's Pizza available.

First pass a herd of buffalo or cows grazing on the grounds of the Domino's Pizza World Headquarters. Across the street is Domino Farms, an early 1900's depiction of Michigan farm life. The Petting Farm has 100+ chickens, goats, sheep, peacocks, pot-bellied pigs, and miniature horses. Take a hayride to buffalo fields and stop and get a close look at their shy, huge faces! Many animal demonstrations throughout the day. One of the cleanest farms you'll ever see. Nice outdoor activity to enjoy with a picnic.

UNIVERSITY OF MICHIGAN MUSEUMS

(I-94 to State Street Exit)

Ann Arbor 48109

- ❑ **Web: www.umich.edu**
- ❑ Admission: FREE (some ask for donations).
- ❑ Tours: Many of these facilities are included in a group tour- by appointment.

SPORTS MUSEUM - 1000 South State Street - (734) 647-2583. Captures the spirit of 100+ years of athletic competition with emphasis on the Rose Bowl, Big Ten and U.S. Olympics. Located in the nation's largest college stadium. Weekdays until 4:00pm.

MUSEUM OF NATURAL HISTORY - 1109 Geddes Avenue - (734) 764-0478. Michigan birds and animals. Face to face with prehistoric allosaurus conquering a stegosaurus or a mastodon from Michigan. Evolution of whale's skeletons. Daily until 5:00 pm. Suggested donation $3.00-$5.00. Planetarium.

<u>MUSEUM OF ARCHEOLOGY</u> - 434 South State Street - (734) 764-9304. 100,000+ artifacts from ancient Egypt, Greece and Rome. See a mummy child! Open Daily until 4:00pm, except Mondays.

<u>STEARNS MUSICAL COLLECTION</u> - 1100 Baits Drive - North Campus - (734) 763-4389. 2000+ musical instruments on display from around the world. Open until 4:00pm weekdays.

<u>BOTANICAL GARDENS</u> - 1800 North Dixboro Road - (734) 998-7061. Tropical, warm-tempered or desert plants. Nature trail. Prairie. Daily 10:00am - 4:30pm. Admission $1.00-$3.00.

ADRIAN & BLISSFIELD RAILROAD

(US 223 - Downtown - leaves from Depot Street), **Blissfield** 49228

- ❑   Phone: (888) GO-RAIL-1 **Web: www.murdermysterytrain.com**
- ❑   Admission: $10.00 adult, $9.00 senior, $6.00 child (3-12).
- ❑   Tours: Family Excursions Saturday afternoon departing at 1:00pm (June-October). Cars are fully heated and air conditioned.

As the powerful "larger than life" diesel engine rumbles into the station, your kids will be standing in awe! The excursion train travels leisurely on a segment of the Erie & Kalamazoo Railroad, which began operations in 1836. Along the way, you'll travel through the rich farmland of Southeastern Michigan, which was once the bottom of a prehistoric lake we now call Lake Erie. Upon arriving at Lenawee Junction, imagine what it must have been like when over forty trains a day stopped there to exchange goods and passengers bound for such places as Chicago, Jackson, Monroe and Toledo. Enjoy a 90-minute scenic train ride that includes two old bridges (or trestles as they're called in railroader lingo) across the Raisin River.

ISLAND LAKE RECREATION AREA

Brighton - *12950 East Grand River (I-96, exit 151), 48116. **Web:** www.michigandnr.com/parksandtrails/parklist.asp Phone: (810) 229-7067. Admission: $4.00 per vehicle.* A canoe livery offers relaxing trips down the scenic Huron River. Hiking trails, beaches, boating, fishing, swimming, bicycle trails, winter sports and cabins available.

MOUNT BRIGHTON SKI AREA

Brighton - *4141 Bauer Road (I-96 - Exit 145), 48116. Phone: (810) 229-9581.* **Web: *http://users.iglide.net/mtbrighton/*** A "family friendly" attraction that offer 26 runs of various skill levels. Snowboarding, lessons and rentals are available.

BRIGHTON RECREATION AREA

Brighton - *6360 Chilson Road (I-96 exit 145 south), 48843.* **Web: *www.michigandnr.com/parksandtrails/parklist.asp*** *Phone: (810) 229-6566. Admission: $4.00 per vehicle.* The area has a combination of high, irregular ranges of hills, interspersed with a number of attractive lakes. Oak forest, thick hedgerows and open spaces blend on the uplands while grassy marshes, shrub masses and dense swamp timber mark the lowlands. Beaches, swimming, and trout fishing are most popular here. Other features include hiking, winter sports, modern and rough camping, boating and bicycle trails.

WALKER TAVERN STATE HISTORIC COMPLEX

13220 M-50 (US 12 & M-50)

Brooklyn 48230

- ❑   Phone: (517) 467-4401
     Web: www.sos.state.mi.us/history/museum/musewalk/index.html
- ❑   Hours: Wednesday-Sunday 11:00am-4:00pm (Memorial Day - Labor Day). By appointment - rest of the year.
- ❑   Admission: FREE
- ❑   Tours: Approximately 1 hour

In the mid-1800's, the journey between Detroit and Chicago (by stagecoach) was a 5-8 day event (one-way, can you imagine?). This farmhouse tavern was the original stopping point (along what is now known as US 12) where travelers could have a meal, relax, or spend the night. Discover how life was in the 1840's with realistic exhibits that show a barroom, dining room, parlor and kitchen. The Visitor's Center also features a movie about a young boy's travels from New York to Chicago in the 1840's. Located in the Cambridge Junction Historic State Park. No camping.

For updates visit our website: www.kidslovepublications.com

MICHIGAN INTERNATIONAL SPEEDWAY

Brooklyn - *12626 US 12 (1 mile west of M-50), 49230. Phone: (517) 592-6666 or (800) 354-1010 tickets.* **Web:** *www.mispeedway.com Hours: Call or visit website for current schedule (Summer). Admission: $30.00 - $95.00 per person.* Gentlemen (and ladies) start your engines! The thrill of world class professional motorsports is alive and well in Michigan. This speedway is a D-shaped, 2-mile oval that offers high-banked (18 degree) turns to a variety of racing vehicles including NASCAR, CART, and the NASCAR Craftsman Truck Series. Also see the fastest 400 mile race, the annual Michigan 400 or Winston Cup series.

CALDER DAIRY FARM

9334 Finzel Road (I-275 - Telegraph Road Exit (south), to Stoney Creek Rd - West to Finzel Rd South - follow signs), **Carleton** 48117

- ❑ Phone: (734) 654-2622 .
- ❑ Hours: Daily 10:00am-8:00pm. Winter hours vary.
- ❑ Admission: FREE
- ❑ Tours: Pre-arranged @ $6.00 per person (includes hayride and ice cream cone). Minimum group is 15.
- ❑ Miscellaneous: Farm Store and Ice Cream Shop. Main Store - watch milk arriving and fed through series of pipes for processing.

See how luscious ice cream is made - right from the Brown Swiss Cow's milk! Pet the Holstein and Swiss Cows plus numerous other animals that you're likely to see on a farm (pigs, ducks, sheep). They make creamy ice cream, chocolate milk, eggnog, plus milk right from the cows - fresh in glass bottles. Check out the milking machines behind the store to see cows milked by the dozen. Take a tour in a hay wagon (horse driven) and you'll see fields of llamas, deer and bright peacocks. At the end of your visit to the land of "Babe", be sure to get a generous souvenir cup of fresh ice cream!

CHELSEA MILLING - "JIFFY MIX"

201 West North Street (I-94 west to Chelsea exit - north - follow signs), **Chelsea** 48118

- ❑   Phone: (734) 475-1361 **Web: www.jiffymix.com**
- ❑   Hours: Monday-Friday 9:00am-1:00pm. Closed Holidays.
- ❑   Admission: FREE
- ❑   Tour: By appointment only. 45 person max. (1 to 1 1/2 hours)
- ❑   Miscellaneous: Souvenir box of Jiffy Mix given with recipe booklet.

In a time when manufacturing tours are minimal or eliminated, this is a good, old-fashioned tour! Inside the world headquarters of the internationally known Jiffy Mix Baking Products, you'll begin in the auditorium with a slide show narrated by your tour guide. Because they're veteran associates, they talk about each operator by name. Learn some history about the company including how they got the name "Jiffy". In 1930, Grandma Mabel Holmes named the famous, low-priced, blue and white baking mix boxes "Jiffy" after hearing cooks exclaim, "The muffins will be ready in a jiffy!". Their flour is from Michigan and is milled using silk material similar to your kid's blanket edging. You'll see the packaging process, first in the slide show, then actually out in the factory. After you have a snack of Jiffy Mix cookies and juice, everyone adorns a hair net and takes a 20 minute walking tour of the packaging process. It's neat to see waxed paper formed in a block, filled, boxed and then sealed. The sealing machine is a cute 8 legged machine. Did you know their #1 selling product is "Corn Muffin" mix? At the end of the tour you can choose from muffin or another mix box to take home…yummies there…yummies at home!

WATERLOO RECREATION AREA

16345 McClure Road (7 miles west off I-94)

Chelsea 48118

- ❑   Phone: (734) 475-8307
      Web: www.michigandnr.com/parksandtrails/parklist.asp
- ❑   Admission: $4.00 per vehicle

The lower peninsula's largest state park, it features cross-country skiing, horse rental and trails, modern and rough camping and cabins, beaches and boating, fishing, bicycle trails, and winter sports. For an additional small charge, you can tour the Farm Museum buildings. There's also long hiking trails and an Audubon Society preserve adjacent. Many visit often to the Eddy Geology center (open Tuesday-Sunday 9:00am-5:00pm, 734-475-3170), where you can view changing samples of geos from the Great Lakes, Michigan and the Midwest. The exhibits include: a "mad scientist lab" with interactive tests of mineral radioactivity, luminescence and computer microscopes; an interactive map of Michigan's bedrock with lift-door samples from prominent sites; and a "fossil graveyard" featuring lift-a-rock models of famous fossilized bones and teeth. Touch-screen computer mineral games challenge users to "where does it come from," and a model ice cave takes the visitor back to the Ice Age through blue-screen technology. There's also a collection station that has rotating rock and mineral collections. Outside, a quarter-mile paved rock walkway features large, outstanding samples of Michigan bedrock. There's also a slide show, hands-on activities and professional demonstrations.

AUTOMOBILE HALL OF FAME

Dearborn - *21400 Oakwood Blvd. (Next to Greenfield Village), 48121. Web: www.automotivehalloffame.org/about/purpose.html Phone: (313) 240-4000 Hours: Daily 10:00am-5:00pm. (Memorial Day-October). Closed Mondays the rest of the year. Closed major winter holidays. Admission: $3.00-$6.00 (age 5+).* A 60-seat theatre giant-screen theatre features a short film, "The Driving Spirit", that takes an amusing look at the individuals responsible for the creation of the automotive industry (follow the "Spirit-ed" boy on this video journey and through the rest of the museum). Before you leave, be sure to start up a replica of the first gasoline-powered car, listen in on a meeting that led to forming the world's largest corporation, look into the Ransom Olds workshop, and visit a classic 1930's showroom.

HENRY FORD MUSEUM & GREENFIELD VILLAGE

20900 Oakwood Blvd. (I-94 to SR 39 north to Oakwood Blvd.)

Dearborn 48124

❑   Phone: (313) 982-6100 or (313) 982-6150 info
Web: www.hfmgv.org

❑   Hours: Daily 9:00am-5:00 pm, Sunday Noon-5:00pm. Greenfield Village is closed in winter (January-March). Closed Thanksgiving and Christmas.

❑   Admission: $13.50 adult, $12.50 senior (62+), $8.50 child (5-12) for each museum. (Combo prices and additional attractions are available). Horse-drawn carriage rides, sleigh rides, steam train or steamboat rides available for additional fee.

❑   Miscellaneous: IMAX Theatre (800-747-IMAX) where you'll learn of fascinating innovations. We recommend children be at least 5 years old to visit and gain from the learning experience. RECOMMENDED LODGING: Holiday Inn Express Hotel & Suites, Allen Park/Dearborn, 3600 Enterprises Drive (off I-94). (313) 323-3500 or www.dialinn.com. The Family Suites have bunk beds w/ Redwing décor and the continental breakfast is massive. The indoor pool area is clean and kid-friendly, too.

America's largest indoor-outdoor museum examines our country from rural to industrial societies. A special focus is placed on accomplishments and inventions of famous Americans.

Greenfield Village highlights:

❑   <u>HENRY FORD BIRTHPLACE</u> - he certainly loved and cherished his mother. See what he played with as a boy.

❑   <u>FORD COMPANY</u> - the hostess recommends you don't buy the model A, but wait for the Model C (better radiator).

❑   <u>COHEN MILLINERY</u> - try on hats of olden days.

❑   <u>GEORGE WASHINGTON CARVER - PEANUTS</u>! A great look at the possibilities of products made with peanuts. Carver helped find industrial uses for peanuts to help poor Southerners find new crops to grow and new uses for the crops they had.

Greenfield Village highlights (cont.):

❑ <u>WRIGHT BROTHERS CYCLE SHOP & HOME</u> - just think of the boys "tinkering" around the shop.

❑ <u>MATTOX HOUSE</u> - Recycling before the work existed! Newspaper wallpaper, license plate shingles, and layered cardboard ceilings.

❑ <u>EDISON'S MENLO PARK LAB</u> - Learn about Edison's brilliant and showy sides. Using a loud child as a volunteer, they demonstrate a real Edison phonograph (it really worked) and souvenir piece of tin foil used as the secret to the phonograph's success.

❑ <u>TASTE OF HISTORY RESTAURANT</u> - try a Railroaders Lunch made with hobo bread just like 19th century railroad workers ate - round raisin nut bread filled with turkey and cheese. Sounds funny but it's really good! In the foyer of the casual restaurant is a machine that, for $1, your child can make plastic model T souvenir cars.

Henry Ford Museum highlights:

❑ <u>HOME ARTS</u> - evolution of home appliances.

❑ <u>MADE IN AMERICA</u> - production of goods in the USA.

❑ <u>INNOVATION STATION</u> - interactively be an innovator or team project player. Really hands-on! Furniture Fun Packs.

❑ <u>YOUR PLACE IN TIME</u> - explore the 1900's from your own life history experiences. Kids find it silly to see what was considered "technology" years ago. For example, The Dymaxion House was built and sold in the mid-1900's as a solution to the need for a mass-produced, affordable, easily transportable and environmentally efficient house. The house was shipped in it's own metal tube and used tension suspension from a central point. From the outside, it looks like a mutated Airstream or flying saucer! A Sales Rep greets you at the entrance and shares the features of the efficient home with your family – want to buy one?

❑ <u>HENRY'S TREASURES</u> - Lincoln's Chair (the rocking chair he was assassinated in). It will stop you in your tracks!

Henry Ford Museum highlights (cont.):

❑   CAFÉ - Check out the Weiner Mobile (even make a Mold-A-
     Rama w/ the kids or grab a snack at the Weiner Mobile Café).

Compared to our visits as children years ago, we noticed a much
more interactive, kid-friendly environment. The guides and actors
really are skilled at engaging the kid's curiosity and use kids, not
adults, as part of their demos.

FAIR LANE

4901 Evergreen Road (On the campus of University of Michigan,
Dearborn - off Ford Rd.), **Dearborn** 48128

❑   Phone: (313) 593-5590. "The Pool" - (313) 436-9196
     Web: www.umd.umich.edu/fairlane
❑   Hours: Monday-Saturday 10:00am-3:00pm, Sunday 1:00-
     4:30pm. (April-December). Monday-Friday tour available only at
     1:30pm (January-March). Closed winter holidays plus Easter.
❑   Admission: (Guided Tours- 90 minutes) $8.00 adult (13+), $7.00
     senior (62+), $5.00 child (5-12).
❑   Miscellaneous: Self-guided outdoor tour: Ford Discovery Trail,
     an Estate walking loop to discover the "Wizards of Fair Lane,"
     includes treehouse, bathhouse, boathouse, and scenic vistas.
     Open daily, mid-June through Labor Day. $2.00 per person.

Much more than just another mansion tour…this was the home of
visionary, Henry Ford. In many ways, our lives have been shaped
and changed by decisions and visions that Henry Ford saw and
created. A 90 minute tour takes you into the fascinating 6-level
mansion which had many innovations. The on-site electric
generating power plant (the Rouge River was the energy source)
produced enough electricity to power the mansion and part of the
university campus! See many of Ford's personal vehicles in the
garage that include the famous Model A and Model T, an early
1900's innovative "camper" (some people say that he started the
RV industry), a "Fordson" tractor, and even an electric car that he
was going to partner into production with Thomas Edison. Kids,
look for the mini- electric cars used by the grandkids to drive

around the property and the one lane bowling alley. Check out the giant wrench in the generator room. What was Mr. Ford's favorite plant? (soybeans). Complete your tour with lunch at "The Pool" restaurant (since it was built over the estate's swimming pool - open weekdays, lunchtime only).

DETROIT SYMPHONY ORCHESTRA

Detroit - *3663 Woodward Avenue #100, 48201. **Web:** www.detroitsymphony.com Tickets: (313) 576-5111 or Office: (313) 576-5100.* Be sure to ask about "Young People Series".

WRIGHT MUSEUM OF AFRICAN-AMERICAN HISTORY

Detroit - *315 East Warren Avenue (off I-94 or I-75), 48201. **www.maah-detroit.org** Phone: (313) 494-5800. Hours: Wednesday -Saturday 9:30am-5:00pm., Sunday 1:00-5:00pm. Admission: $5.00 adult (18+), $3.00 child (17 and under)* A tribute to the history and culture of Detroit's African-American community. The exhibit, "Of the People: The African-American Experience" traces the history and operations of the slave trade. Learn also that Detroit was one of the most active stops in the "Underground Railroad" (a network of safe stops that helped slaves escape from the south before the Civil War). Once reaching Detroit, they could cross the Detroit River into Canada. See the space suit worn by Mae Jemison, the first African-American woman to travel in space in 1992. Other fun and educational exhibits trace the history of African music and how it transformed present American music including the famous Detroit's "Motown Sound".

DETROIT CHILDREN'S MUSEUM

6134 Second Avenue

Detroit 48202

- ❑ Phone: (313) 873-8100
  Web: www.detroitchildrensmuseum.org
- ❑ Hours: Monday-Saturday 9:00am-4:00pm
- ❑ Admission: Usually free.

Your kids (target age 4-9) will be encouraged at this museum to test their imagination and creativity at its various interactive attractions. Be sure to ask for the "Treasure Hunt Game" that gets kids involved in a discovery adventure throughout the building. Younger children will find lots to do in the Discovery Room where they can test their skills with many interactive teaching toys. Parents hang on tight to those little ones!

DETROIT HISTORICAL MUSEUM

5401 Woodward Avenue (Woodward and Kirby. SR 1)

Detroit 48202

- ❑ Phone: (313) 833-1805 **Web: www.detroithistorical.org**
- ❑ Hours: Wednesday-Friday 9:30am-5:00pm, Saturday & Sunday 10:00am-5:00pm.
- ❑ Admission: $5.00 adult, $2.50 senior (62+), $2.50 child (4-18). Children under 4 FREE.
- ❑ Miscellaneous: FREE admission on Wednesdays. Train-cam mini-train setup is new feature where camera displays the view from the little train going around the town.

After you've wondered through Frontiers to Factories: Detroiters at Work before the Motor City; and the Streets of Old Detroit, be sure to plan most of your time in the Motor City exhibits. See the first car in Detroit - a horseless carriage that was driven down Woodward Avenue. Then, around the corner, you can crank up a Model T and then sit in it (great photo op!). The best part of this exhibit has to be the Body Drop! First, watch it happen on video (actual footage from a Ford Assembly plant). Then see the 70 foot section of actual assembly plant and the performance of the final steps of production. Some mannequins are in the pits below, some workers are above one floor as they "drop" the car body onto the chassis below. Did you know that Mr. Cadillac's full name is Antoine de la Mothe Cadillac? - No wonder they're so fancy!

DETROIT INSTITUTE OF ARTS (DIA)

5200 Woodward Avenue (off I-94 or I-75, Cultural Center)

Detroit 48202

❑ Phone: (313) 833-7900, **Web: www.dia.org**

❑ Hours: Wednesday-Friday 10:00am-4:00pm, Saturday and Sunday 10:00am-5:00pm. Friday nights until 9:00pm.

❑ Admission: Donations. Suggested - $4.00 adult, $1.00 child (14 and under).

❑ Tours: 1:00pm Wednesday - Saturday. 1:00 & 2:30 pm, Sunday.

❑ Miscellaneous: Restaurant and café.

Shhhh…we won't tell your kids that this cool place is really an "art museum" if you don't! A great place for kids of all ages to interact and explore (and the museum even likes it when kids come to visit!). Most exhibits are very "kid- friendly" and interactive and there is even a treasure hunt game called "The Mystery of the Five Fragments" that encourages kids to "want to discover" the museum and its treasures. See exhibits such as "The American House", "The Spiral Staircase" and even "The Donkey" (which invites kids to hang, climb, and burn up excess energy) while at the museum. Fun, interactive computer programs also entertain and teach. The Great Hall features many suits of armor from the 13th to 18th century. But, above all, the masked mummy (kept safely in a display case) in the Egyptian art and artifacts exhibit is always a way to get the kids to say "wow" or "wooooo".

NEW DETROIT SCIENCE CENTER

5020 John R Street (I-75 - Warren Exit)

Detroit 48202

❑ Phone: (313) 577-8400 **Web: www.sciencedetroit.org**

❑ Hours: Monday-Friday 9:30am-3:00pm, Saturday 10:30am-6:00pm, Sunday Noon-6:00pm. (extended hours during special exhibits)

❑ Admission: $7.00 adult, $6.00 senior (60+), $6.00 child (2-12). IMAX is additional $4.00.

❑ Miscellaneous: Café.

Just a block away from the Detroit Institute of Arts is another wonderful example of what learning "outside of the books" is all about. Located in the heart of Detroit's Cultural Complex (park once and visit maybe 4-5 museums), the museum still has the IMAX Dome Theatre and Digital Dome Planetarium plus new, dynamic exhibits. Motion Lab has a "stadium" Science Stage and lots of pulling, pushing physics comparing motion, speed and direction (little engineers thrive here). The Life Science Lab focuses on similarities between the rainforest and city ecosystems. The Matter and Energy Lab has a "caged" Sparks Theatre and exhibits exploring electricity, magnetism, energy conversion, etc. Waves & Vibrations has all the funky lights and sounds. There's even an area for the younger set to explore all the things their older siblings are playing with on a larger scale.

BELLE ISLE

(I-75 to East Grand Blvd. Take MacArthur Bridge over to the Isle
on the Detroit River), **Detroit** 48207

- ❑   Phone: (313) 852-4075 **Web: www.detroitzoo.org**
- ❑   Hours: Dawn to Dusk. Specific hours for special parks within the Isle
- ❑   Miscellaneous: FREE admission to Trails, Picnic areas, beach,
      Nature Center. Common to see many deer. There's also a wild
      animal hospital and playgrounds.

The well-used 1000 acre park and playground, still in site of the skyscrapers of Detroit offers:

- ❑   <u>AQUARIUM AND CONSERVATORY</u> - (313) 852-4141.
      Hours: Daily, 10:00am-5:00pm. Admission: $2.00-$4.00. Old
      aquarium focuses on freshwater species found in Michigan and
      the tropics (ex. Electric eel and a stingray). The adjacent
      conservatory explores plants and flowers mostly in desert and
      tropical settings (ex. Cacti, ferns, palm trees, banana trees and
      orchids).

❑   DOSSIN GREAT LAKES MUSEUM - 100 Strand Drive
      (South Shore of Belle Isle). (313) 852-4051. Hours: Wednesday -
      Sunday, 10:00am-5:00pm. Admission: $1.00-$2.00 (age 12+).
      www.detroithistorical.org. You're greeted by two Battle of
      Lake Erie cannons and the actual anchor recovered from the
      Edmund Fitzgerald shipwreck. Stand in the pilot house of an ore
      carrier. As the marine radio sends out requests, turn the ship
      wheel to steer it on course or use the periscope. The 1912 Great
      Lakes Luxury Steamer Lounge Room is handsome (all oak
      carvings) - reminiscent of scenes in the movie "Titanic".

MOTOWN HISTORICAL MUSEUM

Detroit - *2648 West Grand Blvd. (M-10 to West Grand Blvd. Exit),
48208. Web: www.recordingeq.com/motown/motown.htm Phone:
(313) 875-2264. Hours: Sunday & Monday, Noon - 5:00pm,
Tuesday - Saturday, 10:00am - 5:00pm. (Closed holidays).
Admission: $7.00 adult, $4.00 child (12 and under).* In two homes
that are next to each other, the music world was changed forever
by Berry Gordy, composer and producer. The original recording
studio "A" not only helped to build the "Motown" sound, but
discovered and built the careers of the Stevie Wonder, the
Temptations, the Four Tops, Diana Ross, and Marvin Gaye, just to
name a few. A great stop in musical history.

PEWABIC POTTERY

Detroit - *10125 E. Jefferson Avenue, 48214. Phone: (313) 822-
0954. Web: www.pewabic.com Gallery Hours: Monday-Saturday
10:00am-6:00pm. Admission: FREE. Tours: Self-guided tours of
the pottery's kiln room and other production areas are during
regular business hours. Groups must call ahead to make
reservation (small fee).* Nationally renowned for its handcrafted
ceramic vessels and architectural tiles and its unique glazes,
Pewabic Pottery is located in the Detroit area. They make a wide
range of vases, candlesticks and unique embossed tiles. Four of the
13 People Mover stations are adorned with ceramic murals created
at Pewabic.

DETROIT TIGERS BASEBALL

Detroit - *Corner of Brush & Adams Streets (Comerica Park), 48216. Tickets: (313) 471-BALL.* **Web: *www.detroittigers.com*** Admission: General $8.00-30.00. Major league baseball played April-September. Game's biggest scoreboard. Home runs - two huge tigers with glowing eyes growl and aquatic fireworks fountain performs. Outside - 30 hand-painted tigers on carousel and Italian Ferris wheel. Inside - main concourse has a visual tour of baseball and lifestyle history.

DETROIT LIONS FOOTBALL

Detroit - *311 E. Grand River (Ford Field), 48226. Phone: (248) 325-4131.* **Web: *www.detroitlions.com*** Admission: $20.00-35.00. NFL football (over 68 seasons) season runs September-December. Giant glass wall in new dome stadium.

DETROIT RED WINGS HOCKEY

Detroit - *600 Civic Center Drive (Joe Lewis Arena), 48226. Phone: (313) 396-7575.* **Web: *www.detroitredwings.com*** NHL top five teams in the League play September-early April. Call or visit website for ticket availability. HOCKEYTOWN CAFÉ restaurant downtown (2301 Woodward, 313-965-9500, next to Fox Theatre) near all the sporting action is a good stop for food and sports themed meals. You're greeted by the 1962 Zamboni and while you're waiting on your food, take a stroll around and gander at the Statues, The Walk of Fame, or the Ring of Honor. Look for your favorite player's showcase. The kids meals are around the $5.00 range. The adult entrees were delicious and a great value. Ample, well-lit parking nearby in lots or garages. Many "kid-friendly" shows next door at Fox Theatre, too.

DETROIT PISTONS BASKETBALL

Detroit (Auburn Hills) - *2 Championship Drive (The Palace of Auburn Hills), 48326. Phone: (248) 377-0100.* **Web: *www.nba.com/pistons*** Admission: $15.00-65.00. NBA team with all star players.

DETROIT ROCKERS SOCCER

Detroit (Auburn Hills) - *2 Championship Drive (The Palace of Auburn Hills), 48326. Phone: (313) 396-7070.* **Web:** *www.detroitrockers.net Admission: $11.00-16.00.* Soccer team plays October - March.

DETROIT SHOCK WOMEN'S BASKETBALL

Detroit (Auburn Hills) - *2 Championship Drive (Palace of Auburn Hills), 48326. Phone: (248) 377-0100.* **Web:** *www.wnba.com/shock Admission: $8.00-75.00.* WNBA team.

DETROIT VIPERS HOCKEY

Detroit (Auburn Hills) - *2 Championship Drive (Palace of Auburn Hills), 48326.* **Web:** *www.detroitvipers.com Phone: (248) 377-0100. Admission: $5.00-35.00.* IHL Hockey team plays September-April.

RAINFOREST CAFÉ EDUCATIONAL TOURS

4310 Baldwin Road (I-75, exit 84 - Great Lakes Crossing)

Detroit (Auburn Hills) 48326

- ❑ Phone: (248) 333-0280 **Web: www.rainforestcafe.com**
- ❑ Hours: Daily, Lunch and Dinner.
- ❑ Tours: Usually begin at 10:00am and include lunch. Must be scheduled in advance.

A theme restaurant and wildlife preserve filled with live and mechanical animals; ongoing rainstorms (even thunder and lightning); a talking rainforest tree; giant "walk-through" aquarium (really cool!); hand-sculpted "cave like" rock everywhere. Preschoolers and younger love the fish tank but are a little uneasy with the motorized large gorillas and elephants (request seating on the other side of the dining room). Did you know they give Educational Group Tours? What a "light-hearted" way to introduce your kids to the animals, plants and environs of the rainforest! The Fun Field Trip Adventure uncovers why elephants have big ears & why the Café's resident crocodile collects pennies for charity. What is your favorite fish in the coral reef? You can also include a group lunch afterwards in your plans (for an ~$8.00 per person fee).

Nibble on Jurassic Tidbits and Paradise Pizza plus other kid-friendly food, drink and dessert. Although your food bill will be above moderate - it's the epitome of a theme restaurant.

WALTER P. CHRYSLER MUSEUM

1 Chrysler Drive (northwest corner of Featherstone & Squirrel Roads on Daimler-Chrysler campus), **Detroit (Auburn Hills)** 48326

❑   Phone: (888) 456-1924 or (248) 944-0001
      Web: www.chryslerheritage.com
❑   Hours: Tuesday-Saturday 10:00am-6:00pm, Sunday Noon-
      6:00pm.
❑   Admission: $6.00 adult, $3.00 senior, $3.00 child (6-12).

The Museum contains 55,000 square feet and displays 75 vehicles. It tells the stories of Walter P. Chrysler and his love of trains, brothers John and Horace Dodge and their mechanical genius, and such industry notables as Carl Breer, Virgil Exner and Lee Iacocca. It covers everything from the Detroit Tank Arsenal to Roadrunners, Vipers and Prowlers. Several interactive displays explain brake systems, aerodynamics, power steering, platform team design and more. Interactive computer kiosks timeline the decades from 1920-1980 using vintage news footage, classic commercials and audio clips.

CRANBROOK ART AND SCIENCE MUSEUMS

1221 N. Woodward Ave (I-75 exit to Square Lake Rd (West) to Woodward, I-696 exit-Woodward), **Detroit (Bloomfield Hills)** 48303

❑   Phone: (877) GO-CRANB **Web: www.cranbrook.edu**
❑   Hours: Art: Tuesday-Sunday 11:00am-5:00pm. Friday until
      8:00pm. Science: Daily 10:00am-5:00pm. Friday until 10:00pm.
❑   Admission: $5-7.00 adult, $3-4.00 senior(65+), $3-4.00 child (3-17).
❑   Miscellaneous: Picnic areas. Planetarium and Laser Shows. $1-
      2.00 extra. Café. Gift shop. Seasonal gardens with fountains,
      ponds and sculpture.

Different areas to check out are: Our Dynamic Earth (15 foot T-Rex, wooly mastodon), Gem & Mineral Hall, Nature Place (live reptiles, turtles, and bugs - native to Michigan), Art (metalwork, realism sculpture "Body Builder", outdoor sculpture), Physics Hall (hands-on experiments about lasers and light, movement, and air).

LIONEL TRAINS VISITOR'S CENTER

26750 Russell Smith Drive (23 Mile Road) (I-94 to Exit 243)

Detroit (Chesterfield) 48051

- ❑ Phone: (586) 949-4100 **Web: www.lionel.com**
- ❑ Admission: FREE
- ❑ Tours: (For reservation call: (586) 949-4100 ext. 1211)
  Wednesday & Thursday 10:00am, 3:00 and 4:00pm. Friday
  10:00am, 1:30, 2:30pm. Saturday 10:00, 11:00am & Noon. Gift
  Shop is open during all tours.

Since 1900, Lionel has been delighting hearts (both young and old) with the illusionary world of model train villages. Not only will you have fun watching and learning each step of the manufacturing process (by video), but this tour allows plenty of time to "play" with the creations that make Lionel so special. See 10 trains running (on a 14 X 40 layout) simultaneously from village to village, over bridges and through tunnels just like a miniature movie set. Kids can interact with the display by pushing several buttons that create a movement or reaction in the display. There is also a smaller children's layout where kids get to operate the trains. If you're a collector (or about to become one), be sure to buy one of the Visitor's Center boxcars that are available only in the gift shop.

MORLEY CANDY MAKERS

23770 Hall Road (I-94 to Hall Road M-59 Exit)

Detroit (Clinton Township) 48036

- ❑ Phone: (586) 468-4300 or (800) 682-2760.
  Web: www.morleycandy.com
- ❑ Admission: FREE

❑   Tours: Self-guided, Monday-Friday 7:00am-3:30pm (observation
     hallway only). Guided group tours with video are available
     Monday-Friday between 10:00am-1:00pm. Call to schedule
     appointment.

One of Michigan's largest candy makers, this tour is sure to delight
chocolate lovers of all ages. Both educational and fun, see
Morley's cooking chocolate in huge copper kettles (gallons at a
time). Much of that chocolate gets poured over the famous caramel
used to make both vanilla caramels and, when mixed with fresh
southern pecans, their spectacular Pecan Torties® ! Did you know
chocolate doesn't like sudden temperature changes? How do they
keep it from "turning"? The 70 foot long observation hallway is a
great way to see all the candy making in action. Don't leave
without your edible souvenirs!

MARVIN'S MARVELOUS MECHANICAL MUSEUM

31005 Orchard Lake Road (I-696 exit Orchard Lake Road North)

Detroit (Farmington Hills) 48334

❑   Phone: (248) 626-5020 **Web: www.marvin3m.com**
❑   Hours: Monday-Thursday 10:00am-9:00pm, Friday-Saturday
     10:00am-11:00pm, Sunday Noon-9:00pm.
❑   Admission: FREE. Each device takes a quarter to operate.
❑   Miscellaneous: Concessions. Modern pinball and interactive
     games are there too.

Pass back in time to an old-fashioned carnival full of antique slot
and pinball machines, mechanical memorabilia and games. It's a
very busy place with lights flashing and marionette music playing
all around you. Here are some games that were really unique: a
bulldozer mechanical game, Old Time Photos, Marionette and
Clown Dancing Shows, and miniature carrousel and Ferris wheel.
Marvin's is listed in the World Almanac's 100 most unusual
museums in the U.S. Once you're inside, it's hard to know what
game to play first! P.S. - Grandparents can get real sentimental here.

DIAMOND JACK'S RIVER TOURS

25088 Old Depot Court (Hart Plaza, foot of Woodward, downtown)

Detroit (Grosse Ile) 48138

❏ Phone: (313) 843-9376, **Web: www.diamondjack.com**
❏ Hours: Thursday-Sunday (late May-September).
❏ Admission: $14.00 adult, $12.00 senior, $10.00 child (6-16).
❏ Tours: 2-hour leisurely narrated cruise departs at 1:00 & 3:30pm.
❏ Miscellaneous: Snacks and beverages available on board. Safest parking available at the Renaissance Center. After the cruise, try THE BEACH GRILL - St. Clair Shores (Jefferson Beach Marina Complex) - 24420 Jefferson (betw. 9 & 10 mile) - (586) 771-4455. Moderately priced meal and enjoy spectacular views of all the Great Lakes boats. Indoor/Outdoor dining. Trendy...yet family friendly. Kids menu $3-6.00. Open daily for lunch and dinner.

The 65-foot "mini-ship" cruises down the Detroit River around Belle Isle and back to Ambassador Bridge. This is the world's busiest international waterway along the U.S. and Canadian shorelines. There's a good chance that large freighters and ocean ships will pass by. You'll see a great view of both the Detroit and downtown Windsor, Canada skylines and pass by (with stories told by captain) the historic Warehouse District, Mayor's Residence (if he's out back, he'll wave), Yacht Clubs, Islands, Bridges and a Fireboat. See the world's only marble Art Deco lighthouse or one of only two International Marine Mailboats in the world. They told us the mailboat has it's own zip code and delivers mail to the freighters by a pail on a pulley.

MOTORSPORTS MUSEUM & HALL OF FAME OF AMERICA

43700 Expo Center Drive (I-96 - exit 162),

Detroit (Novi) 48375

❏ Phone: (248) 349-7223 **Web: www.mshf.com**
❏ Hours: Daily 10:00am-5:00pm (Memorial Day-Labor Day). Thursday-Friday only (rest of year).
❏ Admission: $3.00 adult, $2.00 senior and child (under 12).

If there is a racing fan in your family this is a "must stop". See over 100 vehicles including powerboats, motorcycles, "Indy style" racecars, NASCAR style racecars, dragsters, and even snowmobiles. Get their photo taken in the driver's seat of an actual Winston Cup racecar and then take the challenge of racing on the 4-lane scale slot car track or video simulation race car.

DETROIT ZOO

8450 West Ten Mile Road (I-75 to I-696 West - Woodward Avenue Exit), **Detroit (Royal Oak)** 48068

❑   Phone: (248) 398-0900 info **Web: http://detroitzoo.org**
❑   Hours: Daily 10:00am-5:00pm. (April & September/October). Daily 9:00am-5:00pm (May-Labor Day). Daily 10:00am-4:00pm. (November-March).
❑   Admission: $8.00 adult, $6.00 senior (62+), $6.00 child (2-12). $4.00 Parking fee.
❑   Miscellaneous: Picnic areas. Strollers/adult roller chairs available for rent. Simulator ride and miniature railroad (additional fee).

Simply put…your family is in for a real day of adventure and fun when visiting the Detroit Zoo. The world's largest polar bear exhibit, the Artic Ring of Life, is a lifelike trek to the North Pole's tundra, open sea and ice mountains. Start outside and curve around the exhibit to the spectacular 70 foot long clear tunnel (Polar Passage) which takes visitors underneath diving and swimming polar bears and seals. Their antics and casual behavior will entertain you for most of the visit (plan 45 minutes to one hour just at this exhibit)! What a fun learning experience for the kids to see the Inuit peoples and their interaction w/ Artic animals. Here's a few of the other, constantly changing exhibits that you'll see: The Mandrill Exhibit (a very colorful baboon), The Wilson Aviary Wing (30 species of birds in a large free-flying building - much like an indoor jungle - there is even a waterfall), The Penguinarium (love that name! - see underwater views of these birds that cannot fly), and The Chimps of Harambee (a forest setting with rock habitats…what a show!), and The Wildlife Interpretive Gallery (huge aquarium, theater, hummingbird and butterfly garden). And if all this wasn't enough…take an excursion on the famous Detroit Zoo Miniature Railroad (it transports over 500,000 passengers a year).

FOUR BEARS WATERPARK

3000 Auburn Road (I-75 - Rochester Road Exit)

Detroit (Shelby Township) 48317

❑   Phone: (586) 739-5860 **Web: www.fourbearswaterpark.com**

❑   Hours: Monday-Friday, 10:00am-3:00pm. Saturday & Sunday,
     11:00am-7:00pm. (Memorial Day-June 15). Daily, 11:00am-
     7:00pm. (June 16 - Labor Day)

❑   Admission: $12.95 general (48+" tall), $5.95 (under 48" tall).
     Non-participating chaperones, $5.00. Children under 2 FREE.

❑   Miscellaneous: Large picnic grounds. Food service is also
     available.

A summer paradise for kids of all ages, this waterpark boasts the
state's largest collection of water slides. Some of the additional
attractions include: A sand-filled beach on a 50 acre lake, paddle and
bumper boats and special slides for non-swimmers. Land attractions
include: (some have a slight additional charge) go-carts, carnival
rides, batting cages, petting zoo, and bird and animal shows.

DELHI METROPARK

Dexter - *Huron River Drive (on the banks of the Huron River),
48130. Phone: (734) 426-8211 or (800) 477-3191.   Web:
www.metroparks.com Hours: Daily 6:00am-10:00pm. Admission:
$3.00 per vehicle (weekends), $2.00 per vehicle (weekdays).*
Fishing, picnic facilities, canoe rentals.

SPRING VALLEY TROUT FARM

Dexter - *12190 Island Lake Road, 48130. Phone: (734) 426-4772.
Web: www.springvalleytroutfarm.com   Because of Michigan
weather, the farm is open Spring and Fall on Saturdays and
Sundays from 9:00am to 5:00pm. Memorial Day to Labor Day
open Wednesday through Sunday from 9:00am-6:00pm. The farm
closes end of September each year.* Natural, organic (non-polluted
water) fed trout in spring-fed ponds are waiting to be caught. There
is even a Children's Trout pond reserved for little anglers under 10
years old. The environment is so perfect in these ponds, they can
even guarantee a catch on every outing! They'll clean the fish and
pack them in ice to take home. Fees charged ($3.00 per person to

fish - age 5+ and a fee per pound of fish caught). Picnic/grilling areas. No license or equipment needed.

GREATER LANSING SYMPHONY ORCHESTRA

East Lansing - *Bogue Street & Wilson (MSU Campus - Wharton Center for Performing Arts), 48824. Phone: (517) 487-5001 or (800) WHARTON.* **Web: www.lansingsymphony.org** Free Young People's Concerts and music for Broadway shows like "Beauty & the Beast". MSU's Act One: Family Series (517-432-2000), Hot Buttered Pops, Jingle Bell Pops, or Play Me A Story.

MICHIGAN STATE UNIVERSITY

West Circle Drive (Off SR 43), **East Lansing** 48825

- ❑   Phone: (517) 355-7474 **Web:http://msutoday.msu.edu/directory**
- ❑   Hours: Monday-Friday 9:00am-5:00pm. Saturday 10:00am-5:00pm. Sunday 1:00-5:00pm. Closed all state holidays.

<u>MUSEUM</u>: West Circle Drive. (517) 355-2370. Natural wonders of the Great Lakes, world cultures, animal diversity. 3 stories of special exhibits. Museum store. They offer numerous family programs focused on the history of inhabitants of Michigan.

<u>KRESGE ART MUSEUM</u>: Culturally diverse art. FREE. (517) 355-7631.

<u>BEAUMONT TOWER</u>: Site of Old College Hall - the first building erected for instruction in scientific agriculture. Recently renovated. Weekly carillon concerts.

<u>FARMS</u>: Observe milking cows mid-afternoon. Also sheep, horse and swine areas. Weekdays only. (517) 355-8383. South Campus.

<u>HORTICULTURE GARDENS AND GREEN HOUSE</u>: Bogue & Wilson Road. (517) 355-0348. American Trial Garden test site. Children's Garden - 63 theme gardens - garden emphasizes the important part plants play in children's daily lives, from the first cereal bowl in the morning to the last popcorn snack at night. Secret Garden (just like movie), Pizza Garden (wheat for dough, toppings and spices, tomatoes), Peter Rabbit Garden (bunny food

favorites), Sensation Garden (guess which plant it is by smell), 2 Treehouses, and a Butterfly Garden. (517) 353-4800. Small Admission donation. Spring/Summer. Parking fee on weekdays. Our favorite garden for kids (in the state and midwest) is so colorful and artistically done (on a kid's level).

DAIRY STORE AND PLANT. South Anthony Hall (Farm Lane & Wilson Road). (517) 432-2479 or **www.msu.edu/user/dairysto**. Hours: Monday-Friday 9:00am-6:00pm, Saturday-Sunday Noon-5:00pm. Closed University holidays. Admission: FREE. Everything you ever wanted to know about "Cheddaring"! This is a great guided (in groups, pre-arranged) or self-guided (with simple explanations) observation deck tour of the pilot plant where students process milk making the famous Spartan cheese and ice cream. After you see the production facility, walk downstairs to the Dairy Store and buy a cone (their Junior cones are still 2 dips) or a light lunch.

BUG HOUSE: Natural Science Building. Farm Lane & East Circle Drive. (517) 355-4662. Noisy cockroaches, millipedes and giant grasshoppers.

ABRAMS PLANETARIUM: Shaw Lane & Science Road. (517) 355-STAR. Small Admission. Weekend matinees are suggested for younger ones.

MERIDIAN TOWNSHIP'S CENTRAL PARK

5150 Marsh Road

East Lansing (Okemos) 48864

❑   Phone: (517) 347-7300 or (517) 349-5777 Nokomis
      Web: www.nokomis.org

❑   Hours: Nokomis Learning Center: Tuesday-Friday 10:00am-
      4:00pm, Saturday Noon-5:00pm. Meridian Historical Village:
      Saturday 10:00am-2:00pm (May-October).

Meridian Township's Central Park (cont.)

NOKOMIS LEARNING CENTER - center for focus of woodland Indians of the Great Lakes; specifically the Ojibwa, Ottawa, and Potawatomi tribes known as the People of the Three Fires. Group tours & programs recommended. Gift shop.

MERIDIAN HISTORICAL VILLAGE - the only known Plank Road Tollhouse still around in the state is part of this small village. It includes a furnished farmhouse and one-room schoolhouse with a school bell ringing the beginning of class.

SEVEN LAKES STATE PARK

Fenton - *2220 Tinsman Road (I-75, exit 101), 48430.* **Web:** *www.michigandnr.com/parksandtrails/parklist.asp* *Phone: (248) 634-7271. Admission: $4.00 per vehicle.* The dam, constructed by the developers, formed one large lake from seven small lakes (historically known as the DeCoup Lake) hence the name Seven Lakes State Park. Camping, hiking trails, boating and rentals, fishing, swimming, bicycle trails, and winter sports.

CHILDS' PLACE BUFFALO RANCH

12770 Roundtree Road, **Hanover** 49241

- ❑ Phone: (517) 563-8249 **Web: www.horsesandbuffalo.com**
- ❑ Hours: Tuesday-Sunday 9:00am-4:00pm.
- ❑ Admission: Buffalo herd visit $5.00 per person. Horseback riding $20.00/ hour. Zipline ride $5.00. Mechanical Bull ride $5.00. FREE Bucking Barrel.
- ❑ Miscellaneous: Be a cowgirl/cowboy for the day (age 10+) or Live on the Ranch overnight. Dress casually.

Here's a visit that your kids are sure to tell their friends about! Take a hay wagon ride out into Gary Childs' pastures to see some of his more than 100 buffalo. The brave kids will usually get the opportunity to reach out and actually touch a live buffalo and feed corn cobs onto their huge tongues! (if the herd is cooperating that day). This ranch was also fortunate enough (1/40 million chance) to have given birth to a white buffalo…(which is a powerful Native American spiritual symbol). The calf died, but they have lots of pictures to show.

WETZEL STATE PARK

Harrison Township - *28681 Old North River (3 miles Northwest from New Haven), 48045. Phone: (810) 765-5605.* **Web:** *www.michigandnr.com/parksandtrails/parklist.asp* An undeveloped park providing areas for cross-country skiing, snowmobiling and hiking. No camping or services.

HOLLY RECREATION AREA

Holly - *8100 Grange Hall Road (off I-75 exit 101), 48442.* **Web:** *www.michigandnr.com/parksandtrails/parklist.asp* Phone: (248) 634-8811. Admission: $4.00 per vehicle.* Approximately 10 miles of hiking and cross country ski trails are in the central portion of the recreation area. Although mountain bikes are prohibited on these trails, there is an extensive mountain bike trail system located in the Holdridge Lakes area of the park, ranging in terrain from easy to advanced. Camping, hiking, boating, fishing, swimming, bicycle trails and winter sports.

MYSTERY HILL

7611 US Highway 12 (opposite Hayes State Park)

Irish Hills 49265

- ❑   Phone: (517) 467-2517 **Web: www.mystery-hill.com**
- ❑   Hours: Daily 11:00am-6:00pm (Summer). Weekends only (May, September, October).
- ❑   Admission: Average $5.00 (ages 4+).
- ❑   Tours: 30 minute guided.
- ❑   Miscellaneous: Gift shop. Miniature Golf Course, RC Race Cars.

Exhibits seem to defy gravity and your sense of balance goes. Water runs uphill and people stand sideways without falling over. The principles demonstrated are studied and applied by psychology departments of universities everywhere. It's an illusion experiment *(or is it real?...)* and you're the assistant!

PREHISTORIC FOREST

8203 US Highway 12 (Across from Hayes State Park. Near M-124)

Irish Hills 49265

- ❑ Phone: (517) 467-2514
- ❑ Hours: Daily 10:30am-7:00pm (Summer). Weekends Only (Rest of year).
- ❑ Admission: Average $5.00 (age 4+). Combo discounts available.
- ❑ Miscellaneous: Food available. Waterslide, arcade, trampolines, maze, Sinking Ship Slide - all for additional fee.

Guided train tours that transport visitors back to the prehistoric age. Go through a tunnel under a giant waterfall (serves as a time tunnel) to a forest maze of 60 life-size dinosaurs. Some even move and growl. You'll meet Professor Otto in his lab and see his museum of fossils. Learn how dinos slept and ate (ate things whole and then ate rocks to crush and "digest" food).

STAGECOACH STOP WESTERN RESORT & FAMILY FUN PARK

7203 US 12, Irish Hills 49265

- ❑ Phone: (517) 467-2300 **Web: www.stagecoachstop.com**
- ❑ Hours: Tuesday-Friday Noon-5:30pm, Weekends 10:30am-6:30pm (Summer). Weekends only (September/October).
- ❑ Admission: $12.00 adult, $8.00 child (4-11).
- ❑ Miscellaneous: Petting zoo, Fort Wilderness playground & picnic area. Food. Jamboree Theatre with country music entertainment. Motel/Cabins on premises (includes park admission, evening hayride, and continental breakfast).

Travel back to the Old West - made to look like an authentic 19th century western village with wooden plank sidewalks and dirt streets. Listen closely to the Marshall when he makes announcements every few minutes about the activity to begin. Maybe start out slow by watching a craftsman blacksmith, glass-blower, or worker in the sawmill. Stop by the petting zoo and then pan for gold with an old prospector (watch out, they're greedy!). Parents can sip on a Sarsaparilla (old-fashioned non-alcohol beverage) as kids play on rides like Runaway Mine Cars or the Incredible Flying Machine. Silly, staged gunfights challenge the Marshall against thieves. Remember, the bad guy always gets it in the end! Wander through the shops of a barber, bank, see magic shows, etc. and stop in a saloon (café) for a chuckwagon meal or treat. Be sure to take a Wild Country Train ride before leaving.

DAHLEM ENVIRONMENTAL EDUCATION CENTER

Jackson - *7117 South Jackson Road (I-94 to exit 138 - south), 49201. Web: www.jackson.cc.mi.us/DahlemCenter Phone: (517) 782-3453. Hours: Tuesday-Friday 9:00am - 4:30pm, Saturday & Sunday Noon-5:00pm. Trails open Daily 8:00am - sunset. FREE admission. Miscellaneous: Gift shop. Cross-country skiing in winter.* Over 5 miles of hiking trails allow you to explore the fields, marshes, ponds, and forest of this "piece of nature" just a short drive from the city. All, regardless of age and physical abilities, can explore on the special needs (1/2 mile) trail. (All-terrain wheelchairs are available on request). Call or visit website for details on upcoming nature programs.

MICHIGAN SPACE CENTER

2111 Emmons Road (Jackson Community College) (I-94 to US 127 south to SR 50), **Jackson** 49201

- ❑ Phone: (517) 787-4425 **Web: www.michiganspacecenter.com**
- ❑ Hours: (Year-round) Tuesday-Saturday 10:00am-5:00pm. Open Sundays Noon-5:00pm (May-October).
- ❑ Admission: $5.00 adult, $3.00 senior (60+) and student (age 5+)
- ❑ Miscellaneous: Picnic areas.

Look for the gold dome and 85 foot Mercury rocket and you'll know you're close. Inside see an Apollo 9 Command module, (memorial to the Challenger), satellites (something you don't see at many museums), spacesuits, a moon rock, a lunar surveyor, and black holes. Be sure to check out these, too: The Astrotheatre - film of Apollo 9 flight or live broadcast of current space shuttle flight; Infinity Room; Hubble Space Telescope model; Space Capsule (climb in); and computer exhibit games. You'll also get to "kid-power" a rocket and learn why an airplane *can't fly in space!*

CASCADES

1992 Warren Avenue (I-94 exit 138, south on West Avenue)

Jackson 49203

❑ Phone: (517) 788-4320

   Web: www.jacksonmich.com/cascades2.html

❑ Hours: Park open 11:00am-11:00pm. Cascades illuminated dusk - 11:00pm in the Summer.

❑ Admission: General $3-4.00 (ages 6+).

❑ Miscellaneous: Snack Bar. Gift store and restrooms. Paddleboats, mini-golf.

It began in 1932 and you can still view the colorful and musical waterfalls and fountains. Sound response programs were developed so that the Cascades lights and fountains change patterns in direct response to pre-recorded or live music. Use seating provided or climb to the top and be refreshed by spraying water. Continuously changing patterns keep it lively. The Cascades Falls history museum is within the park.

SLEEPY HOLLOW STATE PARK

Laingsburg - *7835 Price Road (off US 27 east on Price Road), 48848. Web: www.michigandnr.com/parksandtrails/parklist.asp Phone: (517) 651-6217. Admission: $4.00 per vehicle.* A river winds its way through the woods and fields of the park and Lake Ovid is nestled in the middle of it all. Lake Ovid is a 410 acre man-made lake which was developed by making a dam on the Little Maple River. A "no wake" lake environment is great for fishing and rough camping. Other features include a beach with snack bar, boating, hiking and bike trails, and winter sports.

BALD MOUNTAIN RECREATION AREA

Lake Orion - *1330 Greenshield (I-75 exit SR 24 north approximately 7 miles), 48360. Phone: (248) 693-6767. Web: www.michigandnr.com/parksandtrails/parklist.asp Admission: $4.00 per vehicle.* Bald Mountain Recreation Area consists of 4,637 rolling acres. The picturesque park area has some of the steepest hills and most rugged terrain in southeastern Michigan. Beginning with a great kiddie beach at Lower Trout Lake, the park also features hiking trails, fishing, boating, horseback riding, winter sports, and cabins for camping.

MINIBEAST ZOOSEUM

6907 West Grand River Avenue (1/2 mile east of I-96 exit 90 & I-69 exit 8), **Lansing** 48906

- ❑ Phone: (517) 886-0630
  Web: http://members.aol.com/YESbugs/zooseum.html
- ❑ Hours: Tuesday-Friday 1:00-5:00pm, Saturday 10:00am-4:00pm. Closed holidays and January & February.
- ❑ Admission: $2.50-$3.50 (ages 3+).

Michigan's largest insect and spider museum and outdoor classroom. They have computers and cockroaches, tarantulas and trails, even snails. 1000's of specimens…even some hands-on "bugging", too! Try their many educational (like roller ball bug-can you keep him alive?) games.

MICHIGAN HISTORICAL CENTER

702 West Kalamazoo Street (I-496 exit ML King, exit north follow signs to Capital Loop), **Lansing** 48909

- ❑ Phone: (517) 373-3559. **Web: www.michiganhistory.org**
- ❑ Hours: Monday-Friday 9:00am-4:30pm, Saturday 10:00am-4:00pm, Sunday 1:00-5:00pm. Closed state holidays.
- ❑ Admission: FREE
- ❑ Miscellaneous: Museum store. Snack Shop open weekdays. RECOMMENDED LODGING: Holiday Inn Lansing West Holidome. 7501 W. Saginaw Hwy (I-96 exit 93B). (517) 627-3211. The pool temperature is just right and there are many "little tykes" playthings plus the arcade and ping pong games for older children. We liked having the TGIFridays restaurant right on the premises with their popular food and kids menu (even for breakfast).

A great way to understand Michigan society, land, and industry - and all in one building. If your travel plans around Michigan are limited, this would be a history time-saver. We really enjoy museum layouts with untraditional "real life" settings and odd turns and corners. We've found this keeps children's curiosity peaked! "Don't Misses" include: the look and touch 3840 pound Float Copper that spans 4 feet by 8 feet and is hollow-sounding; entering rooms like the Mine Shaft or Lumber Barons parlor or old-time theater; learning words you may not know like Riverhog; and the Create-A-Car Touch Screen Computer. As you enter the center, you'll find the three-story relief map of Michigan - it's wonderful to gaze at from many angles.

FENNER NATURE CENTER

Lansing - *2020 East Mount Hope Avenue, 48910. Phone: (517) 483-4224. Hours: Tuesday-Friday 9:00am-4:00pm. Weekends 11:00am-4:00pm (year-round). FREE admission.* A visitor's center and gift shop plus self-guided trails. Call or visit website for special seasonal children's programs.

LANSING LUGNUTS

Lansing - *505 East Michigan Avenue (Oldsmobile Park, downtown), 48912. Web: www.lansinglugnuts.com Phone: (517) 485-4500. (Early April - Early September). Admission: $6.50-$8.00. Fireworks/Kids Days. Play area for kids.* Class "A" Midwest League - Chicago Cubs Affiliate.

POTTER PARK ZOO

1301 South Pennsylvania Avenue (entrance is just south of the I-496 Freeway, along Red Cedar River), **Lansing** 48912

❑ Phone: (517) 483-4222, **Web: www.potterparkzoo.org**
❑ Hours: Daily 9:00am-7:00pm (Memorial Day-Labor Day). Daily 9:00am (10:00am Winter) - 5:00pm (rest of the year).
❑ Admission: $5.00 adult, $3.00 senior (60+), $1.00 child (3-15). Parking fee. Lansing residents receive discount.

More than 400 animals (get a virtual visit on the website) await your family at this great educational and family friendly zoo. Snow Leopards, Black Rhinos, Siberian Tigers, Reindeer, and Red Pandas are just a few of the exhibits featured. Pony rides and petting zoo, too.

WOLDUMAR NATURE CENTER

Lansing - *5739 Old Lansing Road (2 miles west of Waverly Rd.), 48917. Phone: (517) 322-0030. Web: www.woldumar.org Hours: Center open Monday-Saturday 10:00am-5:00pm. Park open dawn to dusk.* Nature Center facilities and grounds provide programs year round. Tours of Moon Log Cabin also.

IMPRESSION 5 SCIENCE CENTER

200 Museum Drive (Banks of Grand River, off Michigan Avenue, downtown), **Lansing** 48933

❑ Phone: (517) 485-8116 **Web: www.impression5.org**

❑ Hours: Monday-Saturday 10:00am-5:00pm. Closed major holidays and first week of September.

❑ Admission: $5.00 adult, $3.50 senior (62+), $3.00 child (3-17).

❑ Miscellaneous: Impressions to Go Café. RECOMMENDED DINING: Clara's Lansing Station Restaurant, 637 E. Michigan Avenue. (517) 372-7120. Located in the historic Michigan Central Railroad Station, this place has the look and feel of a Victorian era station. Trains still pass by while you eat…and maybe you'll get lucky enough to eat in the attached dining car for a fun surrounding. Daily lunch and dinner with moderate pricing. Children's Menu with basic American food fare priced between $3.00-$4.00. Nearby Olds Park (Lugnuts).

150 displays challenge all five senses (i.e. the reason for Impression 5 name). Although it's smaller than many science centers, it's well worth the visit and includes many exhibits we haven't encountered before. Highlights include:

❑ THROWING THINGS - using different principles of physics, kids play with different forms of projectiles and balls…even giant slingshots. We've never seen this before - so many different ways to throw things!

❑ HEART WORKS - a walk through Heart Maze with sound effects, push button arteries (clear and clogged), try on a "fat vest" and find out what it feels like to carry an extra 20 pounds around, display of actual horse, cat, and mouse hearts.

Impression 5 Science Center (cont.)

- ❑ **WATER** - Build a water tower, navigate a ship thru locks, assemble a plumbing system and splash.
- ❑ **BUBBLES** - create bubble walls, circles.
- ❑ **SENSORY STREET** - grab a can, close your eyes, walk around a sample house and neighborhood using all your senses except sight - it's really different and a little hard unless you concentrate.
- ❑ **COMPUTER LAB AND REAL CHEMISTRY LAB** - where techs help you make your own experiment -slime! $1.00 extra and you get to take home your experiment! Outside the lab are "Roundtables" - simple experiments you do as a family.

MICHIGAN STATE CAPITAL

Capital & Michigan Avenues (I-496 exit M.L. King Street. Follow Capital Loop), **Lansing** 48933

- ❑ Phone: (517) 373-2353
- ❑ Tours: Monday-Friday 9:00am-4:00pm, Saturday 10:00am-3:00pm. Closed Sundays and Holiday weekends. Tours leave every half hour.
- ❑ Admission: FREE

The House and Senate Galleries are situated inside a building that looks like the US Capital. Recently restored, the building was originally designed by foremost architect, Elijah E. Myers during the Gilded Age. You'll start out under the dome which is a view upward over 160 feet. This gets the kids' attention. Next, you take a peek in the Governor's Office (if he's in, he'll wave or come over to say "hi"). It's a very stately, very large office that was cleaned during the restoration with cotton swabs (at least, the ceiling was). The kids try to imagine doing their cleaning chores with only cleaning solution and cotton swabs - *sounds impossible!* Another highlight of this tour is the Senate Room. Magnificent to view (from the public access balcony), it has so much detail, the kids are mesmerized. They'll also learn about contemporary legislative processes and how citizens get involved.

PLANET WALK

Lansing - *River Trail along Grand & Red Cedar River (Outside Science Center - 200 Museum Drive), 48933. Phone: (517) 371-6730.* Travel 93 million miles from the Earth to the Sun, almost another 4 billion miles to the farthest planet, Pluto. Want to walk it? Begin at the scaled down version of the sun (it's about the size of a giant play ball). Each step further out covers 1 million scale miles. Pass earth, the size of a pea, and Jupiter, the size of an orange. The total walking distance from the Sun to Pluto is 2 miles.

R.E. OLDS TRANSPORTATION MUSEUM

Lansing - *240 Museum Drive (Downtown off Michigan Avenue), 48933. Phone: (517) 372-0422. Hours: Tuesday-Saturday 10:00am-5:00pm, Sunday Noon-5:00pm. Closed major holidays. Admission: $2-4.00 (over age 5).* See the first Oldsmobile (1897), Toronado (1st 1966), Stars, Durants and Olds car advertising. See autographed and experimental motors plus an REO Speedwagon or Cloud. So many "old" cars to look at up close…look for the Spartan car. The museum is a reflection of R.E. Olds life and contribution to the transport industry from 1883 to the present are featured, too.

RIVERWALK THEATRE SHOWS

Lansing - *228 Museum Drive (next to Impression 5 Museum on the river), 48933. Phone: (517) 482-5700.* **Web: http://riverwalk.thetheater.com** *Admission: $5.00 average admission for Children's Shows (usually before Christmas).* Children's theatre shows are Friday evening, and Saturday and Sunday afternoon.

J & K STEAMBOAT LINE

Lansing (Grand Ledge) - *(various departure spots on the Grand River), 48837. Phone: (517) 627-2154. Admission: $8.00 - $49.00 depending on the type of cruise. Children (3-12) are at 50% of adult rate.* This cruise line features 3 riverboats and a variety of cruising options. "Spirit of Lansing", "Princess Laura" and the largest, the "Michigan Princess" (which has three levels and luxurious woodwork and crystal). Be sure to ask about the "Kids Spectacular" cruise.

GREENMEAD HISTORICAL PARK

20501 Newburgh Road (jct. 8 Mile and Newburgh Roads)

Livonia 48150

❑   Phone: (248) 477-7375

      Web: www.ci.livonia.mi.us/Community/Greenmead.htm

❑   Hours: Grounds open Daily 8:30am-4:00pm (May-October, and in December). Closed holidays.

❑   Admission: $1.00-$2.00 per person.

❑   Tours: Guided tours are offered only on Sundays between 1:00 - 4:00pm and during special events.

The 95 acre park site was the 1820's homestead of Michigan pioneer, Joshua Simmons. The Simmon's family lived in a modest frame house, while the barn, a building of primary importance was the first major structure completed. Together, the buildings tell the story of farm life in rural Michigan. Eight historical buildings (some plain, some fancy) outline regional history, especially during scheduled events or Sundays. There is a wide variety of items exhibited in the general store. They have stocked the store with goods from the 1913 ledger. This building is a favorite of children of all ages, who enjoy shopping at its candy and trinket counters.

ALGONAC STATE PARK

Marine City - *8732 River Road (2 miles north of the city on SR 29), 48039. Phone: (810) 765-5605. Admission: $4.00 per vehicle.* **Web: www.michigandnr.com/parksandtrails/parklist.asp** On the St. Clair River you can watch the large freighters pass by from this park. Algonac's lakeplain prairies and lakeplain oak savannas are considered globally significant. These special habitats include nineteen species that are on the state list of endangered, threatened, and special concern species. Other features include winter sports, hiking trails along a prairie area, fishing (walleye), rough camping, and boating.

HEATH BEACH

16339 Cone Road (US 23 to exit 22 - follow signs)

Milan 48160

❑ Phone: (734) 439-1818 **Web: www.heathbeach.com**
❑ Hours: Daily 10:30am-7:30pm (Memorial Day Weekend-Labor Day Weekend).
❑ Admission: $6.00 (weekends), $5.00 (weekdays), $3.00 child (9-12), Under 8 FREE (all the time).

Some people see a hole in the ground (in this case caused by the construction of US-23)...others see opportunity. In 1962, area resident Charles Heath gained a 6-acre lake (in his former cow pasture) along the new construction. For years they used this recreation area as a family swimming hole. With the persuading of friends, Charles decided to make some improvements and open it to the public. Today, this family tradition can easily be spotted everywhere in the region with the help of the bumper sticker campaign promoting this family fun spot.

MILAN DRAGWAY

10860 Plank Road (US 23 to exit 25)

Milan 48160

❑ Phone: (734) 439-7368 **Web: www.milandragway.com**
❑ Hours: Season is April-October. Auto races held in the day, Saturday & Sunday. Motorcycle races held Friday nights.
❑ Admission: Adults $10.00, Children $4.00 (7-12), FREE (ages 6 and under). During special events - rates can be higher. Call or visit website for details.
❑ Miscellaneous: Drag and bracket racing. Events include junior racing, nostalgia days, RAM chargers, Harlet drags and invitationals. There's even a new track for off-road truck races.

A race that lasts 6 seconds or less? Don't blink or you might just miss it! See Michigan (and nationally known) racers compete to see who can travel the fastest on the ¼ mile drag "strip". Special events feature "dragsters" that can reach speeds of over 300 MPH (in a little over 4 seconds!) Be sure to bring earplugs for the kids

(& parents) since these "open header" vehicles can be extremely loud! Hey Moms and Dads... Wednesday and Friday allow you (for an entry fee) to see just how fast the family "dragster" can go! Kids can also compete in special miniature drag cars...wow!

KENSINGTON METROPARK

2240 West Buno Road (I-96 - Next exit past Milford)

Milford 48380

❑   Phone: (248) 685-1561 or (800) 477-3178
       Web: www.metroparks.com/kensington.html
❑   Hours: Daily 6:00am-10:00pm
❑   Admission: Weekends $3.00 per vehicle, Weekdays $2.00 per vehicle.

Spanning over 4,000 acres (including the 1200 acre Lake Kent), this park offers family fun year-round. Some of the educational attractions include the Farm Center (discover and touch numerous animals) and the Nature Center (with wildlife exhibits and nature trails). For a break from the action, step aboard the Island Queen paddlewheel boat for a scenic trip around the lake. Speaking of Lake Kent, it offers great fishing (you can even bring your own boat or use rentals including sailboats which are available) and 2 beaches in the summertime. Golfing is also available on the 18-hole course of the south side of the lake. Winter brings sled riding, tobogganing, cross-country skiing, and sleigh rides (minimum snow base of 4-6 inches required) to the park.

PROUD LAKE RECREATION AREA

Milford - *3500 Wixom Road (I-96 exit Wixom Road north), 48382.* **Web: www.michigandnr.com/parksandtrails/parklist.asp** *Phone: (248) 685-2433. Admission: $4.00 per vehicle.* Including part of the upper Huron River, features include hiking trails, beaches and swimming, boating and canoeing, camping, and winter sports. It is also a great place to be (beginning the last weekend of April) when the site releases large batches of trout for fishing.

RIVER RAISIN BATTLEFIELD VISITOR'S CENTER

1403 East Elm Street (I-75, exit 14), **Monroe** 48161

❑   Phone: (734) 243-7136 or (743) 243-7137
    Web: www.geocities.com/pentagon/quarters/7550/
❑   Hours: Daily 10:00am-5:00pm (Memorial Day - Labor Day).
    Weekends only (Rest of the Year).
❑   Admission: FREE (donations accepted)

An important stop for interesting regional history, this visitor's center focuses on the battle (during the War of 1812) that was the worst defeat for the Americans. The British and Chief Tecumseh's Indians killed over 800 settlers during this battle. A 10 minute presentation (with fiber optic maps, mannequins, and dioramas) summarizes the importance of who was in control of the Great Lakes.

STERLING STATE PARK

Monroe - *2800 State Park Road (off I-75), 48161.* ***Web:*** ***www.michigandnr.com/parksandtrails/parklist.asp*** *Phone: (734) 289-2715. Admission: $4.00 per vehicle.* Camping, hiking trails, boating, fishing and swimming. Boat Rentals Memorial Day - Labor Day. Row boats, canoes, paddle boats.

METRO BEACH METROPARK

Metropolitan Parkway

Mount Clemens 48043

❑   Phone: (586) 463-4581 or (800) 477-3172
    Web: www.metroparks.com/metrobeach.html
❑   Hours: Monday-Friday 8:00am-8:00pm. Weekends & Holidays
    8:00am-Dusk.
❑   Admission: Weekdays $2.00 per vehicle, Weekends $3.00 per
    vehicle.

A lakeside summer beach retreat (with a boardwalk over a mile long) that has several unique attractions including: The Tot Lot (a place for kids as young as 3 can ride their bikes without running over someone), Educational Nature Programs, and a heated pool. Also: VOYAGEUR CANOE Passengers help paddle a 34-foot

(20-passenger) Montreal Canoe that makes trips daily from the North Marina. Advance registration required for individuals and groups. TRACKLESS TRAIN Shuttle service to Huron Point picnic and shore fishing areas, weekends and holidays.

MAYBURY STATE PARK

20145 Beck Road (I-96 to I-275 north, west on Eight Mile Road)

Northville 48167

❑   Phone: (248) 349-8390

       Web: www.michigandnr.com/parksandtrails/parklist.asp

❑   Admission: $4.00 per vehicle

Mostly forest, features include horseback riding, cross-country skiing, hiking trails, bike trails, fishing, winter sports, and a visitors center and living farm featuring a petting area for kids. The Farm represents a small family farm where general farming practices are demonstrated. Maybury Farm is open all year Summer Hours: 10:00am-7:00pm, Winter Hours: 10:00am-5:00pm. Guided Tours by Reservation Phone: (248) 349-3858.

HAYES STATE PARK

Onstead - *1220 Wampler's Lake Road (US-12 west to M-124), 49265.* **Web:** *www.michigandnr.com/parksandtrails/parklist.asp Phone: (517) 467-7401. Admission: $4.00 per vehicle.* W.J. Hayes State Park, in the heart of the Irish Hills, is bordered by a group of inland lakes frequented by anglers and boaters. Camping, boating, fishing, swimming and winter sports are offered.

LAKE HUDSON RECREATION AREA

Onstead - *1220 Wampler's Lake Road (M-156 SE), 49265.* **Web:** *www.michigandnr.com/parksandtrails/parklist.asp Phone: (517) 445-2265. Admission: $4.00 per vehicle.* Nearly 2,700 acres of recreational opportunities around Lake Hudson. The park, which lies in southeast Michigan, offers premier muskie fishing and hunting. A new beach area provides an excellent place for sunbathing and swimming. Camping, hiking, boating, fishing, swimming and winter sports.

ORTONVILLE RECREATION AREA

Ortonville - *5779 Hadley Road, 48462. Phone: (248) 627-3828.* *Web: www.michigandnr.com/parksandtrails/parklist.asp Admission: $4.00 per vehicle.* Camping/cabins, hiking trails, boating, fishing, swimming and winter sports.

LAKELANDS TRAIL STATE PARK

Pinckney - *8555 Silver Hill, Rt. 1, 48169. Phone: (734) 426-4913.* *Web: www.michigandnr.com/parksandtrails/parklist.asp* A 13-mile gravel trail that connects Pinckney and Stockbridge. Along the way, you'll pass through rolling farmland and wooded areas that offer spectacular views. The Pinckney trailhead is a quarter mile north of M-36 on D-19 in Pinckney. The Stockbridge trailhead is on M-52 in Stockbridge.

PINCKNEY RECREATION AREA

Pinckney - *8555 Silver Hill (I-94 exit 159, North), 48169. Web: www.michigandnr.com/parksandtrails/parklist.asp Phone: (734) 426-4913. Admission: $4.00 per vehicle.* Camping, hiking (Lakelands trail is popular), boating, fishing, swimming, bicycle trails and winter sports.

PLYMOUTH HISTORICAL MUSEUM

Plymouth - *155 South Main Street (one block north of Kellogg Park), 48170. Web:* **http://www.plymouth.lib.mi.us/~history** *Phone: (734) 455-8940. Hours: Wednesday, Thursday, Saturday 1:00-4:00 pm. Sunday, 2:00-5:00 pm. Admission: $3.00 adult, $1.00 student (5-17), $7.00 family.* A kid-friendly museum with exhibits that include a scavenger hunt where "every child wins a prize". See the "Images of Abraham Lincoln" exhibit that features Lincoln in 10 phases of life (from boy to hero), wax figures of Abraham & Mary Todd Lincoln, and even displays a lock of Lincoln's actual hair!

WOLCOTT MILL METROPARK
(between 29 and 30 Mile Road)
Romeo 48065

❑　Phone: (586) 749-5997 or (800) 477-3175
　　Web: www.metroparks.com/wolcottmill.html
❑　Hours: Weekdays 9:00am - 5:00pm, Weekends 9:00am - 7:00pm
　　(May - October). Closes at 5:00pm (November - April).
　　Restricted winter hours.
❑　Admission: Weekends, $3.00 per vehicle. FREE weekdays.

A gristmill is always a fun experience (really, explain it to the kids like it is a giant "mousetrap" game inside - full of large gears and rubberbands, etc.). See the mid-1800's era gristmill grind wheat into flour on the huge millstones. (It's interesting to note that in a hundred years, most mills would only wear out maybe one set of millstones). Also featured is the Farm Learning Center (on Wolcott Road) that teaches the methods and importance of farming today. See cow milking, sheep demonstrations, and experimental vegetable plots.

MCCOURTIE PARK

Somerset Center - *(US 12 and US 127 - 11/2 miles west - enter from South Jackson Road), 49282. Open dawn to dusk. Picnic facilities, ballfields.* Walk over 17 concrete bridges (each a different style), visit the underground apartments and garages, see the giant birdhouse and their tree chimneys. All of this concrete! Until you get up close, it will fool you - it looks like wood! Herb McCourtie, a concrete baron, left the park grounds to his hometown. It's unique enough to definitely write home about!

CROSSWINDS MARSH WETLAND INTERPRETIVE PRESERVE

Sumpter Township - *(I-94 to exit 8 - go west), 48111.* **Web:** *www.waynecounty.com/parks/crosswinds_interp_pro.htm Phone: (734) 654-1220. FREE admission (small fee for programs).* Over 100 species of birds (binocular rentals available for $1.00) can be viewed at this 1000 acre artificially created wetland - one of the largest in the country. Learn more about the plants and wildlife

For updates visit our website: www.kidslovepublications.com

that were moved to this area by taking a 2 mile canoe trip that has interpretive markers to describe what you are seeing. (Canoe rentals are available for $5.00 per hour).

COE RAIL SCENIC TRAIN

840 North Pontiac Trail (I-96 - Wixom Road Exit - North)

Walled Lake 48390

❑ Phone: (248) 960-9440

   Web: www.michiganstarclipper.com/scenictr.html

❑ Admission: Averages $8.00 per person.

❑ Tours: Train departs Sundays at 1:00 and 2:30pm. One hour long. (late April-October).

Train rides thru scenic countryside of Walled Lake and West Bloomfield in old-fashioned cars.

PONTIAC LAKE RECREATION AREA

Waterford - *7800 Gale Road (off M-59), 48327. Phone: (248) 666-1020. Web: www.michigandnr.com/parksandtrails/parklist.asp Admission: $4.00 per vehicle.* Archery ranges and horse trails/rentals make this park unique. Camping, hiking trails, boating, fishing, swimming, bicycle trails and winter sports.

DODGE NO. 4 STATE PARK

Waterford - *4250 Parkway Drive (off M-59 west to Cass Elizabeth Road), 48328. Phone: (248) 682-7323. Admission: $4.00 per vehicle. Web: www.michigandnr.com/parksandtrails/parklist.asp* A white sandy beach and a one-mile shoreline on Cass Lake makes Dodge #4 State Park an excellent location for summer and winter water activities. Camping, fishing, boating, swimming and winter sports.

FRIDGE, THE

Scott Lake Road (I-75 to Dixie Highway Exit - South)

Waterford 48328

❑ Phone: In season: (248) 975-4440. Off season: (248) 858-0906

   Web: www.co.oakland.mi.us/parksrec/ppark/fridge.html

❑   Hours: Wednesday-Friday 4:00-9:30pm. Saturday 10:00am-
     10:00pm. Sunday Noon-8:00pm. (All times are weather
     permitting). Closed Christmas Eve and Day. (mid-December to
     mid-March)
❑   Admission: $4.00-$8.00. No riders under 43" tall permitted, and
     riders under age 10 must be accompanied by an adult.

Drop 55 feet (rather quickly) and then travel over 1000 feet as you
and 3 close friends discover the thrill of tobogganing. The park has
2 runs, over 200 toboggans, and even a place to warm up with a
fireplace and food. In the summer you'll find a tennis courts, a 5-
story raft ride, wave pool, and BMX bicycle course.

DRAYTON PLAINS NATURE CENTER

Waterford - *2125 Denby Drive (Jct. Of US 24 and Hatchery
Road, following signs), 48329. Phone: (248) 674-2119. Hours:
Grounds open 8:00am-9:00pm (April -October). Only open until
6:00pm rest of year. Interpretive Center open Tuesday - Friday
11:00am - 2:00pm and Weekends Noon - 4:00pm. FREE
Admission.* 137 acres of trails along the Clinton River plus a nice
Interpretive Center. In the center are displays of mounted animals
in re-created scenes of their natural habitats.

HIGHLAND RECREATION AREA

White Lake - *5200 East Highland Road (off M-59 East), 48363.
Web: www.michigandnr.com/parksandtrails/parklist.asp Phone:
(248) 889-3750. Admission: $4.00 per vehicle.* Camping, hiking,
boating, fishing, swimming and winter sports. Horse rentals and
trails too.

ALPINE VALLEY SKI AREA

White Lake - *6775 East Highland Road (I-96 - Milford Road exit
to M-59 West), 48383. **Web: www.skialpinevalley.com** Phone:
(248) 887-4183.* You'll have a real "Alpine" feeling since this
resort offers 25 runs (some of which have many trees and are
steep). Rental equipment: Skis (also shaped skis to learn easier)
and snowboards.

ROLLING HILLS COUNTY PARK

Ypsilanti - *7660 Stoney Creek Road, 48197. Phone: (734) 482-3866.* Summers: Wave pool, water slide, zero-depth pool, waterfall, picnic area, sports fields, fishing pond, grassy sunbathing area, sandy beach, 9-hole Frisbee golf course, tube rentals. Winter: Dual toboggan chutes, ice skating, and cross-county skiing.

YANKEE AIR FORCE MUSEUM

2041 Willow Run Airport

Ypsilanti 48197

- ❑ Phone: (734) 483-4030 **Web: www.yankeeairmuseum.org**
- ❑ Hours: Tuesday-Saturday 10:00am-4:00pm, Sunday Noon-4:00pm. Closed Mondays & Holidays. Call for Winter Hours - January & February
- ❑ Admission: $3.00-$5.00 (age 5+)

During WW II, B-24 bomber mechanics were schooled here marking one of Michigan's many roles in the war and aviation history. This museum, which was started as a way to commemorate this, has actually grown to one of the most unique in the country (in our opinion) for several reasons. The first is that some of the "relic" museum aircraft (21 aircraft in all) are actually some of the only "still flyable" examples left today. The flyable B-25 Mitchell and B-17 (a large 4 engine bomber) are a couple examples of these planes and are a wonderful way to bring this "conflict in history" to life. Outside, children can see a large B52D jet-propelled (8 engine!) bomber and can even get the chance to climb inside (with a prior appointment). Be sure to see the tribute to Amelia Earhart and other female aircraft pioneers in the "Women in Aviation" room.

1131

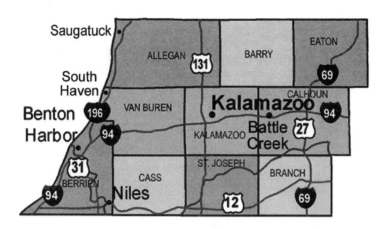

Chapter 6
South West Area

Our Favorites...

Deer Forest

Kalamazoo Nature Center

Kalamazoo Valley Museum

Kellogg's Cereal City

Saugatuck Dune Rides

Silver Beach

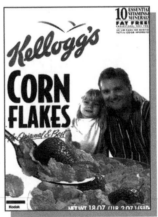

Breakfast Buddies

WHITEHOUSE NATURE CENTER

Albion - *1381 East Erie Street (Albion College), 49224. Phone: (517) 629-0582. Web: www.albion.edu/naturecenter/trails.asp Hours: Monday-Friday 9:30am-4:30pm. Weekends, 10:30am-4:30pm. Closed major and college holidays. FREE Admission.* A 135 acre outdoor facility for education that features 6 nature trails and 168 species of birds. Most of the trails are less than one mile long and each features different opportunities. Includes an observation room with live exhibits.

FORT CUSTER RECREATION AREA

Augusta - *5163 West Fort Custer Drive (M-96 West), 49012. Web: www.michigandnr.com/parksandtrails/parklist.asp Phone: (269) 731-4200. Admission: $4.00 per vehicle.* Area comprises 2,988 acres located between Battle Creek and Kalamazoo. The terrain is typical of southern Michigan farm country, with second growth forests and remnant areas of prairie. The area features three lakes, the Kalamazoo River, and an excellent trail system. Camping, hiking, boating, fishing, swimming, bicycle trails, winter sports.

KELLOGG BIRD SANCTUARY

Augusta - *12685 East C Avenue (13 miles northwest on SR89, between 40th and E. Gull Lake Drive), 49012. Phone: (269) 671-2510. Hours: Daily 9:00am-8:00pm (May-October). Daily 9:00am-5:00pm (rest of year). Small admission.* An MSU experimental facility of birds of prey, wild geese, ducks, swans, pheasants and peacocks. There are displays and observation decks. Several endangered species, like the genetically endangered red jungle fowl and Reeves' pheasant are on display, as well as the rare sharp-tailed grouse and greater prairie chicken (which is no longer found in Michigan).

BINDER PARK ZOO

7400 Division Drive (I-94 to exit 100 - go south)

Battle Creek 49014

❑   Phone: (269) 979-1351, **Web: www.binderparkzoo.org**

❑   Hours: Monday-Friday 9:00am-5:00pm, Saturday & Holidays 9:00am-6:00pm, Sunday 11:00am-6:00pm (mid-April to mid-October).

❑   Admission: $6.50-$8.50 (age 2+).

❑   Miscellaneous: Gift shop with unique animal items.

Natural settings offer over 250 animals in 80 exhibits that you can see while strolling along wooden boardwalks. See exhibits like a Chinese Red Panda, and a Mexican Grey Wolf, interact with insects, and have fun learning at the Conservation Stations (a hands-on exhibit). The hands-on playground at the children's zoo is said to have the world's largest and most accurate dinosaur replicas, a petting zoo, and miniature railroad.

BATTLE CREEK BATTLECATS

Battle Creek - *1392 Capital Avenue NE (I-94 to exit 98B - go north, C.O. Brown Stadium), 49017. Phone: (269) 660-CATS. Web: www.battlecatsbaseball.com Admission:$4.00-$8.00.* This class "A" Midwest League Affiliate for the Houston Astros offers plenty of family entertainment value. Be sure to call about special family "free-bee" nights that include free fireworks, balls, hats, etc. Can't you just smell the hot dogs?

FULL BLAST

35 Hamblin Avenue (I-94 to I-194/M-66 - north)

Battle Creek 49017

❑   Phone: (269) 966-3667

     Web: www.uplanyournight.com/fullblast.htm

❑   Hours: Varies by activity and season but basically 11:00am-7:00pm.

❑   Admission: $7.00 per person with waterpark entry. $4.00 per person without waterpark entry.

A family fun attraction with something for everyone. Attractions include a skateboard park, indoor and outdoor waterparks (with 2 – 100 ft. waterslides, a river float, bubble beach), 3 basketball courts, full-service health club, café and food court, and teen nightclub. Imagination Station (indoor)/Adventure Land (outdoor) - a playground with slides, climbing nets, and endless tunnels. Guest must be 54" or shorter to play.

KELLOGG'S CEREAL CITY USA

171 West Michigan Avenue (I-94 exit 98B to I-194/M 66 north. On the riverfront.), **Battle Creek** 49017

- ❑ Phone: (269) 962-6230 **Web: www.kelloggscerealcityusa.org**
- ❑ Hours: Monday-Friday 9:30am-5:00pm, Saturday 9:30am-6:00pm, Sunday 11:00am-5:00pm (Summer). Tuesday-Friday 10:00am-4:00pm, Saturday 10:00am-5:00pm, Sunday 12:00pm-5:00pm (September-May).
- ❑ Admission: $5.00-$8.00 per person (age 3+)
- ❑ Miscellaneous: Red Onion Grill - a 1930's style diner serves sandwiches. The Factory Store. Half of the facility is for older kids (in all of us) and another half is for younger kids.

Flakes started as an experiment for a new healthy breakfast food by Dr. Kellogg in the late 1800's. Within a couple of years, almost 40 different cereal companies had started in the Battle Creek area - including POST (one of the only surviving still). You'll learn this and more in the theater presentation on the first floor. Adults will find some of their marketing strategies unique - like asking people to stop eating their flakes because they were in short supply. As you go upstairs, don't be surprised to " bump" into Tony the Tiger or Snap, Crackle & Pop (we have video tape of big hugs from our kids to these characters)! The simulated working production line tour is where you can see, smell and taste a warm sample of fresh flakes being made. This is narrated by a "kernel of corn" hoping he becomes a "cereal flake". Cereal City has hands-on interactives in a cobblestone lane setting. The "Tony" and "Tony Jr." is a soft play area where younger sets can climb up inside a cereal box and slide down as you're poured out of the box! There's a ball pit with gym, too. Before you leave, buy a box of special Corn Flakes with your photo on the front - a must souvenir for cereal lovers!

LEILA ARBORETUM & KINGMAN MUSEUM OF NATURAL HISTORY

928 West Michigan Avenue (near 20th St)

Battle Creek 49017

❑ Phone: Museum (269) 965-5117, Arboretum (269) 969-0270

❑ Hours: (Museum) Tuesday-Friday 9:00am-5:00pm, Saturday & Sunday 1:00-5:00pm. (Arboretum) Daily Dawn to Dusk.

❑ Admission: (Museum) $5.00 adult, $4.00 senior (65+), $3.00 student (3-18). The arboretum admission is usually FREE. Planetarium $2.00.

It now features a sunken garden, a visitor's center, a children's adventure garden, and large floral displays (depending on season). The Kingman Museum of Natural History (West Michigan at 20th) has 3 floors of exhibits including dinosaurs and a planetarium.

1839 HISTORIC COURTHOUSE MUSEUM

Berrien Springs - *313 North Cass Street, 49103. Phone: (269) 471-1202. Web: www.berrienhistory.org/square/museum.html Hours: Tuesday-Friday 9:00am-4:00pm, Saturday & Sunday 1:00-5:00pm (May - mid-January). Closed Monday-Wednesday (mid-February to April). Admission: FREE. Small admission for guided tours.* The restored courtroom and courthouse are surrounded by an 1870 sheriff's residence and jail, 1830's log house, and a mid-1800's county office. All focus on local history.

COOK ENERGY INFO CENTER AND DUNES

1 Cook Place (I-94 exit 16 or 23, follow signs - off Red Arrow Highway), **Bridgman 49106**

❑ Phone: (800) 548-2555 **Web: www.cookinfo.com**

❑ Hours: Tuesday-Sunday 10:00am-5:00pm (mid-January to mid-December). Closed all holidays.

❑ Admission: FREE

❑ Tours: 45 minute guided.

❑ Miscellaneous: Picnic areas.

Technology and nature together - sounds impossible. Nuclear power, electricity and future energy sources are explained. From your arrival in the Energy Center lobby, your group will be whisked off to Theater 1 for a private screening of Dr. Nate's nuclear energy video. You'll learn the secrets of nuclear energy and how we use it to make electricity at the Cook Nuclear Plant. Next you're off to Theater 2 to watch a 26-foot 3-D rotating exhibit rise from the floor, rotate, and flash as the intricate working of a nuclear energy plant are displayed. Hike dune trails along Lake Michigan shoreline including forests and wetlands. There are also energy video games and hands-on displays. Schedule a fun "Power Trip" with Dr. Nate for your class or group and learn how nuclear energy is produced and used.

BEAR CAVE

Buchanan - *(4 miles North on Red Bud Trail), 49107. Phone: (269) 695-3050. Hours: Daily 10:00am-4:00pm (Memorial Day-Labor Day). Small admission.* One of the few caves in Michigan that is accessible to the public, Bear Cave (150-feet long) is accessed by a narrow, winding stairway. The temperature is a constant 58 degrees F. so be sure to dress appropriately. A taped narration explains the sights of stalactites, flowstone, and petrified leaves. A warning though…the cave does contain bats. However, if you don't bother them, they usually won't bother you!

TIBBITS OPERA HOUSE

Coldwater - *14 Hanchett Street (South of US 12), 49036. Phone: (517) 278-6029.* **Web: www.tibbits.org** *Admission: "Popcorn Theater" around $5.00 (12 and under). Tickets for other shows vary but begin at around $9.00. Tours: FREE, Monday - Friday, 9:00 am - 6:00 pm (advance reservation required).* An opera and theater since 1882, you can still see community plays year-round and professional summer stock productions in June through August. A family favorite is the "Popcorn Theater" that is specially produced for children ages 5 and older and is scheduled for Friday and Saturday mornings.

DEER FOREST

Paw Paw Lake Road, 6800 Marquette Dr. (I-94 exit 39 north, follow signs), **Coloma** 49038

- ❑ Phone: (269) 468-4961, **www.theimaginaryworld.com/df.html**
- ❑ Hours: Daily 10:00am-7:00pm (Memorial Weekend-Labor Day).
- ❑ Admission: Starts at $10.00 (age 3+)
- ❑ Miscellaneous: Gift shop. Picnic areas. "Wild Child Play Habitat". Santa's Summer Home. Kid's entertainment like magicians. Mostly in the woods and shaded.

Their slogan, "More fun than a zoo" is true, mostly because it's designed as an Animal and an Amusement Park. Fun and different animals to pet are baby zebras and mini-horses (the size of dogs) or sit between the humps of a camel. Most every animal here is tame enough to pet (making it different than a zoo). You can also ride ponies and camels, a treetop Ferris wheel, a carrousel or mini-train. Our favorite part had to be Storybook Lane, a large park within the park, where you meander around the lane. Each setting illustrates a different Nursery Rhyme scene like "3 Men in a Tub" (in a pond with real frogs and small fish) or "Baa Baa Black Sheep" (with what else but, black sheep). To get your money's worth, be sure to spend several hours here and plan a picnic or buy at the snack bar. Also, lots of photo ops everywhere.

SS KEEWATIN

CR A2 (Blue Star Highway & Union Street) (Kalamazoo River near bridge at Harbour Village), **Douglas** 49406

- ❑ Phone: (269) 857-2464
- ❑ Hours: Daily 10:00am-4:30pm (Summers only).
- ❑ Admission: $3.00-$6.00 (ages 6+).
- ❑ Miscellaneous: Extensive nautical gift shop and museum. To keep the kids curious, tell them to look for the captain's boots he left on the ship (Note: you'll find them towards the very end of the tour!)

This visit sure was nostalgic for Michele. As we approached the large vessel (350 feet long), I *(Michele)* remembered the same eerrie feeling it gave me as a child. It went out of service in 1965 and was brought here as a museum in 1967. I was about 10-12 years old when I first visited. Now, with my children and husband in tow, we escaped back to the time of luxury liners, elegant dining rooms, handsome staterooms, and the grand ballroom. Occasionally, pictures from the movie "Titanic" appeared on the walls and with good reason. If you liked the movie, or just the romance of the grandiose "floating hotel" - Keewatin (Key-way-tin) will fill your dreams. However, the ship is not fully restored, and is a mix of pristine wood and etched Italian glass mixed with the smell and look of old upholstery and worn paint. Well, back to reality - your kids will love that they get to go inside the "really huge boat" and even get to climb up to the top deck and turn the ship's wheel.

MUSEUM AT SOUTHWESTERN MICHIGAN COLLEGE

Dowagiac - *58900 Cherry Grove Road (east on SR62 from SR51), 49047. Phone: (269) 782-1374. **Web: www.smc.cc.mi.us/museum** Hours: Tuesday-Saturday, 10:00am-5:00pm. Open until 8:00pm on Wednesdays. Closed on national, state and college holidays. Free admission.* An interactive adventure in local history and an exciting exploration in science and technology. Cass County history is explored through displays on science, agriculture, industry (Heddon lures & Roand Oak Stoves), American Indians, the Underground Railroad. Try on vintage-style clothing of the 19th century, travel thru an archeological time tunnel or solve mysteries of the past by reconstructing pottery from shards. Now, put your energy and curiosity to use in two galleries of sensory stimulation exploration of Science and Technology. Displays of light & minerals, air & motion, generating light, and producing energy. The Kaleidoscope Gallery changes every 3-4 months.

VAN BUREN COUNTY HISTORICAL MUSEUM

Hartford - *58471 Red Arrow Highway (located between Hartford and Lawrence, next to county fairgrounds), 49057. Phone: (269) 621-2188. Hours: Wednesday & Saturday 10:00am-4:00pm. Sunday 1:00-4:00pm.* 30 rooms (former county poor house) including a one-room school, children's room, general store, music room, old-fashioned kitchen, parlor, doctor's operating room, blacksmith shop and dentist's office.

CHARLTON PARK VILLAGE & MUSEUM

2545 South Charlton Park Road (2 miles South on SR 37 then 4 miles East on SR79 - follow signs), **Hastings** 49058

❑   Phone: (616) 945-3775, **Web: www.charltonpark.org**

❑   Hours: Tuesday-Sunday 9:00am-5:00pm. (Memorial Day-Labor Day), plus festivals.

❑   Admission: $2.00-$4.00 (age 5+). Special events can have various admission fees and are the best time to visit (many re-enactors): Civil War Muster or Steam Engine Show (July) & Pow Wow (September).

A very authentic recreation of an 1890's rural Michigan town, this village offers 25 buildings that include a schoolhouse, a blacksmith shop, an 1880's doctor's home, a general store, an 1885 church, a print shop, a cabin and a wigwam. Also find a beach, boat launch, and playground in the recreational part of the park complex.

GILMORE CAR MUSEUM

Hickory Corners - *6865 Hickory Road (M43 at Hickory Road), 49060. Web: www.gilmorecarmuseum.org Phone: (269) 671-5089. Hours: Monday-Friday 10:00am-5:00pm, Weekends until 6:00pm (May-October). Admission: $7.00 adult, $6.00 senior (62+), $4.00 child (7-15).* Have you ever had a dream about finding that "priceless" antique car in someone's barn? See more than 130 unique and rare cars all displayed in antique barns. A few cars that you will see include Cadillacs, Packards, and even a steam powered car. Also, you'll find a reproduction of the Wright Brother's plane and a narrow gauge train. For the "tikes" they have antique pedal cars.

K-WINGS HOCKEY

Kalamazoo - *3600 Vanrick Drive (I-94 - Sprinkle Road exit - Wings Stadium), 49001. Phone: (269) 345-5101 tickets or (269) 345-9772 office. Web: www.kwings.com* You'll experience hard-hitting, fast-paced action, great music, humorous on-ice promotions, contests, and the antics of Slappy, the K-Wings zany mascot. An UHL affiliate team (October - April). $5.00-$15.00. Public skating and rentals at rink, too.

For updates visit our website: www.kidslovepublications.com

ECHO VALLEY

8495 East H Avenue, **Kalamazoo** 49004

- ❑ Phone: (269) 349-3291 **Web: www.echovalleyfun.com**
- ❑ Hours: Friday 6:00-10:00pm. Saturday 10:00am-10:00pm.
  Sunday Noon - 7:00pm. (mid-December to early March)
- ❑ Admission: (Toboggans) $9.00. All day passes $15.00. (Inner
  Tubing) $9.00. (Ice Skating) $5.00
- ❑ Miscellaneous: Lodge and snack bar. Outdoor ice skating rink.
  Parents & Chaperones who prefer to observe all the fun rather
  than participate may enter Echo Valley at NO COST.

Aaah…the feeling of that sled racing down a fresh snow covered hill…and the air getting colder on my face…is a childhood memory that I will never forget. Relive those memories and introduce your kids to the fun of tubing and tobogganing that makes winter a blast. Old wood toboggans have been replaced with super-fast custom made sleds molded from a single piece of polyethylene. The toboggans are equipped with padded seats and Teflon runners. Eight icy and fast tracks await you as you fly down a hill of over 120 feet, at speeds of up to 60 miles per hour. The best part of all is that at this resort there is a tow rope to pull the toboggans back up the hill.

KALAMAZOO NATURE CENTER

7000 North Westnedge Avenue (I-94 to US131exit 44 east)

Kalamazoo 49004

- ❑ Phone: (269) 381-1574 **Web: www.naturecenter.org**
- ❑ Hours: Monday-Saturday 9:00am-5:00pm, Sunday 1:00-5:00pm.
  (Extended summer hours).
- ❑ Admission: $4.50 adult, $3.50 senior (55+), $2.50 child (4-13).
- ❑ Miscellaneous: Nature trails (one is wheelchair and stroller
  accessible). Gift shop - large variety of Insect Inside Candy.

When you enter, either walk over to the Tropical Rainforest (3 stories) environment that's home to parrots, iguanas, tropical plants and exotic fish or walk through Nature Up Close. You'll walk through giant tree trunks and discover nature 10 times the size of life. Imagine 8 foot tall flowers and watch out for that huge frog - it's like the movie *Bugs Life*! We especially liked the pollen exhibit where the kids can try to help bees pollinate flowers. It's a clever demo and we learned bees pollinate by accident. The Expedition Station is outstanding with a collection of stuffed birds and real bones - all hands-on. Outside, walk through 1000 acres of dense hardwood forest and check out the Butterfly House, Hummingbird Garden or Delano Pioneer Homestead - early life in Michigan.

KALAMAZOO CIVIC THEATRE

Kalamazoo - *426 South Park Street (Carver Center), 49007. Phone: (269) 343-1313.* Youth Theatre with productions like Snow White and Sneakers. Civic Theatre performs musicals and dramas, some with family themes.

KALAMAZOO SYMPHONY ORCHESTRA

Kalamazoo - *126 East South Street (Miller Auditorium), 49007. Web: www.kazoosymphony.com or www.kjso.org Phone: (269) 349-7759. Tickets: (800) 228-9858. Admission charged for many concerts.* The season includes family concerts and FREE summer outdoor concerts. Look for the Family Discovery Concert and the Crazy Classics Concert. The youth symphony provides an orchestral experience of the highest quality for talented young musicians in southwest Michigan. Players are drawn from the Kalamazoo metropolitan area and surrounding communities.

KALAMAZOO VALLEY MUSEUM

230 North Rose Street (I-94 Westnedge Ave. exit 76 north to M-43 east), **Kalamazoo** 49007

- ❑ Phone: (269) 373-7990 **Web: http://kvm.kvcc.edu/**
- ❑ Hours: Monday-Saturday 9:00am-5:00pm, Sunday 1:00-5:00pm. Wednesday 5:00-8:00pm also. Closed all major holidays.
- ❑ Admission: FREE

❑   Miscellaneous: Digistar Planetarium. Challenger Mini-Mission
      (5th graders and up as a group actually simulate an astronaut
      mission using working equipment!). $3.00-$5.00 charge for
      Astronomy/Space related activities.

What an unexpected surprise! The Kalamazoo Valley should be
proud. It's interesting to learn that funds for the museum were
raised by the community with the museum artifacts found mostly
by locals in their attics and basements. In an 1860's farm kitchen,
make a seed wreath or search for the lost town of Singapore or test
your spelling skills in a schoolhouse. Our favorite hands-on
displays were: the create your own sand dunes or tornadoes - can
you stop them?... and the Race Cars that show you it's easier to
work together than alone. What impressed us was that most
displays were actual hands-on, not just push buttons. It was also
interesting to learn about all of the products manufactured in the
area over the years. Every young kid loves the Children's
Landscape Play Area. Oops, almost forgot - check out their 2500
year old woman (mummy)!

KALAMAZOO AIR ZOO

3101 East Milham Road (I-94 exit 78 to airport)

Kalamazoo (Portage) 49002

❑   Phone: (269) 382-6555 **Web: www.airzoo.org**
❑   Hours: Monday-Saturday 9:00am-6:00pm, Sunday Noon-6:00pm
      (June-August). Monday-Saturday 9:00am-5:00pm, Sunday
      Noon-5:00pm (September-May).
❑   Admission: $10.00 adult, $8.00 senior (60+), $5.00 child (6-15).
❑   Tours: Ride in an antique plane Ford Tri-Motor for $49.00 per
      person. Call or visit website for schedule.
❑   Miscellaneous: Gift shop. Theater (old war movies)

"It's a land of lions and tigers and bears" – it's an Air Zoo! Enter
the world of imaginative and colorful aircraft with names like Tin
Goose... Gooney Bird... Flying Tiger and the "cats", Wildcat...
Hellcat... Bearcat... Tigercat...and Tomcat. What a great way to
intrigue those little guys who don't find aircraft museums
amusing...until now. Let your kids try to count the number of

different "species" represented. "Would-be aviators" can try a virtual reality ride as a family in a flight simulator (tilt, turns, even engine and wind noise) or cockpit cutaways where you can press, pull and push levers and buttons.

CORNWELL'S TURKEYVILLE USA

Marshall - *18935 15 1/2 Mile Road (I-94 to I-69 exit 42), 49068. Web: www.turkeyville.com Phone: (269) 781-4293 or (800) 28-4315. Hours: Daily 11:00am-8:00pm. (April-October) 11:00am-7:00pm (November-March).* You're invited to the County Fair by Grandma and Grandpa Cornwell where tradition starts with farm-raised, preservative-free turkey. Choose from fun menu items (all contain turkey!) like "Sloppy Tom" barbecue sandwich or "Buttered Tom" cold sandwich. Also Ice Cream Parlour, General Store and Country Junction bakery for dessert. Dinner Theatre with productions like "South Pacific" and "Christmas Memories". Call or visit website for schedule. If your kids need to use restrooms, make sure they know the difference between "Toms" and "Hens". While on the website, be sure to hear the "turkey music" from around the world - hilarious!

WOLF LAKE FISHERY INTERPRETIVE CENTER

34270 County Road 652 (US 131 exit 38, 6 miles west of Kalamazoo on M43), **Mattawan** 49071

❑   Phone: (269) 668-2876
❑   Hours: Monday-Saturday 9:00am-5:00pm, Sunday 10:00am-5:00pm. (Call for Winter hours)
❑   Admission: FREE
❑   Miscellaneous: Picnic Area. Trails.

If you've never been to a "fish farm" it's worth a trip. This one has a museum center with a stuffed sturgeon - it's big - the largest fish caught in the state - 87 inches long and 193 pounds! Learn about fish life cycles and habitats, as well as why they even have fisheries. There's a slide show of hatchery operations and occasional hatchery tours. It looks like a giant scientific engineering lab with all the pipes, basins and valves. Outside, there are display ponds with steelhead, grayling, sturgeon and Chinook salmon - you can feed the fish and watch them jump for food. Kids will love the fishing derbies (June-August). If you want them to have a positive fishing experience, they're almost guaranteed to catch here.

YANKEE SPRINGS RECREATION AREA

Middleville - *2104 Gun Lake Rd (US-131, exit 61. East on A-42), 49333. Web: www.michigandnr.com/parksandtrails/parklist.asp Phone: (269) 795-9081. Admission: $4.00 per vehicle.* Yankee Springs Recreation Area was once the hunting grounds of the Algonquin Indians and the famous Chieftain, Chief Noonday. The site of Yankee Springs was established in 1835 and the village was made famous by Yankee Bill Lewis who owned and operated a hotel along the stagecoach run from Kalamazoo to Grand Rapids. Camping/cabins, hiking trails, boating, fishing, swimming, bicycle trails, and winter sports.

BITTERSWEET SKI AREA

Otsego - *600 River Road, 49078. Phone: (269) 694-2032. Web: www.skibittersweet.com   Hours: Daily (December-March).* 16 runs. Night skiing, lessons, rentals. Food service available.

MOUNT BALDHEAD

Saugatuck - *(by the river near Oval Beach), 49453.* Climb the 279 steps and you'll be rewarded with a great view this huge dune and Lake Michigan.

SAUGATUCK DUNE RIDES

Blue Star Highway (A2) (I-196 exit 41southwest)

Saugatuck 49453

- ❑   Phone: (269) 857-2253 **Web: www.saugatuckdunerides.com**
- ❑   Hours: Monday-Saturday 10:00am-5:30pm, Sunday Noon-5:30pm (May-September). Open until 7:30 (July & August). Weekends only (October)

❑   Admission: $13.00 adult, $8.00 child (3-10). Rides are about 35
     minutes long.

A calm, relaxing dune ride - NOT! An amusement thrill ride is
more like it! The scenic ride on 20-passenger dune schooners (with
airplane tires for "flying") goes over dunes between Lake
Michigan and Goshorn Lake. On a clear day, you'll get a view of
the coastline from a tall peak, speed through woodlands and maybe
get a view of the lost city of Singapore - an old lumber town left as
a ghost town. The trip is well worth the money and very
entertaining. Our driver was hilarious and there were dozens of
comical signs along the way like "Bridge Out" or "Men Working".
Meet the family of beech trees and the tree shaped just like the
number four. Ladies, be prepared for a new hairdo by the end of
your trip. They only go 35 mph but it's enough to give you
butterflies every now and then. It may frighten small pre-school
children - unless they love kiddie roller coasters.

STAR OF SAUGATUCK

Saugatuck - *716 Water Street, 49453. Phone: (269) 857-4261.
Hours: Leaves daily, every 2 hours beginning at 11:00am. Last
trip departs at 8:00pm. (Memorial Day - Labor Day). Weekends in
October. Admission: $5.00-$10.00 (age 3+).* A 90 minute scenic
cruise on the Kalamazoo River. One of the many sights you'll see
is "Singapore", the lumbering ghost town buried under the dunes.
The 67 foot paddlewheeler offers 2 decks, live narration, and can
seat 82 passengers per trip.

GRAND MERE STATE PARK

Sawyer - *12032 Red Arrow Highway (I-94, exit 22 west), 49125.
Web: www.michigandnr.com/parksandtrails/parklist.asp Phone:
(269) 426-4013. Admission: $4.00 per vehicle.* Great sand dunes
and over a mile of shoreline on Lake Michigan. Natural area behind
dunes with 3 lakes. No camping. Warren Dunes State Park is also here
(see separate listing below).

WARREN DUNES STATE PARK

12032 Red Arrow Highway (I-94 exit 16 south)

Sawyer 49125

❑   Phone: (269) 426-4013

      Web: www.michigandnr.com/parksandtrails/parklist.asp

❑   Admission: $4.00 per vehicle

The highlight is obvious - over 2 miles of Lake Michigan shoreline complete with sandy/grassy dunes. The dunes are always changing, so each visitor is greeted by a different formation on each visit. If it's a windy day, you can almost hear the sand sing (or some say, squeak). The park has 2½ miles of shoreline, 6 miles of hiking trails and is open year-round. Also featured are hundreds of modern campsites, cabins, hiking, swimming and winter sports. Grand Mere State Park is also here and administered by Warren Dunes.

DR. LIBERTY HYDE BAILEY MUSEUM

South Haven - *903 Bailey Avenue (off Blue Star Hwy. & Aylworth Avenue on Bailey Avenue), 49090. Phone: (269) 637-3251 or (269) 637-3141. Hours: Tuesday, Friday and Sundays, 2:00-4:00 pm. Saturdays, 10:00am-4:00pm. (May-October). Donations accepted.* The Museum marks the birthplace of world-famous botanist and horticulturist, Liberty Hyde Bailey. He designed the first horticultural laboratory building at Michigan Agricultural College (now Michigan State). You'll find lots of Bailey family artifacts.

KAL-HAVEN TRAIL STATE PARK

South Haven - *23960 Ruggles Road (I-96, exit 22 west), 49090. Web: www.michigandnr.com/parksandtrails/parklist.asp Phone: (269) 637-2788.* Journey onto the 34-mile crushed limestone path connecting South Haven and Kalamazoo. The trail wanders past farm lands, through wooded areas, and over streams and rivers. Along the way, see a camelback and covered bridge.

MICHIGAN MARITIME MUSEUM

260 Dyckman Avenue (I-196 exit 20 west)

South Haven 49090

❑   Phone: (269) 637-8078 or (800) 747-3810.
   Web: www.michiganmaritimemuseum.org
❑   Hours: Monday-Saturday, 10:00am-5:00pm. Sunday, Noon-5:00 pm.
   Closed Christmas & Easter.
❑   Admission: $2.50 adult, $1.50 senior(62+), $1.50 child (5-12)
❑   Miscellaneous: Boardwalk, museum shop. Nearby is the Idler
   Riverboat Restaurant (moored at Old Harbor village) - (269) 637-
   8435 - casual, New Orleans food for lunch or dinner.

Near South Pier Lighthouse - Great Lakes maritime history
showcase tells stories of vessels that passed through these waters
and the people who built them. They have displays featuring
lumber ships, luxury steamboats, Native Americans, fur traders,
and settlers. The kids' favorite part is the US Lifesaving Service
and Coast Guard Exhibit. See actual full-size rescue boats and
stations. The Boat Shed allows visitors to see and ask questions
about actual boats being constructed.

VAN BUREN STATE PARK

South Haven - *23960 Ruggels Road (south of town on Blue Star
Highway to entrance), 49090. Phone: (269) 637-2788. Web:
www.michigandnr.com/parksandtrails/parklist.asp   Admission:
$4.00 per vehicle.* Their main attraction is the large, duned beach
and swimming. A couple hundred campsites and hiking trails, too.

CURIOSITY KIDS' MUSEUM

415 Lake Blvd. (I-94 exit 27 north, downtown)

St. Joseph 49085

❑   Phone: (269) 983-CKID **Web: www.curiouskidsmuseum.org**
❑   Hours: Wednesday-Saturday 10:00am-5:00pm, Sunday Noon-
   5:00pm. (Extended summer hours - open Mondays and Tuesday
   also). Closed major holidays.

❑   Admission: $4.00 general (age 1+)

This fun place has hands-on learning and curiosity building exhibits. From Geo Kids & the Global Child to Dinomania, a TV studio or Bubbles...each exhibit has costumes to wear that match the type of activity. Serve customers in a diner or pick apples from trees, then process them and sell apple products at the market. A really cool room-sized space exhibit features a rocket with a NASA blast-off launch game, a mars rover table with mars surface, virtual planets to visit, a moon surface with extending arm for rock pickup, rocket propulsion blast off, and a mission control center to other areas of the museum. The "Ship" exhibit lets kids try their hand at navigating Great Lakes waters as a captain or pirate. Use coast guard signal flags, machines to load gear, and even build your own fish computer game. What fun!

SILVER BEACH

410 Vine Street & Lake Street (St. Joseph Train Station below the bluff), **St. Joseph** 49085

❑   Phone: (269) 985-9000 restaurant or (269) 983-7111 beach

Web: www.goswm.com/entertainment/silverbeach/go.htm

Silver Beach is below the bluff in downtown St. Joseph on Lake Street. It has a large parking lot, men's and women's bathhouses, park office and visitors' center, bike racks, playground equipment, volleyball nets and 1600-foot beach for swimmers (lifeguard on duty during the summer). This is one of the cleanest family beaches you'll want to visit.

❑   ROXY'S DEPOT RESTAURANT: Daily, Lunch and Dinner
      except Tuesdays. Moderate pricing. Very casual. In a historic,
      and still used, railroad station, you can try Rail Spikes (kabobs),
      Choo Choo Bread, Northwoods Chili (lumber campstyle) or a Silver
      Beach Chicken. The restaurant's motto: "A place in Time with
      People in Mind" - so relax...the next train isn't due for awhile."

THREE OAKS SPOKES BICYCLE MUSEUM

Three Oaks - *One Oak Street & South Central (old train station), 49128. Web: www.applecidercentury.com/bikemus.htm   Phone: (269) 756-3361 or (888) 877-2068. Hours: Daily 9:00am-5:00pm (call ahead on weekdays). Free Admission.* More than two dozen exhibits including an 1860's "boneshaker" to a "monster cruiser" (36 inch balloon tires). It's home to several antique and classic bicycles, information on the history of cycling, history of the city of Three Oaks, and railroad equipment, including a replica of the telegraph room that formerly occupied the train station. The tracks alongside the museum are still in service for Amtrak passenger trains. Available at the museum are maps of 12 area bike routes.

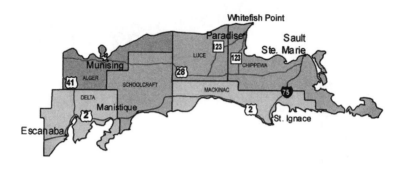

Chapter 7
Upper East Area

Our Favorites...

Great Lakes Shipwreck Museum

Museum of Ojibwa Culture

Pictured Rocks

Soo Locks & Boat Tours

Tahquamenon Falls

Freighter Passing Through Soo Locks

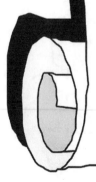

DELTA COUNTY HISTORICAL MUSEUM AND LIGHTHOUSE

(Ludington Park, the east end of Ludington Street)

Escanaba 49829

❑   Phone: (906) 786-3428 or (906) 786-3763
     Web: www.cr.nps.gov/maritime/light/escanaba.htm
❑   Hours: Daily 11:00am-7:00pm (June-Labor Day).
❑   Admission: $1.00 for lighthouse entrance, otherwise FREE.

Chronicles the development of the Upper Peninsula and Delta County, especially logging, railroads and shipping industries. An unusual display of a 1905 motor launch powered by only a one-cylinder engine is there also. Most folks make a point to go nearby to the restored 1867 Sandpoint Lighthouse. The keeper's house is furnished in period with winding stairs leading to the lighthouse tower's observation deck.

HIAWATHA NATIONAL FOREST

2727 North Lincoln Road (shorelines on lakes Huron, Michigan and Superior), **Escanaba** 49829

❑   Phone: (906) 786-4062 **Web: www.fs.fed.us/r9/hiawatha**
❑   Hours: Daily, open 24 hours.
❑   Miscellaneous: Point Iroquois Lighthouse & Maritime Museum, Sault Ste. Marie (906-437-5272).

The forest manages two uninhabited islands, Round and Government Islands which are are accessible by boat. Boating and other outdoor activities are allowed on Government Island. On the northern tip of the forest is the Grand Island National Recreation Area and Pictured Rocks National Lakeshore. Fishing for bass, pike, trout and walleye are good. Cross-country skiing and snowmobiling, camping, canoeing, hiking or bicycling trails, and swimming are available. There is a visitor's center (Munising, open business hours, daily) and cabin rentals too. Near Munising are the Bay Furnace ruins, the remains of an 1870's iron furnace.

FAYETTE STATE HISTORIC PARK (GHOST TOWN)

13700 13.25 Lane (US-2 to M-183 south)

Garden 49835

- ❑   Phone: (906) 644-2603
     Web: www.sos.state.mi.us/history/museum/musefaye/index.html
- ❑   Hours: Daily 9:00am-5:00pm (mid-April - October). Longer evening hours in the summer.
- ❑   Admission: $4.00 per vehicle.

Travel back in time over 100 years as you walk around a preserved industrial community. The Visitor's Center has a scale model of the city when it was buzzing and info on hiking trails around the complex. See docks where schooners tramped and mostly reconstructed iron furnaces and kilns along with support buildings for the then, booming, industry. Camping, boating, fishing, swimming, and winter sports are also available.

MICHIHISTRIGAN MINI-GOLF

US 2 (Halfway between SR 77 and SR 117)

Gould City 49838

- ❑   Phone: (800) 924-8873 **Web: www.michihistrigan.com**
- ❑   Hours: (Late May - late September)
- ❑   Admission: $4.00/round

Locals and visitors stay at cabins and campgrounds on the premises plus eat at the restaurant full of Michigan pride. By accident, the owners "threw" clay creating forms looking like the Upper and Lower Peninsula of Michigan. Using aerial photos of the state, they built a scale model of Michigan covering many acres. Each hole is a different important town. After 18 holes, fish the stocked "Great Lakes" around the course. Snowmobile in the winter right from your cabin. This is one-of-a-kind!

INDIAN LAKE STATE PARK

Manistique - *CR-442 West, 49854. Phone: (906) 341-2355. Web:* ***www.michigandnr.com/parksandtrails/parklist.asp*** *Admission: $4.00 per vehicle.* Located on Indian Lake, the 4th largest inland lake in the Upper Peninsula. It is 6 miles long and 3 miles wide. The lake was once called M'O'Nistique Lake. According to surveyor records dated 1850, Native Americans lived in log cabins near the outlet of the Lake. Camping/cabins, hiking, boating, fishing, swimming, bicycle trails, and winter sports.

PALMS BOOK STATE PARK (BIG SPRING)

Manistique - *(US 2 to M-149), 49854. Phone: (906) 341-2355. Web: www.michigandnr.com/parksandtrails/parklist.asp Admission: $4.00 per vehicle.* Beaching and boating are the only activities offered (no fishing or camping) but most come to board rafts and float across the wide spring. In the middle of the spring, look below at the huge trout being swished around by the hot springs flowing out from below - and yet the water is kept at 45 degrees constantly. The American Indians call this area "kitch-iti-kipi" or "Mirror of Heaven".

GRAND ISLAND SHIPWRECK TOURS

1204 Commercial Street (M-28 west of town - watch for signs)

Munising 49862

❑   Phone: (906) 387-4477 **Web: www.shipwrecktours.com**
❑   Admission: $23.00 adult, $10.00 child. Babies on lap FREE.
❑   Tours: (2 hours) @ 10:00am & 1:00pm (June, September, October). 10:00am, 1:00 & 4:00pm (July & August). Weather permitting.

When you realize that there are over 5000 shipwrecks on the bottom of the Great Lakes…it makes you probably wonder…why are you about to get on a boat? Don't worry, today you can safely voyage (and see) the underwater world of Lake Superior. Board Michigan's only glass-bottomed boat for your chance to see 3 of these wrecks. The clarity of the water is amazing and you will actually see an intact 136', 1860's cargo ship…right under your boat! It's a great idea to visit their website for the complete story (and photographs) of each boat that you will see. Also pass by the South Lighthouse and an original settlement on Grand Island.

PICTURED ROCKS CRUISES

(Boats depart from Munising's harbor - downtown)

Munising 49862

- ❑   Phone: (906) 387-2379 **Web: www.picturedrocks.com**
- ❑   Admission: $25.00 adult, $10.00 child (6-12).
- ❑   Tours: Departure times can vary - generally there are 2-7 trips per day (weather permitting). Call or visit website for schedule. (Memorial Day weekend - mid-October)

A picturesque 37-mile (3-hour) tour that takes you as close to the rocks as you can safely get (you can almost touch them). See colorful and majestic formations along Lake Superior's shore, some are sharp pointed and rise over 200 ft. high. The cruise passes points such as Lovers Leap, Grand Portal, Miners Castle and Indian Head. These rock sculptures are described with legend and lore by your captain.

PICTURED ROCKS NATIONAL LAKESHORE

M-28 and CR-H58

Munising 49862

- ❑   Phone: (906) 387-3700 **Web: www.nps.gov/piro**
- ❑   Hours: (Visitor Center) Monday-Saturday, 9:00am-4:30pm. (year-round). Daily with longer hours (mid-May through October)
- ❑   Miscellaneous: Camping, hiking trails, boating, fishing, swimming, winter sports. Michigan Great Outdoor Culture Tour mini-dramas and special talks/tours (summer).

Tens of thousands of acres of wilderness along over 40 miles of Lake Superior where ice-carved rocks resemble familiar shapes. Look for parts of ships or castle turrets. The rocks are also multi-colored from the minerals that seep into the soil. There are several awe-inspiring platform stops (some 200 foot cliffs) like Miners' Castle or Grand Sable Dunes. Rough camping and rugged backpack hiking is popular for those accustomed to it. There's also a Maritime Museum and Au Sable Light Station in the area.

WAGNER FALLS SCENIC SITE

Munising - *(a mile east of Munising on M-28), 49862. Phone: (906) 341-2355.* A beautiful waterfall is nestled amongst hemlock and virgin pine trees. ½ mile trail. No camping. No services.

GARLYN ZOOLOGICAL PARK

US 2 (40 minutes west of the Big Mac bridge)

Naubinway 49762

❑   Phone: (906) 477-1085, **Web: www.garlynzoo.com**
❑   Hours: Daily 11:00am-7:00pm (April-October). Saturday & Sunday Only 11:00am-5:00pm (November & December).
❑   Admission: $6.00 adult, $5.00 child (3-16), $20.00 family.
❑   Miscellaneous: Gift shop

The UP's biggest collection of animals (25+ species) that includes - black bears, white-tail deer, camels, wallabies, reindeer, llamas, cougar and coyote. Grain can be purchased to hand feed many of the animals.

MUSKALLONGE LAKE STATE PARK

Newberry - *(CR-407), 49868. Phone: (906) 658-3338. Web: www.michigandnr.com/parksandtrails/parklist.asp   Admission: $4.00 per vehicle.*   The 217-acre park is situated between the shores of Lake Superior and Muskallonge Lake and the area is well known for its forests, lakes, and streams. Camping, hiking, boating, fishing and swimming.

OSWALDS BEAR RANCH

Newberry - *Highway 37 (four miles north on M- 123 to Deer Park Road (H-37), 49868. Phone: (906) 293-3147. Hours: Daily 10:00am-8:00pm (Memorial Day weekend-Labor Day weekend). Daily until 6:00pm (September after Labor Day). Admission: $8.00 per carload. Web: www.exploringthenorth.com/oswald/bear.html* Like any proud father, Newberry resident Dean Oswald enjoys sharing the accomplishments of his 23 grown North American Black Bears with visitors. The bears roam freely within their three well maintained natural habitats. Sleeping areas, or "dens", are provided for the animals, as well as plenty of climbable trees and swimming pools. Visitors are able to walk around the entire perimeter of the habitat to view the bears in all areas. While strolling the grounds, Oswald will point to each and list their different personalities, names and even their weight. This is not a drive-thru, it's a walkabout.

GREAT LAKES SHIPWRECK MUSEUM

110 Whitefish Point Road (M-123 north to Whitefish Pt. Road for 11 miles), **Paradise** 49768

❑   Phone: (906) 492-3747 or (877) SHIPWRECK

   Web: www.shipwreckmuseum.com

❑   Hours: Daily 10:00am-6:00pm (May-October)

❑   Admission: $8.00 adult, $5.00 child (12 & under), $22.50 family.

A working lighthouse and restored keeper's quarters are the oldest on Lake Superior since 1849 and a crucial point on the Lake. Gordon Lightfoot's ballad, "The Wreck of the Edmund Fitzgerald", plays as you view the actual bell recovered from the ship! Displays of ships claimed by Lake Superior's storms include the Invincible 1816, the Independence (story of sailor "The Man Who Never Smiled Again" survivor), and the Edmund Fitzgerald in the 1970's (29 sailors aboard, all perished). See the short film on the history of the Edmund Fitzgerald and the raising of the bell honoring a request by surviving family members to establish a permanent memorial. Also, take the time to tour the Lighthouse Keeper's home to discover how a family survived with little contact with the nearby community. To add to what is already an extremely emotional visit, take a reflective walk out on to the boardwalk and beach of Whitefish Point - the "Graveyard of the Great Lakes" as you watch large freighters fight the turbulent waters. Please make the trip to Whitefish Point to see this...we were very "moved" by this visit!

TAHQUAMENON FALLS STATE PARK

41382 West M-123 (Off SR 123, then west 5-12 miles. Watch for entrance signs), **Paradise** 49768

- ❑ Phone: (906) 492-3415 or (800) 44-PARKS
     Web: www.michigandnr.com/parksandtrails/parklist.asp
- ❑ Hours: Daily, Dawn to Dusk.
- ❑ Admission: $4.00 per vehicle
- ❑ Miscellaneous: Modern camping near falls or on river.
     Picnicking. Hiking trails. Fishing. Canoeing. Snowmobiling,
     snowshoeing, cross-country skiing. Gift shop, snack bar & Camp
     33 Restaurant at Upper Falls.

This is the land of Longfellow's Hiawatha - "by the rushing Tahquamenaw" Hiawatha built his canoe.   On the hiking trails, moose, balk eagles, black bear, coyotes, otter, deer, fox, porcupine, beaver and mink may be occasionally spotted. The short 4/10 of a mile walk out to the Upper Falls reveals one of the largest waterfalls east of the Mississippi.   Nearly 50 feet tall and more than 200 feet across, its amber color is a pleasing site. The amber color of the water is not from mud or rust - discover what causes it. The Lower Falls are four miles downstream. They are a series of five smaller falls and rapids cascading around an island. For the best photo-ops, we suggest wide angle lens (or purchase great postcards at the gift shop). May we suggest a stop for a bite to eat at Camp 33 Restaurant.   The replica 1950 logging camp has two focal points - the beautifully displayed animal skins and the warm fireplace.   This is a great place to try UP specialties like whitefish or pasties (*pronounced "pass-tees" - so you'll sound like a local!*).

MUSEUM SHIP VALLEY CAMP

501 East Water Street (east of the locks - waterfront)

Sault Ste. Marie 49783

- ❑ Phone: (906) 632-3658 or (888) 744-7867
     Web: www.thevalleycamp.com
- ❑ Hours: Daily 10:00am-6:00pm (mid- May – June & September –
     mid-October). Extended hours July & August.
- ❑ Admission: $8.00 adult, $4.00 child (6-16).

Walk-in tours are offered of the 1917 steam powered freighter containing the world's largest Great Lakes maritime museum. Many come to see the Edmund Fitzgerald Exhibit - two lifeboats from the actual boat along with multimedia shows of the tragic event. Several mechanical (dormant) parts of the ship are touchable. A long aquarium is along one wall with marine life found in the area. After seeing the large freighters and their crew go through the locks, kids will love to see an actual ship's pilot house, dining rooms and crew's quarters.

RIVER OF HISTORY MUSEUM

209 East Portage Avenue (1st floor of restored Federal Building)

Sault Ste. Marie 49783

- ❑ Phone: (906) 632-1999
- ❑ Hours: Monday-Saturday 10:00am-5:00pm. Sunday Noon-5:00pm (mid-May to mid-October).
- ❑ Admission: $1.50 - $3.00 (age 8+).

St. Mary's River history through exhibit galleries of sight and sound. Join the River as she tells her story of the events she has witnessed, people she has met, and changes wrought along her shores and waters. Follow Chippewa Indians to French fur traders to modern industry. The sound of locks and canals being built is one of the audio enhanced exhibits.

SOO LOCKS PARK

Downtown. Portage Avenue (Within view of International Bridge. Follow signs off I-75), **Sault Ste. Marie 49783**

- ❑ Phone: (906) 632-2394
  Web: www.lre.usace.army.mil/SOO/soohmpg.html
- ❑ Hours: Daily 7:00am-11:00pm (mid-May to November 1).
- ❑ Admission: FREE
- ❑ Miscellaneous: Run by the US Army Corp of Engineers. To view live pictures of the Soo Locks Visit on their website. Theater showing film on history of operations.

The highlights here are:

❑ OBSERVATION PLATFORM - 2nd level or Riverside view of the locks. It's unbelievable how actual freight ships move precisely into concrete locks and then are lowered or raised to the level of the next part of the lake. How do they do it? (Learn how…and they do not use pumps). Now the longest in the world, they are still the largest waterway traffic system on earth. A public address system lets visitors know which vessels are coming through the locks and what their size, cargo, nationality and destination are.

❑ WORKING MODEL OF A LOCK (with real water moving a model boat) is inside the museum building and best to watch before outdoor viewing.

Dress appropriately for weather outside because you'll want to watch the large freighters rise up in the water before your eyes!

SOO LOCKS BOAT TOURS

Dock #1: 1157 E. Portage Ave; Dock #2: 515 E. Portage Ave.

Sault Ste. Marie 49783

❑ Phone: (906) 632-6301 or (800) 432-6301 **Web: www.soolocks.com**
❑ Hours: Daily 10:00am-6:30pm (mid-May to mid-October). Later hours on summer weekends.
❑ Admission: $18.00 adult, $16.00 student (13-18), $8.50 child (4-12).

While watching the ships go through the locks and enjoying the park is fun, it's much more thrilling to actually go THROUGH the locks on a ship. On the Soo Locks Tour, you'll be in for a two-hour live narrated excursion that will actually take you through the Locks, right alongside the big freighters. Your tour boat will ride the water as it is raised twenty-one feet, straight up, to the level of Lake Superior. You will then cruise under the International Bridge and railroad bridge before crossing into Canadian waters where you'll see one of Canada's largest steel plants in operation. You will return to the lower harbor through the historic "newly restored" Canadian Lock and cruise past the St. Mary's Rapids.

TOWER OF HISTORY

326 East Portage Ave (east of the locks), **Sault Ste. Marie** 49783

- ❑ Phone: (906) 632-3658 or (888) 744-7867
  Web: www.towerofhistory.com
- ❑ Hours: Daily 10:00am-6:00pm. (mid-May – mid-October)
- ❑ Admission: $4.00 adult, $2.00 child (6-16).

A 21-story tower offering a panoramic view of the Soo Locks, the St. Mary's River Rapids, and many historical homes. The tower museum has Native American artifacts and a video show depicting the history of the Great Lakes and Sault Ste. Marie. You ride to the top by elevator.

SENEY NATIONAL WILDLIFE REFUGE

Seney - *(M-77, 5 miles south of Seney), 49883. Phone: (906) 586-9851. Web: www.exploringthenorth.com/seney/seney.html Hours: Daily 9:00am - 5:00pm (mid-May - mid-October). Admission: FREE.* Take the family on a driving journey (7 miles, self-guided, starts at Visitor's Center parking lot) that allows the chance to see wildlife such as: nesting loons, cranes, swans, Canadian geese, bald eagles, deer, and others. An orientation slide show is shown every half hour. This show introduces viewers to the variety of wildlife found on the Refuge, as well as management techniques. The center is complete with a natural history book store and children's touch table. Over 70 miles of trails are also available for your hiking adventures.

TOONERVILLE TROLLEY & RIVERBOAT RIDE

Soo Junction Road (North off M-28 - Watch for signs to CR-38)

Soo Junction 49868

- ❑ Phone: (906) 876-2311 or (888) 778-7246
  Web: www.destinationmichigan.com/toonerville-trolley.html
- ❑ Hours: Times vary - call ahead for schedule (mid-June - early October). Train only excursions Tuesday-Saturday (mid-June-August only)

❑   Admission: (Train & Riverboat - 6 1/2 hours) $28.00 adult,
      $13.00 child (6-15). (Train only - 1 3/4 hours) $12.00 adult,
      $6.00 child (6-15). Kids 5 and under are FREE.

Nearly a day (a 6½ hour tour) awaits you as you journey to see
Michigan's largest falls (50' high), The Tahquamenon Falls (see
separate listing). Start with a 5 mile, 35 minute narrow gauge rail
trip, and then connect with a narrated 21-mile riverboat cruise with
lots of chances to see area wildlife. Once the boat docks, take a
short walking trip to see the falls. What's really neat is that the
falls are undisturbed and really do look like Niagara Falls might
have looked to early settlers (smaller, but still very coool!). The
train only tour does not go to the Falls.

CASTLE ROCK

Castle Rock Road (I-75 to exit 348)

St. Ignace 49781

❑   Phone: (906) 643-8268
      Web: www.stignace.com/attractions/castlerock/
❑   Hours: Daily 9:00am-9:00pm. (early May to mid-October)

See and climb (189 steps) the legendary Castle Rock (a limestone
"sea stack" - nearly 200 feet tall) that Native Americans once used
as a lookout. Be sure to check out Paul Bunyan and Babe! A great
piece of history and what a view for a half dollar! There are lots of
Native American gifts in the shop below. This is a difficult climb,
aerobically, so take your time and don't plan on carrying the kids
up...everyone will have to climb the stairs on their own (you'll feel
like "Rocky" when you reach the top)! Don't worry, the walk down
is much easier.

DEER RANCH

St. Ignace - *1510 US Highway 2 West (US 2, 4 miles west of Big
Mac Bridge), 49781.* **Web: www.deerranch.com/main.cgi** *Phone:
(906) 643-7760. Hours: 9:00am – ½hour before dusk. (May-
November) Admission: $3.00 (age 5+).* Gift Shop featuring Deer
skin products including many sizes of moccasins. They have a
nature trail where you can feed and photograph native Michigan
Whitetail Deer and fawns.

MUSEUM OF OJIBWA CULTURE

500-566 North State Street (at the north end of the boardwalk, downtown, across from waterfront), **St. Ignace** 49781

❑   Phone: (906) 643-9161

   Web: www.stignace.com/attractions/ojibwa

❑   Hours: Monday-Saturday 11:00am-5:00pm, Sunday 10:30am-
   5:00pm. (Memorial weekend - late June). Daily 10:00am-8:00pm
   (Late June-Labor Day). Monday-Saturday, 11:00am-5:00pm,
   Sunday 10:30am-5:00pm. (Labor Day - mid-October)

❑   Admission: $1.00-$2.00 general, $5.00 family.

❑   Miscellaneous: Native American Museum Store. Marquette
   Mission Park adjacent is supposed site of grave of missionary
   Father Marquette and also site of archeological discoveries.

The museum is housed in Father Marquette's French Jesuit Mission Church and dedicated to his focus on Ojibwa Indians, the first inhabitants of this region. Learn traditions of the peoples through an 8-minute video presentation that relates the importance of the Ojibwa family, dioramas of an Ojibwa family network, and frequent demonstrations by Native American interpreters (esp. outside in the giant long house or the realistic teepee with weaved bark mats). There is a "kid-sized" longhouse indoors where kids can play, then walk diagonally over to the Interactive Kids Area: felt play, dark boxes, color drawings of Ojibwa symbols or make a paper canoe or scroll stories. The easy to understand descriptions with every display or activity really help you understand their way of life...they often relate it to our modern way of life.

MYSTERY SPOT

150 Martin Lake Road (US-2 West, 5 miles west of Mackinac Bridge), **St. Ignace** 49781

❑   Phone: (906) 643-8322

   Web: www.stignace.com/attractions/mysteryspot/

❑   Hours: Daily 8:00am-9:00pm (mid June - Labor Day). Daily
   9:00am-7:00pm (after Labor Day - late October & mid-May to
   mid-June)

❑   Admission: Average $4.00 (age 5+).

For updates visit our website: www.kidslovepublications.com

O.K. - Illusion or reality. Reality or illusion. That's up for you to decide, but one thing's for sure…you'll sure have fun doing it. See the laws of physics as we know them…and why they don't apply to the "Mystery Spot". The kids will love this science lesson. There's also mini-golf and a maze on the premises.

STRAITS STATE PARK

St. Ignace - *720 Church Street (I-75, exit onto US-2 East), 49781.* *Web: www.michigandnr.com/parksandtrails/Parklist.asp Phone: (906) 643-8620. Season : March thru October. Admission: $4.00 per vehicle.* Great views from an observation platform of the Mackinac Bridge and the Straits of Mackinac. Camping/mini-cabins, picnicking, boating, fishing, swimming and winter sports. A visitor's center highlights Father Marquette exploration in the area. The Father Marquette National Memorial tells the story of that 17th-century missionary-explorer and the meeting of French and Native American cultures deep in the North American wilderness. Current attractions include the National Memorial and an outdoor interpretive trail.

TOTEM VILLAGE

St. Ignace - *1230 US Highway 2 West (US 2, 2 miles west of Big Mac Bridge), 49781. Phone: (989) 643-8888. Hours: Open daily May-October. Small admission charge.* They've set this place up for picture taking. For example, pose your family beside a teepee or next to a giant totem pole. The focus is on scientifically studied lifestyles of the Indian culture and significant contributions of Upper Peninsula people. There's a model of the 1st American Lake Superior sailing ship, a replica of Fort Fond du Lac, a Scale model of the first Soo Locks, a trading post, an old-time sugar camp and live bobcats, foxes and reindeer.

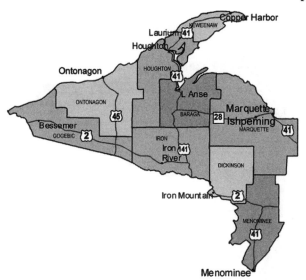

Chapter 8
Upper West Area

Our Favorites...

Copper Harbor Lighthouse

Copper & Iron Mines

Michigan Iron Industry Museum

National & State Parks

U.P. Children's Museum

BARAGA STATE PARK

Baraga - *1300 US-41 South, 49908. Phone: (906) 353 - 6558. Web: www.michigandnr.com/parksandtrails/parklist.asp   Admission: $4.00 per vehicle.* Along the Keweenaw Bay offers modern and rough camping, beach with swimming (water doesn't get much above 50 degrees though), boating, fishing, and hiking.

HANKA HOMESTEAD MUSEUM

Baraga - *Arnheim Road (7 miles west of US 41), 49908. Phone: (906) 353-7116. Hours: Tuesday, Thursday, Saturday & Sunday from 1:00-4:00pm (Memorial Day to mid-October). Donations accepted.* A 100 year old Finnish farming home restored to a 1920's appearance. Guided tours explain life for immigrants starting out in America.

BRIMLEY STATE PARK

Brimley - *9200 West 6 Mile Rd (I-75, take M-28 west to M-221), 49715. Web: www.michigandnr.com/parksandtrails/parklist.asp Phone: (906) 248-3422. Admission: $4.00 per vehicle.* Brimley State Park provides recreational opportunities along the beautiful shore of Lake Superior's Whitefish Bay. Home to the Point Iroquois Lighthouse Station. Available for camping, boating, fishing and swimming.

COPPERTOWN USA MUSEUM

109 Red Jacket Road (2 blocks west of US-41)

Calumet 49913

❑   Phone: (906) 337-4354
     Web: http://uppermichigan.com/coppertown/main.html
❑   Hours: Monday-Saturday 10:00am-5:00pm (mid-June to mid-
     October). Sunday 12:30-4:00pm (in July & August).
❑   Admission: $1.00-$3.00 per person.

Michigan's Copper Industry began thousands of years ago when ancient miners chipped away at exposed veins of pure copper with huge hammerstones. Tools and techniques of mining advanced considerably in the centuries that followed and Coppertown's Mining Museum traces the evolution of miners. More than a copper museum, but rather a Visitor's Center (even includes a walk-in, simulated copper mine) for the Keweenaw Peninsula. See how copper mining has evolved from the early Native Americans who mined with stone hammers to the techniques used during the "Copper Rush". Exhibits include: Early Miners, Two Man Drill, Foundry - Casting Metal Products, The Hospital, Sheffield Pump Car and Loading Ore Cars.

IRON COUNTY MUSEUM

Museum Drive (off M-189 to CR-424)

Caspian 49915

- ❑   Phone: (906) 265-2617 **Web: www.ironcountymuseum.com**
- ❑   Hours: Weekdays, 8:30am-2:00pm (May), Monday-Saturday & Holidays 9:00am-5:00pm, Sunday 1:00-5:00pm (Summer). Monday-Saturday, 10:00am-4:00pm (September)
- ❑   Admission: $5.00 adult, $2.50 child (5-18)

A historic, educational site that has 20 buildings including pioneers' cabins, a logging camp, train depot, and schoolhouse. The community was built here because of the Caspian Mine (during its peak production, it was the area's largest producer of iron ore). The Headframe, or hoisting building, one of the earliest of its type, has been placed on The National Register of Historic Places. The very rare exhibit is the Monigal Miniature lumber camp, over 80 feet long and reputed to be the "largest in the world." The Mining Halls contain early mining tools and equipment, several glass dioramas showing underground ore bodies, tramming tunnels and mine levels, a memorial to the 562 miners killed, and the development of unions. One of the homes featured was the home of Carrie Jacobs-Bond who was a nationally known composer of the 19th Century. Composing over 200 songs, her hits included "I Love You Truly" and "Perfect Day". This success allowed her to become the first female composer to earn a million dollars.

LAUGHING WHITEFISH FALLS SCENIC SITE

Cedar River - *N7670 Highway, M-35, 49813. Phone: (906) 863-9747. Web: www.michigandnr.com/parksandtrails/parklist.asp* One of the Upper Peninsula's many impressive waterfalls. Picnic area, foot trails, and 3 observation decks overlooking the falls. No camping or services.

WELLS STATE PARK

Cedar River - *N7670 Highway M-35, 49813. Phone: (906) 863-9747. Web: www.michigandnr.com/parksandtrails/parklist.asp Admission: $4.00 per vehicle.* J.W. Wells State Park is located on Green Bay approximately 30 miles south of Escanaba, 25 miles north of Menominee or one mile south of Cedar River. Its 678 acres include a 3 mile shoreline with a beautiful sandy beach for swimming, a large picnic area, campground and rustic cabins that are available to rent year round. There are seven miles of trails to hike in summer and cross-country ski in the winter. Also boating, fishing, and bicycle trails.

CRAIG LAKE STATE PARK

Champion - *(8 miles West of Van Riper State Park-on US-41 / M-28). 49814. Web: www.michigandnr.com/parksandtrails/parklist.asp Phone: (906) 339-4461.* Craig Lake is a wilderness area (the most remote state park in the system) and access into the park is somewhat of an adventure. Only vehicles with high ground clearance are recommended due to the rocky conditions of the road. But if you're really into "getting away from it all" the park contains six lakes for fishing and a variety of wildlife such as black bear, deer, loons, beaver, and part of the Upper Peninsula moose herd.

VAN RIPER STATE PARK

Champion - *SR 41 (west of town), 49814. Phone: (906) 339-4461. Web: www.michigandnr.com/parksandtrails/parklist.asp Admission: $4.00 per vehicle.* This 1,200 acre park contains one-half mile of frontage on the east end of Lake Michigamme with a fine sand beach. The water temperature is generally moderate - a pleasant change from Lake Superior temperatures. There is also one and one-half miles of frontage on the Peshekee River.

Camping, boating, and swimming are here but most come hiking to look for Canadian moose imported to this park by helicopters. Cabins and winter sports are also available.

COPPER HARBOR LIGHTHOUSE BOAT TOURS

(Copper Harbor Marina, 1/4 mile west of Copper Harbor on M-26)

Copper Harbor 49918

❑　Phone: (906) 289-4966
　　Web: www.copperharborlighthouse.com
❑　Admission: $12.00 adult, $7.00 child (12 and under). Children sitting on laps are FREE.
❑　Tours: Narrated, 60-90 minutes. Daily every two hours 10:00am - 5:00pm and are subject to weather conditions. (Memorial Day - September)

The only way to see the Copper Harbor Lighthouse (which is actually a part of the Fort Wilkins State Park) is by boat tour. Once ashore, short walking paths wind you among historic signposts and shipwreck artifacts. Such items include the keel of the first shipwreck on Lake Superior, the John Jacob Astor, which was blown onto the rocky shores of Copper harbor in the fall of 1844 while attempting to deliver supplies to those who would spend the winter here. You will then tour the original lightkeeper's dwelling, the oldest remaining lighthouse structure on Lake Superior, which preceded the 1866 building. Recently renovated and made into a lighthouse museum, the dwelling features maritime exhibits including a fourth order Fresnel lens. You can ask questions or listen to stories from the staff historian while enjoying interactive exhibits which tell of lighthouse construction on the Great Lakes. The daily lives of these keepers become real while walking among the period furnishings and hearing actual stories of the people who worked in the United States Lighthouse Service. During this narrated tour, you'll have the chance to not only see the lighthouse, but also the first real attempts at creating a copper mine shaft (dates back to the 1840's).

DELAWARE COPPER MINE TOUR

(12 miles south on US 41), **Copper Harbor** 49918

❑   Phone: (906) 289-4688

   www.copperharbor.org/Business/ads/delawaremine/home.html

❑   Admission: ~$8.00 adult/Half Price child (age 6+).

❑   Tours: Self-guided tours. Daily 10:00am - 5:00pm (mid-May to
    mid-June and September to mid-October). Guided tours depart
    every 20 minutes Daily, 10:00 am - 6:00 pm. (July-August)

This mid-1800's copper mine offers a 45 minute underground
walking tour. The tour will take you down Shaft No. 1 to the first
level (at a depth of 110 ft.) where you'll see pure veins of copper
exposed. Above ground, take the walking trails to the mine ruins,
sawmill, large antique engine display, and train collection featuring
"G" scale and 7 1/2" gauge. Stop by the zoo to visit the miniature
deer or search the rock piles of souvenir copper. Dress for 45-50
degree F. temperatures.

FORT WILKINS HISTORIC STATE PARK

US-41 East, **Copper Harbor** 49918

❑   Phone: (906) 289-4215

   Web: www.michigandnr.com/parksandtrails/parklist.asp

❑   Admission: $4.00 per vehicle.

❑   Hours: Daily 8:00am to dusk (mid-May through mid-October)

Today, Fort Wilkins is a well-preserved example of mid-19th
century army life on the northern frontier. Through Fort Wilkins'
exhibits, audiovisual programs and living history interpretation,
visitors may explore the daily routine of military service,
experience with soldiers' families the hardships of frontier isolation
and discover the life ways of another era. Attractions include 19
restored buildings, costumed interpreters, copper mining sites,
evening slide programs, camping and picnicking. The fort was
built to protect copper miners from local tribes - completely made
from wood. The site also includes the Copper Harbor Lighthouse
with a restored 1848 lightkeeper's dwelling, 1866 lighthouse, 1933
steel light tower and interpretive trails (see separate listing). The
lighthouse is reached by boat.

BEWABIC STATE PARK

Crystal Falls - *1933 US-2 West, 49920. Phone: (906) 875-3324. Web: www.michigandnr.com/parksandtrails/parklist.asp Admission: $4.00 per vehicle.* Camping, hiking trails, boating, fishing, and swimming available. Home to virgin woodlands and a wood bridge to the island.

ADVENTURE COPPER MINE

200 Adventure Road (12 miles east of Ontonagon, off SR38)

Greenland 49929

❑   Phone: (906) 883-3371

     Web: www.exploringthenorth.com/mine/venture.html

❑   Hours: Daily, 9:00am-6:00pm. (Memorial Day weekend - end of color season)

❑   Tours: Guided one hour, 1/4 mile tour. Email or call for current admission prices.

❑   Miscellaneous: Gift Shop with copper crafts. Camping with hookups. Snowmobiling area and underground tours. A jacket and walking shoes are recommended.

Put on your hard hat for the beginning of your tour ride to the mine entrance. Turn on the miner's light as you follow the path 300 feet underground walking through passages worked by miners over 100 years ago. You'll see large clusters of pure copper with silver threads and quartz and calcite crystals. Look down into open mine shafts that run 100's of feet into the earth. The second half of your tour, you emerge from the depths of the mine onto an overlook bluff for a great view of the distant hills and valleys.

MCCLAIN STATE PARK

Hancock - *M-203 West, 49930. Phone: (906) 482-0278. Web: www.michigandnr.com/parksandtrails/parklist.asp Admission: $4.00 per vehicle.* The sunsets at McLain State Park are spectacular and the view of the lighthouse is magnificent. Camping/cabins, hiking, boating, fishing, swimming and winter sports.

QUINCY MINE HOIST

201 Royce Road (along US-41 - part of Keweenaw Peninsula
National Park), **Hancock** 49930

❑   Phone: (906) 482-5569 or (906) 482-3101
     Web: www.quincymine.com
❑   Hours: Monday-Saturday 8:30am-7:00pm. Sunday 12:30pm-
     7:00pm (Summer). Shorter hours Spring & Fall. Call for details.
     Open (mid-May – October)
❑   Admission: (Surface & Underground Tour) $12.50 adult, $7.00 child
     (6-12). (Surface & Tram Ride) $7.50 adult, $3.50 child (6-12).
❑   Tours: Depart every half hour. Hard hats and warm coats are
     provided.
❑   Miscellaneous: Gift shop. As you can expect, this tour might not
     be suitable for younger children who don't like dark places, loud
     noises, etc., however, there are no small or confined spaces.

The "hoist" is where all the ore was hauled to the surface, and what
you will see is the world's largest. The shaft started in the mid-
1800's and operated until the 1960's, eventually reaching a depth
of over 10,000 feet! As you can imagine, at this depth it can get
quite "hot" (with temperatures averaging over 90 degrees F.). On
the outside, you can view the shafthouse which is over 150 feet tall
and has hauled millions of pounds of copper to the surface. You
can also travel over 2000 feet into the hill to view portions of the
mine that were carved during the Civil War era.

ISLE ROYALE NATIONAL PARK

800 East Lakeshore Drive (only accessible by boat or seaplane)

Houghton 49931

❑   Phone: (906) 482-0984 **Web: www.isleroyale.com/isle.htm**
❑   Hours: (mid-April to October)
❑   Miscellaneous: Isle Royale Queen (906-289-4437) offers
     summertime boat trips (4 ½ hours) from Copper Harbor and the
     Ranger III leaves Houghton summer times (6 ½ hours). There's
     also a seaplane that floats over to the Isle.

The nation's only island national park is where roughed campers (no campfires permitted) or woodsy lodgers (only one on the entire island) gravitate. Backpacking hiking, canoeing, charter fishing trips or sightseeing trips are available. With 99 percent of the island still wilderness, many opt for marked trails like Greenstone, Minong, Mt. Franklin, Mt. Ojibwa, or the Rock Harbor Lighthouse. The trails are about 45 minutes in length along cliffs, paths of fir and wildflowers, and past many moose, wolves and beavers. Try to visit Siskiwit Lake's Ryan Island, the largest island on the largest freshwater lake in the world!

CORNISH PUMPING ENGINE AND MINING MUSEUM

Iron Mountain - *(2 blocks west of US-2 on Kent Street), 49801. Phone: (906) 774-1086. Hours: Monday-Saturday 9:00am-5:00pm. Sunday, Noon-4:00pm. (May-October). Admission: $2.00-$4.00 (age 8+).* A discounted combo admission is offered with the Menominee Range Museum. One of the largest steam pump engines built in North America (the flywheel is 40 feet in diameter and weighs 160 tons) plus displays of mining equipment and artifacts related to mining history.

MILLIE MINE BAT CAVE

Iron Mountain - *(Just off East A on Park), 49801. Phone: (906) 774-5480. FREE admission. Always open. Closed during snow months.* Batcave...hummm...must be Batman's home right? Well, not really, but this IS the second largest (known in the North America) home for hibernating bats! The mine is 350 feet deep that has several rooms with a consistent temperature of 40 degrees...just perfect for the furry little creatures. You'll find a walking path, benches, and informational plaques. The bats come in for the winter in September and leave in April (if you're not scared...these are wonderful viewing times). There is a "bat cage" preventing humans from entering the depths of the cave but still allowing bats the freedom to move in and out.

BLACK RIVER NATIONAL FOREST SCENIC BYWAY

Ironwood - *County Road 513 (US 2/SR 28 to CR 513), 49938. Phone: (906) 667-0261.* See the Black River with several beautiful waterfalls. Five waterfalls are 20 to 40 feet high and are named for their characteristics like Sandstone (red rock riverbed), Gorge, and Conglomerate (rock ledges). Paved sidewalks and a kid-friendly swinging bridge, and a pass by Ski Flying Hill (only one in the states) where you might see ski flying (jumping) events (especially late January).

OTTAWA NATIONAL FOREST

(Almost 1 million acres off US 2)

Ironwood 49938

❑ Phone: (906) 932-1330 Visitor Center
    Web: www.fs.fed.us/r9/ottawa
❑ Hours: Dawn to dusk.

More than 50,000 acres of the expanse are designated wilderness with barely untouched lakes and trees. With more than 35 waterfalls within the forest, many plan to take the marked trails to catch a view. The 500 lakes and 2000 miles of rivers provide good fishing for trout and salmon. When the ground freezes, many try snowmobiling, ice fishing and cross-country skiing. In Watersmeet there are two facilities - The J.W. Tourney Forest Nursery and Visitors Center (US-2 and US-45). Great Lakes tree seed and stock are supplied here, as well as, exhibits, audiovisual programs and naturalist-led group walks and talks. Camping, hiking, boating and swimming are also available. Lake Gogebic State Park is included as part of the forest.

DA YOOPERS TOURIST TRAP

490 North Steel Street (US 41)

Ishpeming 49849

❑ Phone: (906) 485-5595 **Web: www.dayoopers.com**
❑ Hours: Daily 9:00am-9:00pm (Memorial Day-September). Times vary rest of the year.
❑ Admission: FREE

The UP life is "unique" to say the least. When talking to locals, we often heard that one of the greatest things about living up here is that you have time for a hobby *(since you can only work 6 months a year)*. Well, "Da Yoopers" actually started as a singing group that promoted the "uniqueness" of this life around the state. They have fun "poking fun" and you'll see and hear it all at the "tourist trap". Not only can you learn how to really talk like a Yooper... but where else will you ever see a snowmmobile that was built for "summer" use, a chainsaw the size of an 18-wheeler (in the Guinness Book...world's largest, really), or the world's largest firing rifle? We agree, be sure to pick up some "Da Yoopers" music before you leave to really get the most from your UP adventure.

TILDEN OPEN PIT MINE TOURS

Ishpeming - *(depart from Ishpeming Chamber of Commerce), 49849. Phone: (906) 486-4841. Admission: $6.00/person. Tours: (Reservations required). Tuesday-Saturday @ Noon (mid-June to mid-August). Miscellaneous: For safety reasons no dresses, skirts, open-toed shoes, or children under age 10 are permitted on this tour.* One thing you'll know for sure after completing this tour is that the iron industry in Michigan is still very much a thriving business. We suggest to go to the Michigan Iron Industry Museum (see separate listing) first to see how it WAS mined. Then, see this huge pit (that is over 500 feet deep!) where the iron ore is mined and refined by some of the largest mining equipment in the world. (We really think it would be fun if they painted "Tonka" on the sides of the equipment!)

US NATIONAL SKI HALL OF FAME AND MUSEUM

Ishpeming - *(US 41 between Second and Third Streets), 49849. Phone: (906) 485-6323.* **Web: *http://skihall.com/www/home.php*** *Hours: Monday-Saturday 10:00am-5:00pm. Admission: $1.00-$3.00 (age 10+).* Watch an 18 minute orientation tape, then explore the gallery of greats of American skiing. Also study the development of the sport through trophies, photos, old grooming equipment and a cable car.

HOUGHTON COUNTY HISTORICAL MUSEUM CAMPUS

5500 State Route 26 (after crossing the Portage Lake Lift bridge, head north on M-26), **Lake Linden** 49945

❑   Phone: (906) 296-4121 **Web: www.habitant.org/houghton**
❑   Hours: Monday-Saturday 10:00am-4:30pm, Sunday Noon-4:00pm (June-September).
❑   Admission: $5.00 adult, $3.00 senior (65+), $3.00 student (12-18), $1.00 child (6-11).

Eight historic buildings including themes of a Country Kitchen, Grandma's Room, Medicinal, Mining Room and Forestry Room. Kids will like trying to figure out what "bull ladle", "fanny", or "kibble" are. There's also a schoolhouse, log cabin, tool shop, church, railroad depot and Copperland sculptures.

LAKE GOGEBIC STATE PARK

Marenisco - *N9995 State Highway M-64 (M-64 between US-2 & M-28), 49947. Web: www.michigandnr.com/parksandtrails/parklist.asp Phone: (906) 842-3341. Admission: $4.00 per vehicle.* Enjoy shaded, waterfront camping on the shore of Lake Gogebic, the largest inland lake in the Upper Peninsula.   Sandy beach, picnic area, boating, fishing.

MARQUETTE COUNTY HISTORICAL MUSEUM

Marquette - *213 North Front Street, 49855. Phone: (906) 226-3571. Web: www.marquettecohistory.org Hours: Monday-Friday 10:00am-5:00pm. Admission: $1.00-$3.00 (over 12).* A pioneer focus on mining and lumbering with changing exhibits of artifacts. Loads of rooms filled with colorful artifacts and stories that bring local history to life…with ease.

MARQUETTE MARITIME MUSEUM

(East Ridge and Lakeshore Blvd.), **Marquette** 49855

❑   Phone: (906) 226-2006 **Web: www.mqtmaritimemuseum.com**
❑   Hours: Daily 10:00am-5:00 pm (day after Memorial Day-September).
❑   Admission: General $3.00 (over 12 only).

❑   Miscellaneous: Lighthouse tours nearby.

Marquette and Lake Superior maritime heritage with antique charts, boats and models. It preserves the unique romance, glamour, and history of the days when topsail schooners, Mackinac boats, fur trading canoes, work-a-day fish tugs, lumber hookers, and mighty steam barges plied the lakes. Children love the hands-on exhibits and recreated dockside offices of a commercial fishing and passenger freight companies. Ever seen a fishing shanty kids?

MARQUETTE MOUNTAIN SKI AREA

Marquette - *4501 County Road 553, 49855. Phone: (800) 944-SNOW.* **Web: *www.marquettemountain.com*** 8 runs, rental equipment, babysitting, and lessons are available. Great children's programs for all skill levels. Also now offering, Ski-by-the-hour rates as low as $4.00/hour (2-hour minimum), and Sunday Family Days.

PRESQUE ISLE PARK

Marquette - *Lakeshore Blvd, 49855. Phone: (906) 228-0461 or (800) 544-4321. Hours: Daily 7:00am-11:00pm. FREE admission.* A beautiful 300+ acre park that is located on a rock peninsula on Lake Superior. Some interesting trivia..."Presque Isle" means "almost an island". As you can imagine, the views are incredible with many lookouts, nature trails along bogs (in winter they are cross-country skiing or snowshoeing trails), and picnic facilities. An outdoor pool and waterslide (160') are also available (FREE admission) in the summer.

UPPER PENINSULA CHILDREN'S MUSEUM

123 West Baraga Avenue

Marquette 49855

❑   Phone: (906) 226-3911 **Web: www.upcmkids.org**

❑   Hours: Monday-Wednesday & Saturday 10:00am-6:00pm.
      Thursday 10:00-7:30pm. Friday 10:00am-8:00pm. Sunday Noon-5:00pm.

❑   Admission: $4.50 adult, $3.50 child (2-17).

A very family friendly place that features exhibits that were suggested by local area kids. Some of the fun programs available *(subject to change)* include:

- ❑   WHERE'S YOUR WATER? Crawl through the drain field and into an aquifer to explore life under a pond. Upon your return to the "real world", use microscopes and computers to examine water elements first hand. Touch tank.
- ❑   WONDER GROUND gives you a glimpse of the underground by digging.
- ❑   ALL ABOARD! RECYCLO-TORIUM, a fun filled creation station filled with different "stuff" to take apart, reassemble and just plain create.
- ❑   Don't forget MICROSOCIETY! Stroll down the kid-sized street and shop at all the wacky businesses along Main Street, USA.
- ❑   In the INCREDIBLE JOURNEY walk thru giant-size parts of the body.

MICHIGAN IRON INDUSTRY MUSEUM

73 Forge Road (on Forge Road off County Road 492)

Negaunee 49866

- ❑   Phone: (906) 475-7857
     Web: www.michiganhistory.org/museum/museiron/index.html
- ❑   Hours: Daily 9:30am-4:30pm (May-October).
- ❑   Admission: FREE

The theme is set for this museum with the "step back in time" approach. Today, the museum tells the story of Michigan's three iron ranges and the people who worked them, through museum exhibits, audio visual programs, and outdoor interpretive trails. Walk on paths that wind you through a forest that gives you a sense of what the UP was like when it was still undeveloped. It's really neat to see how things in this region were changed (both below and above ground) by observing interesting time-line exhibits. The kids have several hands-on exhibits and also get to see a model of the Soo Locks and mining cars and other equipment.

ONTONAGON COUNTY HISTORICAL MUSEUM

422 River Street, **Ontonagon** 49953

- ❑ Phone: (906) 884-6165 **Web: www.ontonagon.com/mi/ochs**
- ❑ Hours: Monday-Saturday 9:00am-5:00pm. Closed Saturdays (January-April).
- ❑ Admission: General $2.00 (over 16)
- ❑ Miscellaneous: Nearby is Bond Falls and Agate Falls (906) 842-3341…perfect for picnics.

County artifacts displays including photos, logging and mining equipment and Finnish items. Kids are amazed at the replica copper boulder found in 1843 and weighing over 3,700 pounds.

PORCUPINE MOUNTAINS WILDERNESS STATE PARK

412 South Boundry Road (SR 107 west)

Ontonagon 49953

- ❑ Phone: (906) 885-5275
  Web: www.michigandnr.com/parksandtrails/parklist.asp
- ❑ Admission: $4.00 per vehicle
- ❑ Miscellaneous: Lookout for black bears and black flies - they both love your food. Follow ranger's posted instructions to prevent unwanted visitors.

Hiking will be most to your liking here especially along the shore of Lake of the Clouds or Mirror Lake. Stop in at the wilderness Visitor Center (open late-May to mid-October, 10:00am - 6:00pm) for a dramatic multi-image program, shown throughout the day. The show takes visitors on a tour of the geologic events that created the Porcupine Mountains, carries them through the magnificent old-growth forests and considers the values of Michigan's wilderness heritage. Camping is rough (even in cabins) but auto campers are permitted at some sites. There's also beaches, boating, fishing, swimming, and winter sports offered.

OLD VICTORIA

Victoria Dam (4 miles southwest of town)

Rockland 49960

❑   Phone: (906) 886-2617
❑   Hours: Daily, 9:00am-6:00pm. (Memorial Day-mid-October)
❑   Admissions: Donations.
❑   Miscellaneous: Picnic areas and hiking trails.

A restored settlement company town that thrived in the late 1800's. Miners from England came to work the copper mines and built many small homes, clubs and a barn for living. By the 1920's, Upper Peninsula mining sharply declined due to low copper prices and competition from out West. Guided tours explain the history of the village and its decline.

TWIN LAKES STATE PARK

Toivola - *(M-26 South), 49965. Phone: (906) 288-3321. **Web:** www.michigandnr.com/parksandtrails/parklist.asp   Admission: $4.00 per vehicle.* Camping/cabins, boating, fishing, swimming and winter sports.

IRON MOUNTAIN IRON MINE

(US-2 - 9 miles east of Iron Mountain - Look for "Big John!")

Vulcan 49852

❑   Phone: (906) 563-8077 **Web: www.ironmountainironmine.com**
❑   Hours: Daily 9:00am-5:00pm (Memorial Day - mid-October).
        Tours are 45 minutes long.
❑   Admission: $6.00 + per person (age 6+).

"But Mom and Dad, why do we need a raincoat...it's not raining outside?". Well...you explain as you're buttoning up their raincoats... that it' is probably raining INSIDE! Begin your journey by getting dressed properly for it with a raincoat and hardhat. Then you'll take a train ride through tunnels (over ½ mile long) into the mine on the same tracks that the miners used until 1945 (The mine actually produced over 22 million tons of iron ore). As you travel into the mine (over 400 feet deep), your kids will start to see the "rain" inside (the dripping water) and will be glad that they are dressed properly. Learn the drilling methods that were used like "Double Jack" or "Water Liner" and see demonstrations of both.

INDIANHEAD MOUNTAIN SKI AREA

Wakefield - *500 Indianhead Road, 49968. Phone: (800) 3-INDIAN. Web: www.indianheadmtn.com* A favorite of many Michiganders (state's largest vertical drop of over 600 feet), this resort offers 22 runs, rentals, on-slope lodging, babysitting, and lessons. (mid-November to mid-April).

Seasonal & Special Events

JANUARY

TIP-UP TOWN, USA

NE - Houghton Lake. (800) 248-LAKE. Chilly festival. Ice fishing with tip-up rigs (hence, the name of the town), parade and games such as ice softball, snow mobile racing or snow eating contests. Admission. (last two weekends in January)

INTERNATIONAL ICE SCULPTURE SPECTACULAR

SE - Plymouth, Downtown. (I-275 to Ann Arbor Road west to Main Street). (734) 459-6969 or **www.plymouth.mi.us** Up to 500,000 people walk the streets of downtown Plymouth to gaze at hundreds of blocks of carved ice (each several hundred pounds). Probably more ice to see here than anywhere and they even have a section for kids' make-believe carvings of delightful characters. Cozy shops and restaurants line the streets, plus many food vendors are on hand. Open 24 hours. FREE Admission. (mid-January week)

JANUARY/ FEBRUARY

WINTER CARNIVALS/ FESTIVALS

Things like polar bear dips, skating, snowmen building contests, ice bowling, broomball hockey, sleigh rides, cardboard tobogganing, sled dog races, snow mobile races and plenty of warm food and drink. (late January / early February)

- ❑   **CW – Grand Haven** (800) 303-4097. Area towns celebrate the last week in January.
- ❑   **NE – Alpena** (800) 582-1906.
- ❑   **NE – Mackinaw City / St. Ignace** (800) 666-0160. Mackinaw Mush Sled Dog Race, Mackinaw City 300 Snowmobile Race and Battle of the Straits Gumbo Cook-off.
- ❑   **NW – Petoskey** (231) 347-2500.
- ❑   **SW – Gun Lake** (269) 672-7822.
- ❑   **UW – Houghton** (906) 487-2818. Michigan Tech campus. Early February for 4 days.

FEBRUARY

ICE HARVEST

CE - Flint, Crossroads Village, Genesee County Parks. (800) 648-PARK. Visitors help cut ice from Mott Lake for the Village Ice House. The event is dependent upon the weather because only traditional tools and techniques are used. Weather pending. Admission. (Second Saturday in February)

PERCHVILLE USA

NE - East Tawas. (800) 55-TAWAS. Ice and shorelines. Ice fishing contests for all ages, ice demolition derby, all-you-can-eat perch dinners, and the annual Polar Bear Swim where adults cut a giant hole in the frozen bay, jump in and swim. Children's ice/snow games. Admission. (first weekend of February)

INTERNATIONAL 500 SNOWMOBILE RACE

UE – Sault Ste. Marie. (906) 635-1500 or **www.i-500.com**. Admission. (first weekend in February)

UP 200 SLED-DOG CHAMPIONSHIP

UW - Marquette to Escanaba (finish in Mattson Park). (800) 544-4321. Mushers race their teams across 200 miles of the Winter Upper Peninsula. Visitors can race through steaming stacks of pancakes and syrup served throughout the day. (mid-February)

MARCH

MAPLE SUGARING WEEKENDS

❑   **CE - Midland**, Chippewa Nature Center. (989) 631-0830. With a naturalist along, tour the 1000 acre center, looking for maple sap. Learn how the sap is turned into syrup in the Sugar Shack. Donation admission. (begins the third Saturday in March)

Maple Sugaring Weekends (cont.)

❑ **CW - Grand Rapids**, Blandford Nature Center, 1715 Hillburn NW, 49504. (616) 453-6192. Observe maple sap being gathered, taken inside the Sugar House, and boiled into maple syrup. Finally it is bottled and available for sampling and purchase. (weekends in March)

❑ **SE – Detroit (Bloomfield Hills)**, Cranbrook Institute of Science, (1221 North Woodward Avenue). (248) 645-3200. See maple sap extracted from trees and then taken to the sugar shack to be made into maple products. (Usually a late weekend in February + first weekend in March)

❑ **SE - Jackson**, Ella Sharp Museum. (517) 787-2320 or **www.ellasharp.org**. Maple tree tapping at a turn-of-the-century farm. Watch sap being processed and help make maple sugar candy. Sheep-shearing demos. (fourth Saturday in March)

❑ **SE – Lansing**, Fenner Nature Center, 2020E Mount Hope. (517) 483-4224. Walk into the woods and watch maple syrup being made. FREE. (mid-March weekend)

❑ **SW – Kalamazoo**, Nature Center. (269) 381-1574 or **www.naturecenter.org**. Visit Maple Grove and old-time sugar house. Pancake brunch. Hike trails to visit pioneer sugar shack. (weekends in March)

CLARE IRISH FESTIVAL

CW - Clare. (888) AT-CLARE. Admission charged to some events. Everyone's Irish. Parade, leprechaun contest, Irish stew, music and dancing. (second weekend in March)

ST. PATRICK'S DAY PARADES

❑ **CW - Grand Rapids**, Downtown. (616) 631-6953. Parade with marching bands, clowns, pipers and floats presented by the Ancient Order of Hiberians. (March)

❑ **NW – Manistee**, First Street. (231) 362-3480.

❑ **SE - Ypsilanti**. Travels from the Water Tower to Historic Depot Town. (734) 483-4444. An annual tradition, the parade features authentic costumes and antique autos. (Begins 2:00pm, March 13th)

For updates visit our website: www.kidslovepublications.com

POW WOW

SE - Ann Arbor. (734) 763-9044. For several decades now, more than 1000 champion Native American singers, dancers, artisans and drummers gather for competitions. Nearly 12,000 people attend this event. Admission charged (mid-March)

APRIL

COTTONTAIL EXPRESS

Bring the family for a fun-filled ride, including treats and children's activities. (near Easter weekend, usually April)

- ❑   **SE - Blissfield**. Adrian & Blissfield Railroad. (800) GO-RAIL-1.
- ❑   **SE – Walled Lake**. (248) 960-9440.

EASTER EGG HUNTS

- ❑   **SE - Ann Arbor**, Domino's Farms, (US-23 at Ann Arbor-Plymouth Road east). (734) 930-5032. Come Easter, it's the annual egg hunt when youngsters scour the grounds for plastic eggs that contain candy, stickers, or coupons redeemable for prizes. The Easter Bunny "pops" in and there's also face-painting, hayrides, clowns, and entertainment. (Easter weekend, usually April)
- ❑   **SE – Detroit (Royal Oak)**, Detroit Zoo. (248) 541-5835. Celebrate with a zoo theme and prizes and entertainment. Admission.
- ❑   **SE – Lansing**, City Parks. (517) 483-4293. Some are at dark by flashlight. Admission.
- ❑   **SE – Lansing**, Woldumar Nature Center, 5739 Old Lansing Rd. (517) 322-0030. Celebrate Spring with games, crafts and outdoor egg hunts. Admission.
- ❑   **SW – St. Joseph**, Lake Bluff Park. Egg hunt, Bunny Walk & games.

BLOSSOMTIME

SW - Benton Harbor & St. Joseph. (269) 925-6301. 20 plus neighboring Southwest Michigan communities celebrate Michigan's fruit-growing country making pilgrimages into the countryside to see the orchards in bloom. Carnival, youth parade, and the finale Grand Floral Parade with its 100-plus flowered floats and their queens. (last Sunday in April for one week)

MAPLE SYRUP FESTIVAL

SW - **Vermontville**. (517) 726-0394. Michigan's oldest maple-syrup festival. Parade, petting zoo, carnival and maple-sugar treats sold. (last weekend in April)

MAY

ALMA HIGHLAND FESTIVAL AND GAMES

CE - **Alma**, Alma College, downtown. (989) 463-8979. **www.mach7.com/highlandfestival**. More than 600 costumed bagpipers and drummers march onto the athletic field for performances and competitions. Dancers perform the sailor's hornpipe and Highland fling. Highland shortbread and briddies (pastries stuffed with ground meat). Competitions include border collie sheep-herding and tossing capers. Admission age 6+. (Memorial Day weekend)

MOTHER'S DAY CELEBRATION

CE - **Flint**, Crossroads Village & Huckleberry Railroad, 6140 Bray Road. (800) 648-PARK. Free village, train and Genesee Belle cruise admission for Mom. Special buffet dinner offered (reservations recommended). (Mother's Day - May)

FEAST OF THE SAINTE CLAIRE

CE – **Port Huron**, Pine Grove Park. **www.phmuseum.org**. (810) 982-0891. Historic camps from French & Indian War, American Revolution, War of 1812, and Fur Trade. Admission. (Memorial Day Weekend)

GREAT LAKES SPORT KITE CHAMPIONSHIPS

CW - **Grand Haven**, Grand Haven State Park Beach. (800) 303-4097. Sponsored by the Mackinaw Kite Company, this event fills the air with brightly colored, high-flying kites everywhere. One of the largest kite festivals in the Nation, you'll find up to 40,000 spectators, pilots flying kites (some craft up to 40 foot long), kite ballet events and lessons for beginners. (3rd long weekend in May)

GREEKTOWN ARTS FESTIVAL

SE - Detroit, Greektown, (Monroe and Beaubien Streets). (877) GREEK-TOWN. Contemporary craftspeople demonstrations offer the public a chance to learn about the artists' ideas, techniques and materials. Also Greektown's famous food. (third weekend in May)

EAST LANSING ART FESTIVAL

SE - East Lansing, Downtown between Abbott and Mac Streets, 48823. **www.ci.east-lansing.mi.us**. (517) 337-1731. Especially for kids are the performing dancers, storytellers, clowns and jugglers. Creative art project areas for kids include face painting and making a contribution to the Chalk Art Mural. Shuttles available from many parking sites nearby. (third weekend in May)

FIESTA

SE – Lansing, Cristo Rey Church, 201 W. Miller Road. (517) 482-7550. Mid-Michigan's largest Hispanic festival. Admission. (last long weekend in May)

MICHIGAN PARADE

SE – Lansing, downtown. (517) 323-2000. Celebrates events and people from Michigan's rich traditions in agriculture, industry, recreation, education, athletics and government. FREE. (third Saturday in May)

TULIP TIME

SW - Holland. (800) 822-2770. **www.tuliptime.org**. 8 miles of tulips (6 million red, yellow and pink blooms), Klompen Dancers, fireworks and top entertainment. To start the festival, the town crier bellows "the streets are dirty" and youngsters begin cleaning with brooms and pails. Volksparade is next with the Kinder Parade of 5000 children dressed in costume. There are Dutch treats like pigs in blankets and pastries galore (the Queens Inn Restaurant is open), a Muziekparade and Kinderplasts - music, clowns, puppets, petting zoo, arts & crafts for kids. Admission charged to some events. (begins week before Mother's Day in May)

JUNE

FREE FISHING WEEKEND

STATEWIDE - Inland and Great Lakes Waters. (800) 548-2555. All weekend long, all fishing license fees will be waived for resident and nonresident anglers. All fishing regulations will still apply. (second weekend in June)

FATHERS DAY SPECIALS

- ❏ **CE – Bridgeport**, Junction Valley Railroad. (989) 777-3480. Dads ride FREE with paying children.
- ❏ **CE – Flint**, Crossroads Village and Railroad. (800) 648-PARK. FREE admission for Dad to village, railroad and Genessee Belle.

MICHIGAN LOG CABIN DAY

CE – Port Huron & Statewide. Log House at Port Huron Museum. (810) 982-0891, **www.phmuseum.org**. Celebrate with old-fashioned house party & square dance. FREE. (last Sunday in June)

MICHIGAN SUGAR FESTIVAL

CE – Sebewaing. (800) 35-Thumb. How sweet it is…visit the sugar beet capital of the state for a parade, fireworks, sweet foods and the crowning of the sugar queen. (last weekend in June)

SCREAMIN' ON THE STRAITS PERSONAL WATERCRAFT RACES

NE - Mackinaw City, Straits of Mackinac. (800) 666-0160. Personal watercraft compete for top speeds in various class races. Short distance races one day and long distance "Enduro Race" the next day. (third weekend in June)

LILAC FESTIVAL

NE - Mackinac Island. (800) 4-LILACS. Lilacs were first planted by French missionaries a couple of hundred years ago and the bushes still bloom full of white and purple flowers each year. Dancers, famous fudge, Grand Lilac Parade (100+ horses pulling lilac-theme floats with clowns and marching bands. (June)

NATIONAL STRAWBERRY FESTIVAL

SE - Belleville, Wayne County Fairgrounds and downtown, (I-94 Belleville Road exit south into town). (734) 697-3137 or **www.nationalstrawberryfest.com.** If they're ripe, local farms can be visited heading in or out of town (Rowe's or Potter's). The festival draws 100,000 berry lovers, mostly families. A family circus, kids carnival and games, pony rides, and a parade Saturday. (Father's Day Weekend in June)

INTERNATIONAL FREEDOM FESTIVAL

SE - Detroit/Windsor, Detroit Waterfront & Downtown Museums/Windsor Downtown Waterfront. **www.theparade.org**. Take the kids over the bridge or through the tunnel to Canada for the carnival rides, Canada's largest parade (July 1), or the Great Bed Race. On the U.S. side you'll find a children's carnival, food fair, tugboat race, international tug-of-war with Windsor, and finally fireworks on July 4th (said to be the largest pyrotechnic show in North America). (mid-June through July 4th)

MICHIGAN CHALLENGE BALLOONFEST

SE - Howell, Howell High School area, (I-96 exit 133). **www.michiganchallenge.com.** 60,000 or more folks will share space with you watching skydiving, stunt kites, music, fireworks, and spectacular balloon launch flight competitions. There's also a carnival for the kids and bright balloon glows in the evening. Admission by carload ($9.00) or by entire weekend per person (slightly more). (third or fourth weekend in June)

CEREAL FEST

SW - Battle Creek, Downtown along Michigan Avenue, (I-94 exit 98B). (800) 397-2240 or (269) 962-2240. *Hours:* Thursday parade @ 6:00 pm. Children's activities Saturday 8:00am - Noon (games, FREE samples / literature). Farmers Market, Festival Park. The World's Longest Breakfast Table began in 1956 (*celebration was set up for 7,000 people – 14,000 showed up!*). They could see it was a hit and so competitors Kellogg's, Post, and Ralston Foods team up each year to serve over 60,000 people. Over 600 volunteers serve complimentary cereals, milk, Tang, Pop Tarts, donuts and Dole bananas on more than 300 tables lining one street. It's really a treat for the whole family and very well organized. We were pleasantly and promptly served within minutes and the variety of food choices was abundant. If you haven't already, be sure to stop by Kellogg's Cereal City USA, just a block away. (second week of June)

JULY

4TH OF JULY CELEBRATIONS

Independence Day is celebrated with parades, carnivals, entertainment, food and fireworks.

- ❑ **CE - Bay City**. Bay City Fireworks Festival. 888-BAY-TOWN. Three days around the 4th.
- ❑ **CE - Bridgeport**. Valley of Flags, Junction Valley Railroad. (989) 777-3480. Rides through display of flags. Five days around the 4th.
- ❑ **CE - Flint**. Crossroads Village and Huckleberry Railroad. (800) 648-PARK. Parade through park and American flags everywhere.
- ❑ **CW - Grand Haven** Area. (800) 250-WAVE.
- ❑ **CW – Hastings**, Charleton Village (989) 945-3775. Old-fashioned late 1800's BBQ.
- ❑ **NE - Mackinaw City**, A Frontier Fourth, Historic Mill Creek. (231) 436-4100. 1820's style Independence Day with games, music, sawmill demonstrations, patriotic speeches and reading of the Declaration of Independence.
- ❑ **NE - Mackinac Island**, A Star Spangled Fourth, Fort Mackinac. (231) 436-4100. 1880's celebrations include cannon firings. Admission to Fort.
- ❑ **NE - Mackinac Island**, Old Fashioned Mackinac, Grand Hotel. (800) 33-GRAND.
- ❑ **NW – Boyne**, Veterans Park. (231) 582-6222.
- ❑ **NW – Cadillac**. (800) 369-3836.
- ❑ **SE - Detroit**. International Freedom Fest. (313) 923-7400. Late June-early July. More than 100 festivals.
- ❑ **SE – Lansing**, Riverfront Park. (517) 483-4277.
- ❑ **SW - Jackson**, Cascade Falls Park. (517) 788-4320.

For updates visit our website: www.kidslovepublications.com

☐   **SW - Marshall,** 4th of July Celebration. Cornwell's Turkeyville USA and downtown. (800) 877-5163.

☐   **SW - Saint Joseph** Pavilion. Patriotic Pops. (616) 934-7676.

BATTLE & ENCAMPMENT

CE - Flint, Crossroads Village & Huckleberry Railroad, 6140 Bray Road. (800) 648-PARK. See authentic war battle re-enactments and an encampment. (second or third weekend in July)

RIVERDAYS FESTIVAL

CE - Midland, Chippewassee Park and area surrounding the Tridge. (989) 839-9661. 17th and 18th century voyageurs reenactment, Valley Fife & Drum Corps music and pageantry. Paddlewheel cruises aboard the Princess Laura or get "hands-on" experience paddling the 32 foot canoe. Milk Jug Raft Race, Pancake Breakfast, Dinners, children's activities and concerts. (third weekend in July for 4 days)

NATIONAL BABY FOOD FESTIVAL

CW - Fremont, Downtown. (800) 592-BABY. Five days of baby contests and people acting like baby contests.   Try entering a Gerber (headquartered here) baby food eating contest (*1st one to down 5 jars wins*) or enter a baby in the baby crawl race (imagine what parents hold as prizes to get their babies to move towards the finish line!).   A baby food cook-off, top live entertainment, a midway, and 2 downtown parades. (third long weekend in July)

COAST GUARD FESTIVAL

CW - Grand Haven. (888) 207-2434 or **www.ghcgfest.org**. A Coast Guard tradition filled with family entertainment day and night leading up to the final Saturday. Saturday starts with the biggest and best parade in all of West Michigan, a carnival on Main Street, all leading up to the fantastic fireworks late at night. (begins last weekend in July for 10 days)

July (cont.)

MUSKEGON AIR FAIR

CW - Muskegon, Muskegon County Airport. (800) 250-WAVE or **www.muskegon-air-fair.com**. Solo aerobatics, barn-storming Red Baron Squadron and racing ground vehicles, and parachute teams. Admission. (third weekend in July)

MICHIGAN BROWN TROUT FESTIVAL

NE - Alpena, Downtown and Alpena Mall. (800) 4-ALPENA or **www.oweb.com/upnorth/btrout/**. The Great Lakes' longest continuous fishing tournament. Anglers vie for top prizes and all can enjoy Art On the Bay, a Kid's Carnival, Fish Pond, and FREE concerts. (mid-to-end of July)

ALPENFEST

NE - Gaylord, Downtown. **www.gaylordmichigan.net** or (989) 732-4000. The featured activity is a Swiss tradition of the burning of the Boogg - where residents place all their troubles on slips of paper and throw them into a fire. Many parades and the world's largest coffee break. (third week in July)

AU SABLE RIVER INTERNATIONAL CANOE MARATHON & RIVER FESTIVAL

NE - Grayling to Oscoda, Downtown and along Au Sable River. (800) 937-8837. Called the world's toughest spectator sport - why? Probably because it's tough to follow canoes by land and a good chunk of the race is through the night until daybreak. Because the kids might only be able to catch the beginning or end of this canoe race, downtown areas are prepared to fill the time with family activities like Youth Canoe Races, Children's Fishing Contest, a Festival Parade and Dance, and a tour of Camp Grayling - the nation's largest National Guard training facility. (last full weekend in July)

AMON ORCHARDS

NW – Acme, 8066 US 31N. (231) 938-9160 or (800) 937-1644 or **www.amonorchards.com**. Cherry and fruit farm with motorized carriage rides through farm and area. (summer)

For updates visit our website: www.kidslovepublications.com

LITTLE RIVER BAND OF OTTAWA INDIANS POW-WOW

NW – Manistee, Little River Gathering Grounds (US 31 & M22). (231) 723-8288. 300+ tribes are together to display Native American singers, dancers, crafts and food. (first weekend in July)

NATIONAL FOREST FESTIVAL

NW - Manistee, Downtown. **www.manistee.com/~edo/chamber**. (800) 288-2286. Visit the open houses of the Lymon Building and Water Works with local history artifacts, parades, dances, midway, boat parade and fireworks. (4th of July)

NATIONAL CHERRY FESTIVAL

NW - Traverse City. (800) 968-3380. Cherry treats, three parades, two air shows, turtle races, band contests, mountain-bike rides, live performances and beach volleyball to begin with. There's also a Very Cherry Luncheon, Cherry Pie Eating Contest, cherry grove tours and fireworks above Grand Traverse Bay. (begins right before/after July 4th for eight days)

ANN ARBOR STREET ART FAIR

SE - Ann Arbor, Burton Carillon Tower on North University Ave. (734) 994-5260 or **www.artfair.org**. 1000+ artisans from across the nation set up booths. There are face-painting experts, beginner watercolor stations with try-it easels, Family art activity center, magicians, jugglers, and lots of American and ethnic food. (third long weekend in July)

EATON COUNTY FAIR

SE – Charlotte, County Fairgrounds. (517) 543-4510. Carnival, animals, demo derby, truck and tractor pulls, and live entertainment. (six days near the middle of July)

SPIRIT OF DETROIT THUNDERFEST

SE - Detroit, Detroit River. **www.thunderfest.com**. (800) 359-7760. 500,000 plus fans gather to watch aerodynamic turbine or piston-powered hydroplane racing. Speeds can exceed 200 mph. Admission. (mid-July weekend)

July (cont.)

MICHIGAN TASTEFEST

SE - Detroit, New Center on West Grand Blvd., (between Woodard and the Lodge Freeway). **http://comnet.org/tastefest**. (313) 872-0188. World-wide flavored smorgasbord of food and entertainment, a Kid Zone, walking tours. FREE. (first week on July)

HOT AIR JUBILEE

SE - Jackson, Reynolds Municipal Airport. Launches mornings & evenings, flight demo teams, stunt kites, Kids Kingdom, aircraft displays and carnival. **www.hotairjubilee.com**. (third weekend in July)

INGHAM COUNTY FAIR

SE – Mason, County Fairgrounds. (517) 676-2428. Exhibits, grand stand entertainment, midway and petting zoo. (late July for nine days)

SALINE CELTIC FESTIVAL

SE - Saline, Mill Pond Park. 48176. **www.salineceltic.org** or (734) 944-2810. A free shuttle to the park brings you Highland athletic competitions, children's activities, thematic reenactments, Celtic music and dancing and food. (second Saturday in July)

TEAM US NATIONALS BALLOON CHAMPIONSHIP AND AIR SHOW

SW - Battle Creek. W.K. Kellogg Airport, (I-94 exit Helmer Road). (269) 962-0592 or **www.bcballoons.com**. 200 plus balloons (some shaped like Tony the Tiger, flowers, bears or fruit) take off in competitions, a top-level air show, fireworks choreographed to music, and many ground displays of aircraft. Parking fee. (eight days starting the Saturday before the 4th of July)

PICKLEFEST

SW - Berrien Springs, Grove Park. (616) 471-9680. Craft show, helicopter rides, midway for kids, pickle smash, pickle fling, pickle tasting, pickle decorating, pickle recipe contest, family pickle games, pickle parade and lots of pickle fun. FREE. (last Saturday in July)

INTERNATIONAL CHERRY PIT SPITTING
CHAMPIONSHIP

SW - **Eau Claire**, Tree-Mendus Fruit Farm, (East on M-140 on Eureka Road). (612) 782-7101 or **www.treemendus-fruit.com**. The world record is almost 73 feet! Can you compete or do you just want to watch? Playground and petting corral too! (weekend before/after July 4th)

GOOD OLD DAYS & KNIGHTS AT THE SILVER
LEAF RENAISSANCE FAIRE

SW – **Kalamazoo**, River Oaks County Park (I-94 exit 85). Over 100 scheduled events each day, transporting you back to a medieval village, populated by ladies and their knights in shining armor, artisans, sword battles, Celtic tunes, live theatre, peasants, fairies, dragons, merchants, storytellers and peasant-powered rides. Admission. (last three weekends in July)

VENETIAN FESTIVAL

SW - **St. Joseph**, St. Joseph River. (269) 983-7917 or **www.venetian.org**. Two parades, one on land, and the other a lighted boat parade on the river. Live entertainment, fireworks, and food fair. (third long weekend in July)

AUGUST

COLONIAL DAYS

CE – **Flint**. Genesee County Parks, 5045 Stanley Road, 48506. (800) 648-PARK. Re-enactment of Revolutionary War Battles, drills and skills. Admission. (last weekend in August)

HISTORIC FARM FEST

CE – **Frankenmuth**, Grandpa Tiny's Farm, 7775 Weiss Street. (800) 386-8696. Tractor display, stagecoach rides and steam machinery show. (first weekend in August)

August (cont.)

NATIONAL PICKLE FESTIVAL

CE - Linwood, Downtown, (east of M-13). (989) 697-3790. Cucumber pickles are ripe and moving out by the truckload this time of year. Entertainment, a pickle parade with Petunia Pickle as mascot plus 100+ floats, a kiddy bike parade, food, and carnival. $3.00 admission button. (third weekend in August)

OLD GAS TRACTOR SHOW

CE - Oakley, Corner of Brennan & Ferden Roads. (989) 845-7221. Step back in time as unique tractors and steam engines demonstrate old-fashioned threshing, sawmilling, and bailing techniques...only using steam power. (third weekend of August)

ANTIQUE TRACTOR AND STEAM ENGINE SHOW

NE - Alpena. (800) 4-ALPENA. Return to yesteryear to see a hay press, sawmill, thresher motors, antique chain saws, stone crushers and a shingle mill. Food available. (second weekend in August)

FOREST FEST

NE - Grayling, Hartwick Pines State Park, (I-75 & M-93). (989) 348-2537. Renaissance Forester performance of logging songs, visit by Smoky Bear, displays of DNR fire-fighting equipment, a tree giveaway, pine walks and Logging Museum (second Saturday in August)

THE FLAT BELT FESTIVAL

NE - Grayling, Wellington Farm Park, (I-75 to exit 251). (888) OLD-FARM. Park farmers demonstrate preparations for the upcoming harvest including threshing, blacksmithing, preping tractors, sawmill operations, and mill grinding grain to flour. (last weekend in August)

IRONWORKERS FESTIVAL

NE - Mackinaw City, Mackinac Bridge. Ironworkers from around the world come here annually to test their skills in the column climbing, knot tying, rivot toss and spud throw. The prize is the coveted gold belt buckle. Also a celebration of the building of the Mackinac Bridge in 1957. (800) 666-0160. (second weekend in August)

For updates visit our website: www.kidslovepublications.com

AFRICAN WORLD FESTIVAL

SE - Detroit, Hart Plaza. (313) 494-5800. Sponsored by the Museum of African American History, this outdoor festival features cultural and educational programs, music, global cuisine, and storytellers at the Children's Village. FREE. (third long weekend of August)

MICHIGAN STATE FAIR

SE - Detroit, State Fairgrounds, (Woodward and Eight Mile Road). (313) 369-8250 **www.michigan.gov/mda**. Open 10:00am - 10:00pm, this fair has a midway, baby animal birthing areas, champion animal contests, fair food, and free concerts daily by nationally famous artists. DNR Pocket Park (world's largest stove), pig races and children's theatre productions. Admission. (last 10 days of August)

GREAT LAKES FOLK FESTIVAL

SE – East Lansing. (517) 432-GLFF. Celebrating traditional visual and performing arts with musicians, dancers, craftspeople, storytellers, parades and lots of ethnic food. FREE. (mid-August weekend)

MICHIGAN RENAISSANCE FESTIVAL

SE - Holly, Festival grounds near Mount Holly, (I-75 north exit 106). **www.renaissance-faire.com**. (800) 601-4848. Beginning in mid-August and running for seven weeks, the "Robinhood-ish" woods of Holly take you back to the sixteenth century. See knights in shining armor, strolling minstrels or Henry VIII characters. If you like, your family can dress as a lord or lady. Don't dress the kids too fancy though, all the food served is eaten with only your hands and fingers (ex. Giant turkey legs, cream soups served in bread bowls). Watch a mock jousting tourney, run from the friendly dragon, see jugglers and jesters, listen to storytellers, and best of all, ride on human-powered fair rides (it's hilarious). Admission $6-15.00 depending on age. Discount coupons available at area supermarkets. (mid-August weekend for seven weekends through September)

CIVIL WAR MUSTER

SE - **Jackson**, Cascades Park, 1992 Warren Avenue, 49203. (800) 245-5282 Midwest's largest Civil War Battle re-enactment with Union and Confederate soldiers, artillery and infantries. (last weekend in August)

MICHIGAN FIBER FESTIVAL

SW - **Allegan**, Allegan County Fairgrounds. (616) 945-2816. Meet llamas, rabbits, alpacas, goats, and sheep who all grow great coats that are sheared and processed. Come learn spinning, weaving, and see border collies herd sheep. Hundreds of merchant booths too. (third weekend in August)

ABBOTT'S MAGIC GET-TOGETHER

SW – **Colon**, Abbott's Magic Shop and downtown. (269) 432-3235. **www.abbottmagic.com** Nearly 1000 illusionists from around the world appear in town. Nightly magic shows, trick shop, daytime workshops at Abbotts (124 St. Joseph St). (early August)

KALAMAZOO SCOTTISH FESTIVAL

SW – **Kalamazoo**, County Fairgrounds. **www.iserv.net/~ksfa/**. Ceud Mile Failte – "A Hundred Thousand Welcomes". Ceilidh contests, Celtic fold entertainment all afternoon, a history tent, expanded activities for younger Scots, and an informal pipe band competition. Admission. (last Saturday in August)

NATIONAL BLUEBERRY FESTIVAL

SW - **South Haven**, Lake Michigan shores. (616) 637-5171. Visit the "World's Highbush Blueberry Capital" with every blueberry food concoction, sand-sculpting contests and beach volleyball. (second long weekend in August)

UPPER PENINSULA STATE FAIR

UE - **Escanaba**, (Fairground - east side of Escanaba – US-2), 49829. (906) 786-4011. All the usual fun is here from tractor pulls, motorcycle racing, live entertainment, great food, and rides for the whole family. Can't you just smell the barbecue? Admission. (mid-August)

SEPTEMBER / OCTOBER

GRANDPARENT'S DAY TRAIN

CE - **Bridgeport**, Junction Valley Railroad. (989) 777-3480. Grandparents Day (Sunday) in September. When accompanied by paying grandchildren, grandparents are given a discount rate. Bring young and old to ride on the largest quarter size railroad in the world. (September)

BALLOON FEST

CE - **Midland**, Midland County Fairgrounds. (989) 832-0090 (RE/MAX office). 3rd weekend in September, Friday - Sunday. "Lift-off" to the United Way campaign with daily morning launches of 50 or so balloons. "After Glows" both Friday and Saturday nights. Skydiver shows. FREE admission. (September)

UNCLE JOHN'S CIDER MILL

CE - **St. Johns**, 8614 North US-27. www.ujcidermill.com. (989) 224-3686. Apples in September, pumpkins in October. Walk along the nature trail, take a tractor ride tour through the orchards, play in the fun house or check out the petting zoo and train rides. Small admission per activity. Farm store open daily 9:00am-dark, May-December. (Weekends in September and October)

RED FLANNEL FESTIVAL

CW - **Cedar Springs**, Main Street and Morley Park, downtown, (US-131 exit 104). (616) 696-2662 or (800) 763-3273 Shoppe. Lumberjacks and clowns wore them - the original trapdoor red flannels made in this town since the early 1900's. They're still made here (purchase some at Cedar Specialties Store). An historical museum in Morley Park is usually open and features the history of red flannels (ex. Why the trapdoor?). A warning to visitors: be sure to wear red flannel (pajamas, long johns, shirts) as you walk the downtown streets or else the Keystone Cops might arrest you! Lumberjack food served. Parade. There's plenty of red flannel (many still with trapdoors) for yourself or your teddy bear to purchase. They're so adorable on our teddy! On your way up US131, stop for a meal at an authentic diner...Rosie's (M57, exit

101 east, **www.rosiesdiner.com**). (end of September or beginning of October)

HONORING OUR ELDERS POW-WOW

CW – Hart, Fairgrounds. (800) 870-9786. Traders, dancers, drums and "Entering the Circle" spiritual ceremony. (Labor Day weekend)

MACKINAW FUDGE FESTIVAL

NE - Mackinaw City, Downtown. (800) 666-0160. "Fudgies" from this state and neighboring states and countries come to taste and judge the area's famous fudge. Numerous "fudge-related" events include eating contests (got milk?). (last long weekend in September)

PAUL BUNYAN DAYS & OCTOBERFEST

NE - Oscoda. (800) 235-4625. Lumberjacks and loggers go blade-to-blade in the chainsaw competition plus other contests. (third weekend in September)

KNAEBE'S MMMUNCHY KRUNCHY APPLE FARM

NE - Rogers City, 2622 Karsten Road, 49779. (989) 734-2567. Saturdays. Watch them press cider, then slurp some along with homemade donuts, apple pies or caramel apples. In October, they have goat and pony rides for kids. (September / October)

LABOR DAY BRIDGE WALK

NE - St. Ignace to Mackinaw City. This annual crossing draws an average of 50,000 participant walkers. Starting in St. Ignace, the walkers head south across the Mackinac Bridge to the other side in Mackinaw City. This is the only time civilians are allowed to walk over the bridge. If you complete the 5 mile walk, you'll receive a Bridge Walk Certificate and enjoy a celebration in town. Labor Day. (800) 666-0160. (Labor Day - September)

PARKER MILL

SE - Ann Arbor, 4650 Geddes, (east of US-23). (734) 971-6337. Weekends. FREE admission. This restored 1800's gristmill is one of the country's few remaining completely functional mill and log cabin. Picnicking is recommended. (September / October)

For updates visit our website: www.kidslovepublications.com

FESTIVAL OF THE ARTS

SE - Detroit, University Cultural Center. (313) 577-5088 or **www.detroitfestival.com**. International arts festival held in a 20-block area and has a gigantic children's fair, street performances and great varieties of food. Admission. (long weekend in mid-September)

APPLEFEST

SE - Fenton, Spicer Orchards, (US-23 to Clyde Road exit). (810) 632-7692. Take a hayride out to the orchards for apple picking, pony rides, Victorian Carriage House (storage for 10,000 bushels, a sorting machine, cider mill and shops) highlight this free event (weekends in September and October)

RIVERFEST

SE - Lansing, Riverfront Park. (517) 483-4499. Highlights are the Electric Float Parade, live music performances, children's activities and a great carnival. (Labor Day Weekend)

APPLE CHARLIE'S ORCHARD AND MILL

SE - New Boston, 38035 South Huron Road. (734) 753-9380. Open mid-August to January. Call for seasonal hours. Apples, cider press, petting farm, hayrides and a country store with farm gifts and freshly-made donuts. (September / October)

PLYMOUTH ORCHARDS AND CIDER MILL

SE - Plymouth, 10865 Warren Road, (Ford Road west to Ridge Road, follow signs). (734) 455-2290. Petting farm, hayrides to orchards to pick apples, lots of fresh squeezed cider or cinnamon-sugar donuts or caramel apples available to eat there or take home. (September)

RUBY CIDER MILL AND TREE FARM

SE - Ruby, 6567 Imlay City Road, (I-69 west exit 96). (810) 324-2662. A cider mill, carnival rides, wax museum (presidential), a Christmas gift shop, pony & wagon rides, and a petting zoo await you. (Weekends September through October)

September / October (cont.)

COUNTRY FAIR WEEKENDS

SE - Ypsilanti, Wiard's Orchards, 5565 Merritt Road, (I-94 exit 183 south to Stony Creek south, follow signs. (734) 482-7744. **www.wiards.com** Apple orchards, cider mill, fire engine rides, pony rides, wagon rides out to the apple-picking or pumpkin patch areas, face-painting and live entertainment. (September / October)

JOLLAY ORCHARDS

SW - Coloma, 1850 Friday Road, (I-94 exit 39). (269) 468-3075 or **www.jollayorchards.com**. Hayrides through enchanted / decorated orchards to u-pick apples. Make your own warm caramel apples and bakery with pies baked in a brown paper bag. (September/October weekends)

FOUR FLAGS AREA APPLE FESTIVAL

SW – Niles. (269) 683-8870. Southern Michigan's apple-growing region showcases its harvest with apple-peeling and apple-baking contests. Lots of apple pie, dumplings and doughnuts. Parade, carnival, fireworks and entertainment. (last weekend of September)

MICHINEMACKINONG POW WOW

UE – St. Ignace, Hiawatha National Forest / Carp River campground. The Ojibwa people host gathering songs, dances and crafts demos. (800) 338-6660. Admission. (Labor Day Weekend)

OCTOBER

FALL HARVEST FESTIVALS

Join the rural farm environments at these locations as you help perform the tasks of harvest and the celebration of bounty. Old-fashioned foods, living history dramas and music. Pumpkins and crafts.

- ❏ **CE – Midland,** Chippewa Nature Center.
  www.chippewanaturecenter.com. (second weekend in October)
- ❏ **CE – Millington,** Parker Orchard. (989) 871-3031 (first weekend in October)
- ❏ **CW – Coopersville,** Farm Museum. (616) 997-8555. Kids crafts, scarecrow decorating, pig roast. Small fee. (first Saturday in October)
- ❏ **CW – Grand Rapids,** Blandford Nature Center. (616) 453-6192. Wagon rides. Fee. (mid-October)
- ❏ **CW – Middleville,** Historic Bowen Mills/Pioneer Park. (269) 795-7530. (weekends in September/October)
- ❏ **NE - Alpena,** Jesse Besser Museum. (989) 356-2202. (first Saturday in October)
- ❏ **NE – Levering,** Romanik's Ranch. Re-enactors, corn maze, pumpkin patch. (third long weekend in October)
- ❏ **SE - Dearborn,** Henry Ford Museum & Greenfield Village, 20900 Oakwood Blvd. (313) 271-1620.
- ❏ **SE - Jackson,** Ella Sharp Museum, 3225 Fourth Street. (517) 787-2320.
- ❏ **SW – Battle Creek.** (269) 962-6230.
- ❏ **SW – St. Joseph,** downtown. (269) 982-0032. Pumpkin patch, petting zoo, face paint, sawdust scramble and sing-alongs. (second Saturday in October)

ANDY T'S FARMS

CE - St. Johns, 3131 South US-27. (989) 224-7674. Open, daily 9:00am - 8:00pm (April-December). Family fun farm with fresh veggies and fruit (esp. apples and pumpkins), U-pick tours, hayrides, a petting barn, holiday decorations and bakery. (October)

HILTON'S APPLE ACRES

CW – Caledonia, 2893 108th Street. (616) 891-8019. Apple and pumpkin products, u-pick, play barn, hayrides, fall crafts. (weekends in October)

October (cont.)

PUMPKIN TRAIN

CW - Coopersville, Coopersville & Marne Railway. (616) 997-7000. Twice a day in the afternoon. Take a train with the Great Pumpkin. On board entertainment and refreshments. Pick your own pumpkin from the giant pile. Admission. (Weekends in October)

KLACKLE ORCHARDS

CW – Greenville, 11466 W. Carson City Road (M59). (616) 754-8632 or www.klackleorchards.com. Corn maze, labyrinth, wagon pumpkin rides, elephant rides, inflatable play, u-pick apples/pumpkins, hayrides, pony rides, petting zoo, straw barn fort, kids crafts and music. (weekends in October)

ORCHARD HILL FARM

CW – Lowell, 9896 Cascade Road SE. (616) 868-7229. Pumpkin & apples, play barn, hayrides, fall crafts and u-pick. (weekends in October)

PUMPKINFEST

CW - Remus, 5100 Pierce Road, (south of M-20), 49340. (989) 967-8422. A Centennial Farm with plenty of animals and harvest crops. Country Store with cider, donuts, etc. Swinging Hay ropes, tractors, hayrides to pumpkin field. (Month long in October)

GREAT LAKES LIGHTHOUSE FESTIVAL

NE - Alpena, Old and New Presque Isle Lighthouses. (800) 4-ALPENA. Plan to make it annually to tour and climb the famous short & spooky Old Presque Isle Lighthouse or the three times as tall - New Lighthouse. Keeper's quarters are open too. U.S. Coast Guard exhibits recall tales of disasters and valiant rescues. Some Admissions. (mid-October)

PUMPKINFEST

NE - Grayling, Wellington Farm Park, (I-75 to exit 251). (888) OLD-FARM. Visit the pumpkin patch, watch cider-making, corn-husking, wood-carving, milling and blacksmithing demos. (weekends in October)

A MAIZEN FUN

SE – Lansing, Loniers Shady Lodge Farm, 6275 Clark Road (I-96 exit 90). (517) 719-5636. Tricycle Maze, corn maze, cow train rides, pumpkin patch and wagon rides. Admission. (October)

THE MAIZE & GOOSE FESTIVAL

SW – Fennville, Crane Farm, 6054 124th Avenue. (269) 561-8651 or **www.cranespiepantry.com**. You're invited to witness the annual migration of Canada Geese. Some 300,000 geese pass through the palate of fall colors in this area. Grand parade, music, games and food, corn maze, hayrides, u-pick. (mid-October long weekend – Festival. September/October - Maize)

NOVEMBER

CHRISTMAS FANTASYLAND TRAIN RIDE

CE - Bridgeport. Junction Valley Railroad, 7065 Dixie Highway, 48722. (989) 777-3480. 2 mile evening rides through land aglow with 100,000 lights. Travel through Candlestick Trail, Candy Cane Pass, Santa Claus Lane, Soldier Alley, Valley Station Lit Highway, and Railway to Heaven. Elves will guide you to Santa and kids get to decorate their own ornament as a keepsake of their visit. Admission. (weekend evenings after Thanksgiving through the third weekend of December)

AMERICA'S THANKSGIVING DAY PARADE

SE - Detroit. (along Woodward Avenue from the Cultural Center to downtown). (313) 923-7400 or **www.theparade.org**. Buy a ticket for a grandstand seat ($15) or rent a room downtown along Woodward or get there early (6:00am) for free space streetside. Signaling the traditional kickoff to the holidays, you'll see floats, marching bands, giant balloon characters, and finally, at the finale, Santa and his sleigh. The parade starts at approximately 9:15am. Hob Nobble Gobble® includes entertainment, thrilling games and magnificent food as the celebration of a "Journey to a New Land!" moves the location of Hob Nobble Gobble® from Cobo Center to The Wintergarden at the Renaissance Center. Also spine-tingling experiences in Adventureland, Boogieland, Playland, Starland,

Glamland, Paradeland and all the other lands of Hob Nobble Gobble® (day before Thanksgiving) -(Parade -Thanksgiving Day)

NOVEMBER / DECEMBER

CHRISTMAS PARADES

- ❏ **CE – Saginaw**, downtown. (989) 753-9168. (fourth or fifth Saturday in November)
- ❏ **CW – Grand Rapids**, Santa Claus Parade. (616) 954-9409.
- ❏ **NW – Manistee**. (800) 288-2286. Sleighbell Parade with horse-drawn entries. (first weekend in December)
- ❏ **NW – Petoskey**, downtown. (231) 347-4150.
- ❏ **SW – St. Joseph**, Reindog Holiday Parade. Costumed pets, Santa, carolers and horse-drawn trolley rides. (first Saturday in December)
- ❏ **UW – Sault Ste. Marie**. (800) MI-SAULT. Parade of Lights.

CHRISTMAS AT CROSSROADS

CE - Flint, Crossroads Village. (800) 648-7275. Over 400,000 lights light up Crossroads Village and trackside displays. (Drive-thru viewing Monday nites in December). Craft demos, train rides, live entertainment in the Opera House, and festive traditional buffets (Sundays). Discounted admission. (Tuesday-Sunday evenings beginning Friday after Thanksgiving)

YULETIDE ZOO LIGHTS

CE – Saginaw, Children's Zoo and Celebration Square. (989) 752-6338. See Santa and his reindeer along with wolves, bobcat and eagles. Ride the carousel. Lights. Refreshments. FREE. (Friday & Saturday evenings beginning day after Thanksgiving until weekend before Christmas)

WILDLIGHTS

SE – Detroit (Royal Oak). Detroit Zoo. (8450 West 10 Mile Road). (248) 541-5835. This annual holiday lighting of nearly 300,000 sparkling lights and lighted animal displays is a delight for kids and the animals. Warm refreshments available. Admission. (evenings beginning Thanksgiving weekend through December)

WAYNE COUNTY LIGHTFEST

SE – Detroit (Westland). Hines and Merriman, (I-96 exit Merriman). (734) 261-1990. Nearly one million lights of arcs and tree-lined straights billed as the Midwest's largest holiday light show. More than 35 displays and a refreshment shelter, gifts, and visits with Santa. Admission $5.00 per car. Runs between (mid-November & January 1 - closed Christmas night).

WONDERLAND OF LIGHTS

SE - Lansing. Potter Park Zoo. (517) 483-4222. Thousands of lights create a "Wildlife Wonderland" of unique zoo animal displays. Evenings beginning at dark. Admission. (Thanksgiving through December)

NITE LITES

SE - Jackson, 200 West Ganson Street, Jackson County Fairgrounds, (I-94 exit 139). (800) 245-5282. A one-mile drive with 100,000 lights of "Candyland" (a candy cane treat is included with admission). They even have a drive up animated manger scene. Admission per vehicle ~ $5.00. (Wednesday - Sunday weekly beginning the week of Thanksgiving through Christmas)

ZOOLIGHTS FESTIVAL

SW - Battle Creek. Binder Park Zoo. (800) 397-2240. 1000's of lights and specially theme-lighted animal displays. Parade and Train Village. Admission. (evenings mid-November thru December)

DECEMBER

CHRISTMAS OPEN HOUSES

Museum homes are decorated for the holidays, mostly with Victorian themes. Visits from old Saint Nick, cookies and milk, and teas are offered for kids and parents. A great way to see local history with the focus on old-fashioned toys and festivities instead of, sometimes boring to kids, old artifacts.

- ❑ **CE – Frankenmuth** Historical Museum. (989) 652-9701. (long weekend after Thanksgiving)
- ❑ **CW – Grand Rapids**, Frederik Meijer Gardens. (616) 957-1580.
- ❑ **CW – Grand Rapids,** Public Museum of Grand Rapids. (616) 456-3977. (week after Christmas)
- ❑ **CW – Holland,** Cappon House, 228 W. 9th St. (888) 200-9123. (week after Christmas)
- ❑ **SE – Detroit (Grosse Pointe Shore)**. Edsel & Eleanor Ford House. (313) 884-4222 or **www.fordhouse.org**.
- ❑ **SE – Detroit (Rochester),** MeadowBrook Hall, 280 South Adams, Oakland University campus. (248) 370-3140. Admission for some activities. (all month-long)
- ❑ **SE - Jackson**, Ella Sharp Museum, 3225 Fourth Street. (517) 787-2320.
- ❑ **SW – Hastings,** Charleton Village. (989) 945-3775. (second weekend in December)

HOLIDAY MUSICALS

Admission charged.

- ❑ **CW** – The Nutcracker – **Grand Rapids** Ballet, DeVos Hall. (616) 454-4771.
- ❑ **SE - Ann Arbor** Symphony Holiday Concert. Michigan Theatre. (734) 994-4801. Favorite holiday music and a family sing-along.
- ❑ **SE -** The Nutcracker Ballet - **Detroit** Opera House. (313) 576-5111. Music supplied by the Detroit Symphony Orchestra.
- ❑ **SE –** A Christmas Carol, **Detroit (Rochester Hills)**, MeadowBrook Theatre. (248) 370-4902.

For updates visit our website: www.kidslovepublications.com

❑   **SW** - "A Christmas Carol". **Saugatuck**. (269) 857-1701. After
the show, climb aboard a ride in a horse-drawn buggy thru town.

LONGWAY PLANETARIUM HOLIDAY SHOWS

CE - **Flint**. (810) 237-3400 or **www.longway.org**. Friday evenings
at 8:00 pm, Saturday afternoon and evening, Sunday afternoon
throughout December. Night sky shows with traditional
(Nutcracker Fantasy) and contemporary (The Alien Who Stole
Christmas) themes. Admission. (December)

SANTA EXPRESS TRAIN RIDES

Santa and his helpers ride along and play games and sing songs to
get everyone in the holiday spirit. Admission.

❑   **CW** - **Coopersville**, Coopersville & Marne Railway. (616) 997-
7000. (Saturday mornings, the first three weekends in December)
❑   **SE – Blissfield**, Adrian & Blissfield Railroad. (800) GO-RAIL-1.
❑   **SE – Walled Lake**, Coe Rail Family Train, 840 N. Pontiac Trail.
(248) 960-9440. (departures twice an afternoon on second and
third Saturday of December)

MUSICAL FOUNTAIN NATIVITY

CW - **Grand Haven**, Grandstand at Harbor and Washington
Streets on the riverfront. (800) 303-4096. A 40 foot nativity scene
on Dewey Hill offers evening performances focused on the "spirit"
of the holiday. Donations. (Evening performances in December)

JINGLE BELL JUBILEE & CHRISTMAS VILLAGE

CW – Rothbury, Double JJ Resort. (800) 368-2535. Carolers,
Holiday lights, sleigh rides, crafts and Santa's workshop.
Admission. (weekend evenings in December)

KWAANZA

SE - **Detroit**, Museum of African American History, 315 East
Warren Avenue. (313) 494-5800. Weeklong during Kwaanza.
Kwaanza (first fruits) is an African celebration of the harvest and
the fruits of the community's labor. Each day has a special focus:
unity, self-determination, collective work and responsibility,
cooperative economics, purpose, creativity and faith. (December)

December (cont.)

FIRST NIGHT

SE - Detroit, Birmingham Principal Shopping District. (248) 258-9075 or **www.technomasters.com/firstnight**. First Night is an alcohol-free festival of arts for children and adults. Many booths have kids crafts, storytelling, musical entertainment and dancing, kid-friendly food and a big Midnight celebration. Admission. (December 31 - Beginning mid-day New Year's Eve)

FEST EVE

SE - Lansing and East Lansing. Downtown and Michigan State University Campus. (517) 483-4499. Alcohol-free new year activities and live entertainment plus midnight fireworks. (New Years Eve - December)

NEW YEAR JUBILEE

SE - Ypsilanti, Depot Town. (734) 480-1636. Alcohol-free evening of entertainment and fun for families. More than 45 performances in town churches and buildings. (December - Begins mid-day on New Year's Eve)

MIDNIGHT AT THE CREEK

SW - Battle Creek, Downtown. (800) 397-2240. Ring in the New Year with a family-oriented evening of activities, storytellers, kid-friendly food and beverage, and musical performances of all different types. (December 31)

CHRISTMAS PICKLE FESTIVAL

SW - Berrien Springs, Downtown, I-94 to US-31 south. (616) 471-3116. Do you know about a German tradition at Christmas? The first child to find a glass pickle hidden in the tree gets an extra present! This is the town's inspiration for a holiday parade, street lighting, and pickle tastings. Pickle and non-pickle foods and gifts. Admission. (first week of December)

Master
Index

Activity
Index

OUTDOORS

Unique Recommended Resorts

Travel Journal & Notes:

Travel Journal & Notes:

_____
_____
_____
_____
_____
_____
_____
_____
_____
_____
_____
_____
_____
_____
_____
_____
_____
_____
_____
_____
_____
_____
_____
_____
_____
_____
_____
_____
_____
_____
_____
_____
_____

Travel Journal & Notes:

Travel Journal & Notes:

Travel Journal & Notes:

_____
_____
_____
_____
_____
_____
_____
_____
_____
_____
_____
_____
_____
_____
_____
_____
_____
_____
_____
_____
_____
_____
_____
_____
_____
_____
_____
_____
_____
_____
_____
_____
_____
_____
_____
_____

GROUP DISCOUNTS & FUNDRAISING OPPORTUNITIES!

We're excited to introduce our books to your group! These guides for parents, grandparents, teachers and visitors are great tools to help you discover hundreds of fun places to visit. Our titles are great resources for all the wonderful places to travel either locally or across the region.

We are two parents who have researched, written and published these books. We have spent thousands of hours collecting information and *personally traveled over 20,000 miles* visiting all of the most unique places listed in our guides. The books are kid-tested and the descriptions include great hints on what kids like best!

Please consider the following Group Purchase options: *For the latest information, visit our website:* **www.kidslovepublications.com**

❑ **Group Discount/Fundraising** – Purchase books at the discount price of $2.95 off the suggested retail price for members/friends. <u>Minimum order is ten books</u>. You may mix titles to reach the minimum order. Greater discounts (~35%) are available for fundraisers. <u>Minimum order is thirty books</u>. Call for details.

❑ **Available for Interview/Speaking** – The authors have a treasure bag full of souvenirs from favorite places. We'd love to share ideas on planning fun trips to take children while exploring your home state. The authors are available, by appointment, *(based on availability)* at (614) 792-6451. A modest honorarium or minimum group sale purchase will apply. Call or visit our website for details.

<u>Call us soon at (614) 792-6451 to make arrangements!</u>
Happy Exploring!

YOUR FAMILY MEMORIES!

Now that you've created memories with your family,

it's time to keepsake them by scrapbooking

in this unique, family-friendly way!

Check Out These Unique Features:

* **The Book That Shrinks As It Grows!** - Specially designed pages can be removed as you add pictures to your book. This keeps your unique travel journal from becoming too thick to use.

* **Write Your Own Book** - The travel journal is designed to get you started and help you remember those great family fun times!

* **Design Your Own Book** - Most illustrations and picture frames are designed to encourage kids to color them.

* **Unique Chapter Names** - help you <u>simply</u> categorize your family travel memories.

* **Acid Free Paper** - was used to print your book to keep your photos safe for a lifetime!

Writing Your Own Family Travel Book is This Easy...

Step 1 - Select, Cut and Paste Your Favorite Travel Photos

Step 2 - Color the Fun Theme Picture Frames

Step 3 - Write about Your Travel Stories in the Journal (We get you started...)

Step 4 - Specially Designed Pages are removed to reduce thickness as you add photos

Remove This Page
(to reduce binding thickness as you add personal photos)

The Perfect Companion to the Best-Selling "Kids Love" Travel Series!

Create Your Family Travel Book Today!

Visit your local retailer,

use the order form in the back of this book,

or our website: www.kidslovepublications.com

Attention Parents:

All titles are "Kid Tested". *The authors and kids personally visited all of the most unique places* and wrote the books with warmth and excitement from a parent's perspective. Find tried and true places that children will enjoy. No more boring trips! Listings provide: Names, addresses, telephone numbers, websites, directions, and descriptions. All books include a bonus chapter listing state-wide kid-friendly Seasonal & Special Events!

❑ **KIDS LOVE INDIANA** - Discover places where you can "co-star" in a cartoon or climb a giant sand dune. Over 500 listings in one book about Indiana travel. 8 geographical zones, 213 pages.

❑ **KIDS LOVE KENTUCKY** - Discover places from Boone to Burgoo, from Caves to Corvettes, and from Lincoln to the Lands of Horses. Over 500 listings in one book about Kentucky travel. 6 geographic zones. 224 pages.

❑ **KIDS LOVE MICHIGAN** - Discover places where you can "race" over giant sand dunes, climb aboard a lighthouse "ship", eat at the world's largest breakfast table, or watch yummy foods being made. Almost 600 listings in one book about Michigan travel. 8 geographical zones, 229 pages.

❑ **KIDS LOVE OHIO** - Discover places like hidden castles and whistle factories. Over 800 listings in one book about Ohio travel. 9 geographical zones, 260 pages.

❑ **KIDS LOVE PENNSYLVANIA** - Explore places where you can "discover" oil and coal, meet Ben Franklin, or watch your favorite toys and delicious, fresh snacks being made. Over 900 listings in one book about Pennsylvania travel. 9 geographical zones, 268 pages.

❑ **KIDS LOVE THE VIRGINIAS** – Discover where ponies swim and dolphins dance, dig into archaeology and living history, or be dazzled by record-breaking and natural bridges. Over 900 listings in one book about Virginia & West Virginia travel. 8 geographical zones, 262 pages.

❑ **KIDS LOVE TRAVEL MEMORIES!** – The Perfect Travel Journal & Scrapbook Companion. – See display page (or our website) to learn more about the features of this unique book.

ORDER FORM

KIDS LOVE PUBLICATIONS

1985 Dina Court
Powell, Ohio 43065
(614) 792-6451
Visit our website: **www.kidslovepublications.com**

#	Title		Price	Total
	Kids Love Indiana		$13.95	
	Kids Love Kentucky		$13.95	
	Kids Love Michigan		$13.95	
	Kids Love Ohio		$13.95	
	Kids Love Pennsylvania		$13.95	
	Kids Love the Virginias		$13.95	
	Kids Love Travel Memories!		$14.95	
COMBO PRICING* - *Indicate Titles Above*				
	Combo #2 - Any 2 Titles*		$23.95	
	Combo #3 - Any 3 Titles*		$33.95	
	Combo #4 - Any 4 Titles*		$42.95	
			Subtotal	
*Note: All combo pricing is for **different titles only.** For multiple copies (10+) of one title, please call or visit our website for volume pricing information.		*(Ohio Residents Only)*	5.75% Sales Tax	
		$2.00 first book $1.00 each additional	Shipping	
			TOTAL	

[] Master Card   [] Visa

Account Number _ _ _ _ - _ _ _ _ - _ _ _ _ - _ _ _ _
Exp Date: _ _ / _ _ (Month/Year)
Cardholder's Name _____
Signature *(required)* _____

(Please make check or money order payable to: KIDS LOVE PUBLICATIONS)

Name: _____
Address:_____
City:_____State:_____
Zip:_____Telephone:_____

All orders are shipped within 2 business days of receipt by US Mail. If you wish to have your books autographed, please include a legible note with the message you'd like written in your book. Your satisfaction is 100% guaranteed or simply return your order for a prompt refund. Thanks for your order. Happy Exploring!

"Where to go?, What to do?, and How much will it cost?", are all questions that they have heard throughout the years from friends and family. These questions became the inspiration that motivated them to research, write and publish the "Kids Love" travel series.

This adventure of writing and publishing family travel books has taken them on a journey of experiences that they never could have imagined. They have appeared as guests on hundreds of radio and television shows, had featured articles in statewide newspapers and magazines, spoken to thousands of people at schools and conventions, and write monthly columns in many publications talking about "family friendly" places to travel.

George Zavatsky and Michele (Darrall) Zavatsky were raised in the Midwest and have lived in many different cities. They currently reside in a suburb of Columbus, Ohio. They feel very blessed to be able to create their own career that allows them to research, write and publish a series of best-selling kids' travel books. Besides the wonderful adventure of marriage, they place great importance on being loving parents to Jenny & Daniel.